Praise for *Might Lever to Punt*

'Gu[ar]ment[ee]d to make you yearn for days of yore . . . don't be su[rprised] to find yourself laughing at more in-jokes than you ca[n ad]mit'   – *Focus*****

'A[mu]s[ing] and amusing . . . a glimpse into the world of fandom cra[zines], on holiday, given licence to be sillier than usual'
– *Daily Telegraph*

'Fu[nny an]d affectionate'   – *Time Out*

'A [witty,] irreverent celebration of Britain's secret love of the biz[arre]'   – *Gay Times*

'It'[s hilar]ious . . . For anyone who has ever liked any of this stu[ff the]re's laughter and nostalgia aplenty'
– *Nottingham Evening Post*

'Pe[rceptive] and engaging . . . anyone who agrees that "*Star Wars* wa[s the de]fining moment of our collective childhood" will love thi[s book]'   – *The Times*

'W[ill give] anyone from the era of Spam fritters and Blue Riband bis[cuits a] Prustian rush . . . a witty, heartwarming exploration of [the gea]nt side of SF fandom'   – *SFX*

'W[ill ha]v[e] you hitching aboard the Millennium Falcon to a gal[axy o]verflowing with infinite possibilities'   – *Metro*****

Bob Fischer is a lifelong science-fiction and fantasy fan who has previously enjoyed careers as a record shop owner, a solo singer-songwriter and a short-lived Elvis impersonator (one gig). He works as a writer and broadcaster, presenting full-time for his local radio station BBC Tees, and occasionally popping up on national radio too. He has written for the Fortean Times about North Yorkshire folklore and unsettling 1970s TV, lost a fortune staging an Edinburgh Fringe show about his ongoing Last of the Summer Wine obsession, and since 2012 has been frontman with Teesside's least ambitious rockabilly synthcore band, Old Muggins.

WIFFLE LEVER TO FULL!

DALEKS, DEATH STARS AND
DREAMY-EYED NOSTALGIA AT THE
STRANGEST SCI-FI CONVENTIONS

BOB FISCHER

HODDER

First published in Great Britain in 2008 by Hodder & Stoughton
An Hachette UK company

This paperback edition published in 2018

2

A CIP catalogue record for this title is
available from the British Library

Paperback ISBN 978 1 473 68095 1
eBook ISBN 978 1 848 94329 2

Typeset in RotisSerif by Palimpsest Book Production Ltd,
Falkirk, Stirlingshire

Printed and bound by CPI Group (UK) Ltd, Croydon, CR0 4YY

Hodder & Stoughton policy is to use papers that are natural,
renewable and recyclable products and made from wood grown
in sustainable forests. The logging and manufacturing processes
are expected to conform to the environmental regulations of
the country of origin.

Hodder & Stoughton Ltd
Carmelite House
50 Victoria Embankment
London EC4Y 0DZ

www.hodder.co.uk

Dedicated with love to the memory of
Doug Simpson, 1972–2008.
Nothing is forgotten.

FOREWORD

You are about to pass through a wormhole.

Don't get too excited; it isn't going to bring you out in some remote, exotic corner of the universe, or spirit you away to an exciting, futuristic time zone. It's going to transport you to Teesside, North-Eastern England, in 2005. . . so brace yourself to emerge from the only portal in the cosmos with 'Up The Boro' written in permanent marker on its exit, and the Planet Burgerland van parked up nearby.

I was in my mid-thirties when I wrote *Wiffle Lever To Full!*, and that can be a difficult age. Not quite ready to settle into domesticated adulthood, I frequently found myself peppering my work and home life with half-remembered fragments of my rapidly receding childhood; putting the car's headlights on full beam in heavy snow to emulate the Millennium Falcon's passage though hyperspace; or lying in bed with my sleeping girlfriend and dreaming us both into Doctor Who's TARDIS, Time Lord and Time Lady, embarking on impossible adventures throughout the galaxy, and leaving the bills and the housework far behind.

With the benefit of hindsight, embarking on a year of utterly irresponsible freewheeling through some of the UK's most bizarre and brilliant cult TV conventions was a heartfelt attempt to realise those fantasies . . . and, absolutely, an effort to reconnect with those carefree days of childhood reverie for a final fling of utterly escapist nostalgia. It was a period of my life when obtaining a DVD box set signed by the entire main cast of *Blake's 7*, or spending a night in a hotel bar with the *actual Friar Tuck from Robin of Sherwood* became far more important preoccupations than turning up for work on time or maintaining a healthy relationship.

Selfish? Yes. But then that's the nature of obsession, and this book is often about the tipping point between fandom and obsession, and those – including me – who have walked the line between them.

I didn't embark on this quest with the intention of writing a book, but it quickly became obvious that there was one to be written. And, reading it back, I feel like I've passed through a wormhole too . . . again, not to a far-flung corner of the universe or to some exotic time zone, but definitely to an era that now seems oddly quaint and carefree in itself. *Doctor Who* had returned, and David Tennant was (just) a household name, but nobody had heard of Facebook or Twitter, and even the seemingly monolithic YouTube had barely celebrated its first anniversary. I suspect all of these seismic cultural phenomena have contributed – in the last thirteen years – to the transformation of science fiction and cult TV fandom into a global, multi-million pound industry, but when this book was written it still felt like the reserve of wistful thirtysomethings emerging from small, provincial hotel bars with a rumpled Tesco carrier bag filled with childhood memories.

That was me.

I had lots of fun, and I hope you do, too.

Your wormhole awaits you . . .

Bob Fischer, Teesside, 2018

CONTENTS

THE BATTLE TO SAVE EARTH

By Robert Fischer (Aged Eight And A Third)
Saturday 21 March 1981
PART ONE

One day Richard Moxham and I were
walking down Yarm High Street when a
ray of light shot down from the sky
and formed a kind of force field on the
pavement. I held Richard back and
looked at the force field for a moment.
  Then I walked into it. Richard
followed me. As soon as we felt the
force field we fell unconscious on the ground. Then the force
field dissapered into thin air. I woke up in a strange room.
I stood up and looked around. There was white walls and lots
of screens around me. On one of the walls was an electronic
door. Then I saw Richard laid just at my feet. I pushed him
and said 'Wake Up Richard,' Richard opened his eyes and stood
up. 'What are we doing here?' He asked. 'That's what I want
to know,' I answered. Suddenly I spotted a control box by the
electronic door. I pulled a lever down and the door opened. We
  both went through the gap. Behind the door was a long
corridor. There was twelve doorways down each side. Suddenly I
heard footsteps. I pulled Richard into a doorway. A strange
white robot with a laser gun in its hand came walking down
the corridor. I ran out of the doorway, kicked the robot in
the chest and grabbed the gun. 'Now we have to find you a
gun,' I said to Richard. I saw a trapdoor in the floor. I
  said to Richard 'Look, a trapdoor'. 'What's down there?'
Richard asked. I opened the trapdoor and looked down. It was
too dark to see anything. 'It's too dark to see anything,' I
answered. I put my foot on the trapdoor and fell down it.

To be continued . . .

INTRODUCTION

FOUR THINGS I'VE LEARNED recently about my eight-year-old self:

1. I can spell virtually any word in my modest vocabulary apart from 'disappeared'.
2. I can use quotation marks, but I've yet to be convinced about these new-fangled 'paragraph' things.
3. I have a habit of stating the very bleeding obvious to Richard Moxham.
4. Richard Moxham might be my best friend, but if we've been transported to a strange alien netherworld with only one laser gun between us, then – clearly – bollocks to him.

I'm thirty-two years old, and I'm sitting on the edge of the hatchway to the attic, my legs dangling precariously over the landing floor below. I've just discovered *The Battle to Save Earth*, neatly handwritten twenty-four years previously in a WHSmith exercise book and painstakingly punctuated with surprisingly detailed illustrations – all lustily drawn in black felt-tip and owing a substantial debt to the cartoon strips in

Star Wars Weekly, reserved for me every week by Mr Murray, the elderly newsagent whose dark, enticing corner shop was a wonderland of comics and stickers. The book was at the bottom of a cobweb-strewn cardboard box, lost under a hundredweight of old *Whizzer and Chips*es and a battered, time-worn, Sellotape-strewn KerPlunk, and it's the first time I've clapped eyes on it for almost two decades. I've recently bought my first house and moved into it with my first long-term girlfriend, and my parents have seized the opportunity to transport a small lorry-load of long-forgotten childhood relics from their dusty attic to mine.

Flicking through the book's crinkled pages, I feel like I've once again fallen into a swirling, mysterious force field, this time emerging unscathed on a breezy Saturday afternoon in March 1981. I'm at my gran's bungalow in Acklam, a leafy, modern suburb of Middlesbrough that contemporary Polaroids reveal to have been constructed entirely from brown and orange blobs. And, coincidentally, I've just had beans-on-toast for my dinner. A long, lazy afternoon stretches before me, and I prise open the front page of my pristine new 'writing book', the Biro gripped in my tiny right hand – the key to unlocking an eager imagination. 'This one's going to get published,' I tell my mum, as she brings in a small tray of tea and almond slices.

'I'm sure it is.' She smiles, but I can tell she doesn't believe me. Hah.

Like most of my friends at Levendale Primary School, a modern, open-plan seat of learning in my staunchly middle-class home town of Yarm, I'm obsessed with science fiction. It's that kind of era. *Doctor Who* is a fixture of Saturday teatimes, unless you switch over to ITV, in which case it's *Buck Rogers in the 25th Century*. The only other TV channel available is BBC2, and *nobody* watches BBC2. It's less than a year since the release of *The Empire Strikes Back,* and the influence of *Star*

Wars is, well . . . universal. For Richard Moxham's birthday in October, we went to see *Battle Beyond the Stars*, a low-budget knock-off starring a grizzled George Peppard and Richard 'John Boy Walton' Thomas. There was only one King Cone left in the freezer in the foyer and Richard got it – so let's call it quits with the laser gun, eh? More recently, I've dragged my poor, overworked dad back to Middlesbrough's ABC Cinema to see a deliciously camp and gaudy reworking of that cheesy old sci-fi staple *Flash Gordon*. Although to me, there's nothing remotely cheap or arch about these movies – their stories are as vital and immutable as the Bible, and Brian Blessed is my new god. When my uncle Trevor pays a fleeting visit to my gran's house that afternoon, he talks enthusiastically about *The Adventure Game*, a new BBC quiz show, seemingly aimed squarely at pale, well-spoken boys in parkas. It transports the likes of Maggie Philbin and Michael Rodd to the dreaded, far-away, surreal planet Arg, where they're frequently menaced by a growling aspidistra. Sci-fi is everywhere I go, and, as far as I'm concerned, it's only a matter of time before the entire population of the UK dresses in shiny, tin-foil space suits and communicates in strange, unearthly bleeps and groans. Gary Numan has started already.

It doesn't last, of course. Within a few short years, admitting you like science fiction carries as much cultural credibility as, well . . . admitting you like Gary Numan. But, diligent to the end, I keep the flame alive in my heart. Long after the rest of my generation has lost interest, hit puberty and discovered something called 'girls' (and more on those later), I continue to have *Star Wars Weekly* reserved for me at the newsagent's, even after Mr Murray has ascended to the great magazine rack in the sky.

In fact my obsession with science fiction and the darker corners of cult TV becomes so all-pervading that, even as a thirty-two-year-old man flicking gleefully through *The Battle to Save Earth*, the significance of the date 21 March 1981 is immediately and obviously apparent to me. A matter of hours after writing that breathless opening chapter, my eight-year-old self had almost choked on a corned-beef sandwich as Tom Baker's Doctor Who had plummeted from the top of a towering radio telescope, raised a wearisome arm into the air, and regenerated amidst a halo of light into a youthful and rather surprised-looking Peter Davison. Yes, that fateful Saturday – with its almond slices and beans-on-toast and the first exciting instalment of *The Battle to Save Earth* – was a pivotal day in sci-fi history. I had little idea that Baker was leaving the show, and only a vague inkling that there'd even been previous Doctors. We were halfway through *Little and Large* before I recovered my senses.

It was a seismic communal cultural experience, and back at school on Monday morning, even our kindly supply teacher Mrs Curtain (a woman whom my dad, attending a parents' evening, once told to 'pull herself together') had asked us if we'd seen the Doctor's regeneration. It was the first time I'd ever heard anyone use the word, and the school was aflame with gossip and speculation as to what might happen next in the show. It was all anyone wanted to talk about – until, of course, I revealed that Richard Moxham had been sucked into a force field in Yarm High Street and stranded on an alien oligarchy without a laser gun to his name. Hope you enjoyed that King Cone, *mate*.

I'm not bitter.

I fumble my way down the stepladder and close the hatch

to the attic, still clutching *The Battle to Save Earth* to my chest, which I toss onto a desk in my ramshackle spare-room office. And then, purely on a whim, I boot up the PC and go online to read a little more about Tom Baker's swansong story, 'Logopolis', and, entirely by chance, discover that – in a matter of months – a *Doctor Who* convention, Dimensions, is arriving five miles up the road in Stockton-on-Tees. A town roughly equidistant between my gran's old house in Acklam and my dusty new attic in Teesside force-field hotspot Yarm, packed with yellowing *Whizzer and Chips*es and myriad other delights.

Resistance, to coin a phrase, is useless.

I buy a ticket and start counting down the days.

A couple of weeks later, I do something incredibly reckless. My ticket for Stockton's impending Dimensions convention is still winging its way through the Royal Mail's time vortex to my new front door, but – worryingly – it's got me thinking. I start to wonder, almost to my own disquiet, whether similar celebrations are held for my other childhood sci-fi obsessions. I'm irresistibly drawn again to the PC upstairs (with *The Battle to Save Earth* still plonked unceremoniously on the desk) and – checking nervously around the room to ensure that my brain isn't watching – my fingers type 'Cult TV' and 'Convention' into Google, dancing their way around the keyboard and pressing 'Enter' before the sensible part of my mind has a chance to raise a single, rational objection.

Within seconds I'm lost in a mire of nostalgia, as long-lost and once-loved TV shows leap out of a maze of windows on my wheezing, overworked computer screen. Look, there's *Blake's 7* – the show that made sitting through the last five minutes of *Nationwide* almost worthwhile. Here comes *Red Dwarf*, the space-age sitcom that – as a seventeen-year-old – I found tickling my smeg receptors in a way that no other comedy had done since the glorious teenage evening I'd discovered *Monty Python*. And, inevitably, *Python* is there as well – no longer deceased and gone to join the choir invisible, but alive and kicking in the hearts of hundreds of fans who descend on a remote Scottish castle every autumn for their annual coconut-clopping party. There's *The Hitch Hiker's Guide to the Galaxy*, the TV adaptation that I could recite virtually word for word until it was beaten out of me in spring 1988 by a gang of marauding wizards from Terry Pratchett's Discworld books. Is Discworld there as well? You bet your twenty-sided role-playing dice it is. They're enticing, intriguing and irresistable, like half-forgotten lovers, luring me away for filthy weekends in strange provincial hotels.

While my girlfriend, Sorcha, sleeps soundly beside me, I spend the night lying bolt awake in bed, the rational side of my mind presenting to the courtroom of my conscience a string of irrefutable evidence as to why indulging this ludicrous nostalgic streak at a string of sci-fi and cult TV conventions would, in essence, be a terrible idea. Credit-card demands in red ink are presented with stern, furrowed brows, mortgage statements tutted over and thrown in desperation at my feet. But it's a losing battle. Rationale is prodded into a dark, secluded corner of my mind by the motley rabble of wizards, time-travellers, alien warlords and paranoid androids that have now sectioned off the larger part of my brain and are vigorously protecting its borders with staffs, lances and phasers set to stun. At 4.30am, they erect a deadly force field around my last remaining bubble of sanity, and declare a state of martial law. Five hours later, I'm back in front of the computer screen again – wide-eyed and wired, and shamelessly booking a ticket for a *Robin of*

Sherwood convention in Retford. Oh, and *Red Dwarf*, in Peterborough. And *Blake's 7* as well – that's in Stockton too, so it would be churlish not to attend. Wouldn't it?

I slump, exhausted, in front of the PC. I feel like Lady Macbeth after King Duncan's murder, and want to race into the bathroom to wash the green Dalek blood from my guilty, fevered hands. I'm a broken man, and the eight-year-old boy who sat down one breezy Saturday afternoon to write *The Battle to Save Earth* has reasserted control over my psyche.

And this time, no power in the universe can stop him.

THE BATTLE TO SAVE EARTH

By Robert Fischer (Aged Eight And A Third)
Sunday 22 March 1981
PART TWO

I found myself falling down a round
chute. I landed in another room.
Then I heard voices. I looked up
and saw an army of robots stood
round me. All their guns were
pointing at me. 'You are a prisoner
of klebba . . .' they said. The room
I was being held prisoner in had
now turned into a battleground.

Several laser blasts were being fired
at me, but I returned the fire and was shooting the robots
down one by one. I ran to a doorway and ducked into it. But
I was caught again by a strange hooded man. 'Who are you?'
I asked him. 'I am Commander of all the robots, Captain
Zero,' the man answered. 'Who are you?' 'I'm Robert Fischer
from Earth,' I replied. 'You will be taken prisoner by
klebba,' Zero said. I was taken down a dark passageway and
into a huge hall. There was some steps up to a platform.
Suddenly I saw someone smiling at me. 'Richard!' I shouted. I
kicked Zero off my arm and ran to Richard. 'When this klebba
appears, we'll start a fight,' I whispered to him. 'Ok,
Robert,' Richard said. Suddenly a light appeared on the platform. A man dressed in yellow, green and black walked onto it.
A large group of creatures including Snakemen and Birdmen
saluted him. Zero again grabbed hold of Richard and I. 'Get
lost,' I shouted at Zero. Zero kicked me in the leg so I
thumped him in the jaw. 'Told you we'd start a
fight,' I said to Richard.

To be continued . . .

DOCTOR WHO

DIMENSIONS CONVENTION
SWALLOW HOTEL, STOCKTON-ON-TEES
FRIDAY 11 – SUNDAY 13 NOVEMBER

'Peter Davison is currently at the Chiswick Roundabout.'

LET'S GO BACK EVEN further in time. Back beyond even almond slices and mine and Richard's ripping adventures in *The Battle to Save Earth*. It's Saturday 30 August 1975, just after teatime, and I'm screaming. Not the ordinary, everyday, casual screaming of the average three-year-old (and I am, at this point, a *very* average three-year-old) but a full-blooded, milk-curdling, hands-over-the-ears scream that rattles the double glazing and threatens to generate a tsunami in a nearby bowl of Butterscotch Angel Delight.

The cause of my distress is one no doubt being shared by a legion of similarly tearful toddlers nationwide. It is, of course, Doctor Who. I'm once again at my gran's bungalow in Acklam, and my resident sci-fi guru Uncle Trevor is watching his favourite programme. An amiable twentysomething sporting hair the size, shape and colour of an autumnal laburnum bush and a beige nylon ensemble that generates enough static electricity to power a small African village for a month, Uncle Trevor is rapt in front of a Rediffusion TV. The episode he's watching is part one of 'Terror of the Zygons', a creepy Tom Baker potboiler that culminates, terrifyingly, in the Doctor's companion, Sarah Jane Smith, having her first gruesome encounter with a Zygon – an orange, baby-faced alien covered in more weeping pustules and snot than the average Bay City Rollers audience.

It's all too much for my delicate three-year-old psyche. At this stage in my life, there are only three things in the world that truly scare me, and all three of them are on TV. The first is Ron Mael, the Hitler-moustached keyboard player in oddball glam-rockers Sparks, whose bug-eyed sideways stare into the *Top of the Pops* cameras once sent me into a convulsive fit of terror so pronounced that I almost choked on a *Wombles* Easter egg. The second is Fred Harris, an innocuously bearded *Play School* presenter whose every appearance sends me scurrying behind the hostess trolley, praying for the comfortable familiarity of Johnny Ball or Floella Benjamin. Both Ron Mael and Fred Harris have one factor in common – facial hair. Yes, I'm a pre-school pogono-phobic, liable to soil my terry-towelling dungarees at the slightest exposure to a beard or moustache. Even the pres-ence of a modest pair of sideburns is enough to make me twitch nervously in my rompers. Given the nature of my condition, it's unfortunate that I've been born into an era when growing extravagant facial hair falls somewhere between eating and sleeping in the list of human priorities. And that's just for the women.

The third is, of course, *Doctor Who*. And yet, buried some-where deep beneath the head-chilling terror and the crockery-rattling screams, the show has a hint of fascination for me, too. It scares the 1970s ab-dabs out of me, but I'm always in the room when it starts, and I've never once asked to be removed for my own safety. Although, on this occasion, it's providence that comes to the rescue, and the episode is inter-rupted by a textbook 1970s power cut. My mum dashes to the kitchen to root out candles and matches in case the failure lasts beyond daylight hours. My gran rubs a balloon against Uncle Trevor's shirt front. There are still six years to go before *The Battle to Save Earth* and the start of my true obsession, but the foundations for creating a lifelong fan have already sunk firmly to the bottom of my consciousness.

A BLUFFER'S GUIDE TO . . . DOCTOR WHO

Launched in 1963 to fill the gap between the football results and *Juke Box Jury*, Doctor Who is the great-grandaddy of British TV sci-fi, albeit a great-grandaddy that's outlived most of its younger, flashier descendents and ended up having extensive plastic surgery to make itself, against all odds, a flagship show for BBC1 in the early part of the twenty-first century. And it's *still* on after the football results. The central character – who's actually called 'the Doctor' and not 'Doctor Who', lest you risk the wrath of a million irate fanboys – is a rogue but kindly Time Lord who deserted his dreary home planet Gallifrey in search of galactic adventure, travelling in an unreliable time machine called the TARDIS (capital letters, please), and often joined by one or more travelling companions who are usually human, usually female and usually happy to desert their day jobs (which have ranged from Warrior of the Sevateem to cabin crew with Air Australia) to embark on a year or two of inter-galactic derring-do and monster-bashing. Oh, and the TARDIS is – naturally – disguised as a 1960s police box, primarily because its 'chameleon circuit' – which would otherwise allow it to change shape to blend in with its surroundings – has been broken for the best part of fifty years. We're not sure exactly why, but suspect it might have something to do with a shoestring BBC budget.

The Doctor has so far been killed nine times, and on each occasion has handily 'regenerated' into an entirely different actor. To date, we've seen William Hartnell (the grumpy, white-haired one); Patrick Troughton (the impish, tramp-like one); Jon Pertwee (the dashing one with the big nose); Tom Baker (the mad one with the scarf); Peter Davison (the shy one in the cricket gear); Colin Baker (the shouty one in the loud suit); and Sylvester McCoy (the Scottish one who rolled his 'rrrrr's). In 1989, at the end of McCoy's third series, the show was cancelled, returning briefly in 1996 as a glitzy American TV movie with Paul McGann (the handsome one in the frock coat) and then permanently to BBC1 in 2005, first with Christopher Eccleston (the Northern one in the leather jacket) and then David Tennant (the skinny one with the trainers) in the lead role.

Popular *Doctor Who* catchphrases include 'Exterminate', 'Reverse The Polarity Of The Neutron Flow', 'I'm Pretty Sure That's Cromer' and 'Of Course, It's Not As Good As It Used To Be'. If you want to impress a *Doctor Who* fan, tell him (and it almost certainly *will* be a him) that you might be able to lay your hands on the missing 1968 story 'Fury From the Deep'. If you want to annoy a *Doctor Who* fan, tell him that 'Fury From the Deep' was rubbish, and not a patch on anything written by Russell T. Davies. If you want to go to a *Doctor Who* convention, make sure you're prepared to spend a weekend in a hotel with four hundred people who would genuinely kill a man to get their hands on *any* of the missing episodes.

November 2005. It's a bitterly cold evening in Stockton-on-Tees, and I'm sitting by the window of a first-floor hotel bar watching a scuffle break out between two women in the High Street below. Thankfully, should the violence escalate, reinforcements are at hand. Perched on the bar-stool opposite me is a Cyberman. To my right, a man in the full, flowing regalia of a Prydonian Chapter Time Lord is eating a packet of prawn cocktail crisps and reading the local paper.

I'm at the *Doctor Who* convention, and the culture shock has hit me faster than a Dalek on a dry ski-slope. A turn of phrase that, in the simmering, violent atmosphere of the High Steet outside, might just earn me a good kicking. But in the secluded alternate universe of the Swallow Hotel this weekend, it's hardly likely to raise an eyebrow.

Although to be fair, Cybermen aren't especially noted for their facial hair. Which is more than can be said for the two mini-skirted harridans trading punches in the taxi queue outside.

The convention – called Dimensions, and taking up an entire floor of this towering red-brick construction, a venue normally reserved for conferences, wedding receptions and extra-marital naughtiness – hasn't really started in earnest. This is the Friday-night get-together, a relaxed precursor to the weekend's activities. Sign in, pick up your name tag, and take part in a *Doctor Who*-themed pub quiz in which questions like 'What is the rank of the Time Lord in charge of Gallifreyan security in "The Deadly Assassin"?' are greeted with snorts of derision from men in Edwardian cricketing costumes who are already grumbling that last year's quiz was far more of a challenge.

For some time now I've been keenly people-watching, mentally placing my fellow attendees into shamefully stereotypical categories.

Making up a sizeable – and very vocal – minority of the punters are the fancy-dressers, hardy convention veterans to a man. And, with much less frequency, a woman. They're loud and brash and they all seem to know each other. They're dressed up as their favourite Doctor, or their favourite monster, or their favourite companion, or the Time Lord in charge of Gallifreyan security in 'The Deadly Assassin'. (Just in case the suspense is too much to bear any more, it's the Castellan.)

Then there are the fanboys: the pale, nervous, skinny men – and these are, without exception, all men – who fulfil the classic stereotype of sci-fi fans. They're not loud, they're not brash, and they don't appear to know anybody. At all. Most of them probably spend far too much time logged onto internet message boards, calling themselves *The_Castellan* and complaining that the question should have specified that their namesake in 'The Deadly Assassin' was only in charge of security in *The Capitol*, and that his jurisdiction didn't extend across the *whole* of the planet Gallifrey.

They're not dressed up, unless you consider Undertones-era Feargal Sharkey to be a *Doctor Who* character. Which he isn't, although The Fall's Mark E. Smith does bear more than a passing resemblance to Davros.

There's also a sizeable strata of fandom that places the convention into a dimension even further removed from the shirt-sleeved, Smirnoff Ice-fuelled gritty Northern madness outside. *Doctor Who* has a massive gay following. Darting between Doctors, Cybermen and bespectacled internet Castellans are dozens of stunningly handsome young men dressed in designer gear so immaculately tasteful and tight that it makes Jon Pertwee look like . . . well, Worzel Gummidge. Even the Cyberman sitting opposite has put the conquest of the galaxy on the back burner and is eyeing up a sculpted Jude Law lookalike swigging Blue WKD over by the lifts.

I'm deep in conversation with Nathan, gleefully swapping

stories of our respective childhood screaming fits. Slouched in louche, crimson armchairs by a television on which *EastEnders* is merrily burbling to itself, we realise that we're being loomed over by a tall, brightly ginger, serious-looking fan, eyeing the room with an imperious gaze and holding a fluorescent-pink rucksack at a fully extended arm's length. It's difficult to decide whether he has the look of a trained killer about him or simply the traumatised thousand-yard stare of a man who's seen 'Terror of the Zygons' just that one time too many.

'What do you think is in his bag?' I ask.

'Peter Davison's severed head,' replies Nathan.

I've come to know Nathan primarily through Outpost Gallifrey. Yes, the dreaded internet message board, an addictive online community that has stolen my soul and around half my waking hours. He's wiry and garrulous, with a shock of unruly, sandy hair and an infectiously loud laugh that ack-acks round the bar like a World War I machine gun. He seems to have spent much of the last twenty years immersed in sci-fi fandom, and – like a grizzled Vietnam veteran – has seen sights that no man should ever have to endure. Later in the weekend, he'll produce his collection of late 1980s Janet Ellis fanzines. I love him.

It took me a few days to reveal to Sorcha that I'd spent several hundred pounds of what we'd tacitly agreed was 'holiday money' on a handful of sci-fi and cult TV conventions, in some vague, weak-minded attempt to recapture the freewheeling, fantasy-loving innocence of my childhood. There can't be many men on Teesside who have had to utter the phrase 'Do you fancy Peterborough for your holidays this summer?' to their loved one, especially when the follow-up rationale concerns a weekend in a Holiday Inn with Craig Charles and Danny John-Jules. She wasn't enormously enthusiastic, and the week of eye-rolling and monosyllabic conversations that followed began to drag me back into the real world. And this from a woman who – the first time I'd met her – was serving behind the bar of my local pub brazenly sporting a *Red Dwarf* 'Smeg Off' T-shirt. She was the first woman I'd ever seen wearing any item of sci-fi memorabilia, and only the second woman I'd ever met who could drink a pint of Flying Herbert in less than twenty seconds. We were living together within months, despite her best friend's solemn warning that I looked 'like a young Fred West'.

Since then, however, she seems to have entered something of a state of sci-fi denial. *Doctor Who*, she'd declared, is the refuge of 'geeks and weirdos', although – with the kind of resigned sigh that often accompanies packed suitcases and hastily scribbled letters of farewell – she had reluctantly agreed to transport me home at the end of the inevitable beer marathon with Nathan, on the strict proviso that I'd be ready for collection at midnight on the dot. Like a sci-fi Cinderella, I'll cast off my Time Lord robes and revert back to my usual corduroy ensemble, then jump into the TARDIS, shimmering back into its workaday appearance of Sorcha's mud-splattered Toyota Starlet.

I told her this with a sense of irresistible boyish enthusiasm. 'Whatever,' she'd replied, and gone back to poring over our mortgage statement.

I push our troubled relationship to the very back of my mind. As the doof-doof of drums sounds the end of *EastEnders*, Nathan and I chat about the new series of *Doctor Who*, which we've both watched with a sense of shameless, child-like, open-mouthed wonder. The weeks leading up to Christopher Eccleston's debut episode had been almost unbearable for me. With over a month to go, I'd lain awake in bed next to

Sorcha, furtively counting down the number of sleeps to the blessed day itself. The last time I'd remembered doing this was in the run-up to Christmas 1984, when leaked reports from my parents' clandestine shopping expeditions suggested that a brand-new ZX Spectrum might be heading my way. Much to Sorcha's chagrin, I'd spent the day of broadcast itself ensuring that everything in the house was ready, and that nothing could possibly taint my forthcoming viewing experience. I'd cleaned and tidied the front room with a terrifying missionary zeal, while she stomped angrily away, muttering under her breath a phrase that might – just *might* – have been 'fucking obsessive compulsive disorder'. But I just couldn't allow a stray pile of clothes or an un-vacuumed laminate floor to detract from the magical moments to come. When the opening credits rolled, and that unmistakable tunnelled vortex sucked me into the TV screen for the first time in sixteen years, I cried.

As we speak, I notice that a nervy Castellan is now lurking behind us, staring nervously at the lifts and fumbling with a flashing sonic screwdriver.

'He's probably concerned about the basement,' says Nathan. 'It says "Minus One" on the button in the lift. I met one fan last year who was worried it would take him to a different dimension.'

At this point, noting through the window that the customary air of simmering unpleasantness in the High Street is also in danger of entering a different dimension, I decide to make good my escape, tramping downstairs into the cold night air. It's 10pm, and the High Street is packed with revellers, with scantily clad queues snaking out from the busiest clubs and bars, and a heavy police presence already apparent. The Toyota TARDIS awaits, hidden under a tree in a deserted pay-and-display car park behind the Swallow

Hotel. Taking a last furtive glance to ensure Rucksack Man hasn't followed me out onto the street, I dematerialise for the night.

The next morning is, if anything, even colder. The sky – as *The_Castellan* would undoubtedly point out – is roughly the same shade of grey as a Special Weapons Dalek, and stinging flecks of hard-edged Teesside rain are whistling horizontally through the air. I cross the choppy River Tees via the wobbly Millennium Bridge, which shakes and rattles its way into the back of the Castlegate Shopping Centre, with its permanent aroma of butchers' shops and floor polish.

The babble of excited chatter hits me as I ascend the hotel stairs just after 9am. The convention has started in earnest.

And the fancy-dressers are out in force. Amid the usual parade of Tom Baker and Peter Davison outfits are some admirable attempts to create more recent *Doctor Who* costumes, including a couple of laudable stabs at the tight demob suit and Converse trainers ensemble that new incumbent David Tennant has adopted. Although, unfortunately, few of the brave Tenth Doctors at Dimensions come within a whisker of matching Tennant's slimline figure, and it's hard to look at any of them without thinking of Alexei Sayle.

I've dressed up as the Doctor myself, but not for twenty-three years. In 1982, I'd persuaded my long-suffering primary-school teachers Mrs Moore and Mr Millward to allow me to write and produce a short *Doctor Who* play to be staged in our school assembly. Shamelessly casting myself as the Doctor, I'd stolen a black curly wig from the middle school dressing-up box, and draped myself in one of my grandad's old scarves, liberated from the back of the wardrobe for the first time in decades. I recorded sound effects myself, trying to emulate the wheezing, groaning mechanics of the TARDIS by breathing heavily into a portable tape recorder on our dining-room table, despite my dad's earnest protestations that I was 'spitting on his chips'. The play itself never came to fruition, my brave new vision for 1980s *Doctor Who* eventually falling apart in a flurry of script problems, ego clashes and disastrous production decisions. We were nothing if not authentic.

I still remember the feeling of authority and well-being that stepping into the Doctor's clothes gave me as a child, and can only imagine that today's adult dresser-uppers feel the same sense of empowerment. I wonder if their choice of Doctor somehow reflects their own character traits – the would-be Tom Bakers feeling bohemian and flippant, the pseudo Peter Davisons more gentle and fair-minded. Although one skinny fan in a Jon Pertwee cape falls someway short of his own Doctor's unflappable persona when he emerges from the gentlemen's toilets to find a fully functional Dalek racing towards him with alarming velocity. 'Did you have a nice wee?' it barks, pinning him to the wall as the colour drains from his cheeks. 'I hope you washed your hands.'

Trooping diligently through the hotel, I emerge blinking into the Swallow Hotel's ironically titled Summer Room, a vast, cold function space being used this weekend to host the convention's Q&A sessions. Rows of neatly arranged plastic chairs fill the room, and at the far end is a makeshift stage, behind which hangs a backdrop of the new TARDIS console room, its vivid green and orange tones like the aftermath of an explosion in some lurid 1970s sweetshop.

The room is playing host to a panel with two of the old series' best-remembered monsters. Like a tousle-haired Greek god sprayed from head to foot in gold body paint and – crucially – sporting ping-pong balls for eyes, Bernard Holley appeared in 1971's 'The Claws of Axos', playing the villainous Axon Leader opposite Jon Pertwee as the Doctor and Roger Delgado's impeccably sinister Master. Tall and suavely dignified, with swept-back silver hair and a navy blue blazer, he now cuts an equally impressive figure, with the effortless authority of a rural GP or a recently retired magistrate. As I take my seat in the main hall, he's waiting in the wings to make his entrance. Hastily deserting his own seat with a terrifying velocity, a bearded Tom Baker-alike muscles past him. 'I'll be back in a minute, Bernard. I'm just going to the toilet,' he shouts, in a Geordie accent so thick and impenetrable that anyone attempting to wade through it would be well advised to first invest in a sturdy rope and a carbide lamp. The erstwhile Axon Leader looks on, bemused.

He's accompanied by the shorter, slightly frailer-looking figure of David Gooderson, whose one shot at portraying Davros – the twisted scientific genius behind the dreaded Daleks – came in 1979's 'Destiny of the Daleks'. I'm suddenly swept back twenty-six years in a Stockton-based time eddy, arriving at a crucial juncture in my history of sci-fi obsession . . .

CRUCIAL MOMENTS IN FANDOM HISTORY NUMBER ONE: THE DAY I STOPPED BEING SCARED OF DOCTOR WHO

It's Saturday 1 September 1979, and guess where I am? That's right, I'm in the Atlantic lowlands of Nicaragua, on the banks of the Rio Coco, attempting to aid the newly established Sandanistas establish political stability in the face of adversity from the deposed Somoza regime. No, not really. I'm at my gran's bungalow in Acklam once again. It's just after teatime, so there'll be a tray of Blue Riband biscuits on the coffee table next to my customary mug of cold milk, and it's the start of the football season, so my dad will be moaning about Middlesbrough's results. But I don't care – I'm curled in the armchair by the front-room window, and *Doctor Who* is about to start.

It's been months since the programme was last on air, and the Doctor and I are still enjoying a fractious love-hate relationship. Even though I'm now a sturdy six-year-old, there have still been moments when the programme is too much for me. But with the dawn of this new series I'm prepared to wipe the slate clean and offer the Doctor a fresh start in his bid to claim my affections. The title of the story alone sends a frisson of excitement through my skinny, tracksuit-clad body. 'Destiny of the Daleks'. I've heard of the Daleks from Uncle Trevor, but I've never seen one on TV until now.

From the opening sequences I'm gripped. The humour – crowbarred in, I later discover, by jobbing script editor Douglas Adams – goes a little over my head, but it's the setting that intrigues me more than any of the dialogue. The TARDIS (capital letters, remember) lands in a bleak, desolate landscape of dust-blown boulders and scrubby gorse, and I'm convinced that the location is a remote beauty spot on the local moors that we regularly visit with my outdoors-loving dad, whiling away the Sunday afternoons after toasted scones and *Weekend World*. It's known to all on Teesside as 'the Sheepwash', and it isn't difficult to guess what it's used for. Clue: it isn't for scrubbing pigs, drying cows or combing horses.

By the time the end credits roll, I've had my first glimpse of a genuine TV Dalek (completely failing to notice that the pepperpots in this episode have been visibly battered around in a dusty BBC store-room. They have more peeling grey paint on their bodies than my dad's rusting Triumph Toledo) and – even more significantly – I've managed, for the first time ever, to make it to the end of an episode without being scared at all. I feel like punching the air and celebrating, which is more than any Middlesbrough player has managed in recent memory. Within a week or two, it's my first day back for a brand-new term at school, and I write a breathless story about the Daleks invading the Sheepwash – no doubt menacing myself and Richard Moxham, even at this early stage the butt of my sci-fi malevolence. I'm late out from my dinner for some reason (probably choking on a block of Spam fritter, or rendered immobile by a glob of pink custard) and, by the time I arrive on our sun-bleached school field, Richard and the rest of my chums are prowling around a rustling hedgerow, arms outstretched, barking threatening commands in a high-pitched staccato.

'What are you playing?' I ask as he passes.

'DA-LEKS,' he retorts, in a monotone shriek.

I decide, with an admirable eye for the contrary, to take on the role of David Gooderson's Davros – the evil, half-Dalek tyrant confronted by the Doctor at the end of episode two – and trundle around the football pitch accordingly, mouthing gravelly, motor-mouthed monologues to myself. If you'd told me that, twenty-six years later, I'd be standing in a corridor with the genuine article, I'd have had your Blue Riband biscuits checked for hallucinogenics. Although it's hard to imagine there'd be much of a result – everyone knows it's Jaffa Cakes that are the trippy shit.

Back in the real world, Holley and Gooderson are warmly convivial, with a well-rehearsed selection of sepia-tinted stories. Bernard repeats, to the fans' delight, his immortal Axon war cry 'I will suck the Earth dry.' David, meanwhile, talks warmly of working alongside Tom Baker, and his lengthy career as a jobbing actor in the long-ago likes of *Bergerac* and *Tenko*. It's like watching a touring stage revival of *Pebble Mill at One*. I expect an Aran-sweatered Bob Langley to emerge from the shadows at any moment, clutching a handful of knitted Daleks and introducing Elkie Brooks.

Afterwards, I toy with the idea of joining the autograph queue and asking the erstwhile Axon Leader to sign 'To Bob, I will suck the Earth dry. Best wishes, Bernard Holley' on my crumpled Dimensions programme. But, to my surprise, I find myself mortified with fear at the very prospect. *Doctor Who* has been such an integral part of my childhood that it feels somehow immoral to steal even a second of time away from its associated actors, blighting their day with my stammering requests for autographs and clumsily posed photos. Even though, irrationally, I know perfectly well that's why they're here.

I'm interrupted in this guilty stream of consciousness by Nathan, who apparently has no such qualms and is happily brandishing a glossy picture of himself, his five-year-old daughter and Nicola 'Peri' Bryant, taken in the convention's photo studio on the second floor of the hotel in exchange for fifteen pounds. It looks disturbingly like a family portrait, and he jokes that he'll be placing it on the mantelpiece in his front room and telling unsuspecting visitors to the house that Bryant was his first wife.

As the afternoon lengthens, and pints of beer in varying shades of brown start to appear in the hands of the more daring attendees, I watch Bryant and Mark 'Turlough' Strickson

– the undisputed sex bombs of 1980s *Doctor Who* – being quizzed by the masses. This time, the onstage interviewer could scarcely be a more appropriate choice to draw to a close *Doctor Who*'s first major convention day since the programme's glorious return to the Saturday-evening schedules. It's Avon from *Blake's 7*.

A natural successor to *Doctor Who* on my great, lifelong sci-fi journey, *Blake's 7* was the tricky A-level to *Doctor Who*'s breezy GCSE. Although admittedly, in later series, modules on sci-fi grittiness were replaced by lessons in advanced campery and practical, vocational scenery-chewing. It occupied a vital part of the Monday-night TV landscape, and gave brilliantly charismatic actor Paul Darrow the chance to shine as the scheming, sneering computer genius Avon, a character who – in the words of my dad – 'looked like he had a crisp up his arse and was trying hard not to break it'.

As the trio elicit questions from the crowd, a minor microphone malfunction reduces one otherwise articulate-sounding fan to a stammering Norman Collier impersonation. '. . . like . . . ask Mark about . . . Mike Read . . . TARDIS Wendy House . . .' is the resulting enquiry. Strickson uses all of his convention experience to translate, and returns with a seamless stream of 1980s-themed showbiz anecdotes that begin with his incarceration in the aforementioned Wendy House, live on BBC1's sprawling kids' magazine show *Saturday Superstore* and end with an affectionate tribute to veteran radio actor Valentine Dyall.

Known to a generation of terrified youngsters as 'the Man in Black', Dyall had shot to fame in the 1940s, his brilliantly velvet and sinister tones providing the narration to popular horror anthology series *Appointment With Fear*. In 1983, in failing health, he'd made his final television appearance in

Strickson's debut story 'Mawdryn Undead', portraying the Black Guardian, a cosmic avenging angel whose dark and all-pervading nature was only slightly undermined by the presence of a badly stuffed crow perched wonkily on his head. 'We had to organise filming around him,' smiles Strickson, 'because he lived in Brighton and would only travel to London between ten o'clock and three o'clock, when his pensioner's railcard came into operation.'

Back in the bar, Nathan has started drinking in earnest. As I arrive, he's deep in conversation with John, a bearded and erudite fan who curiously manages to bear a passing resemblance to both a young John Peel and Whispering Bob Harris. He's also, I notice immediately, the man who said, '. . . like . . . ask Mark about . . . Mike Read . . . TARDIS Wendy House . . .' to Mark Strickson. We shake hands warmly and, as more and more pints of John Smith's bitter arrive at the table, I find my eyes starting to sink pleasantly into the back of my head, my backside starting to sink pleasantly into the back of the chair, and my tongue – for reasons I can't quite recollect – embarking on a passionate defence of Stephanie de Sykes and her immortal *Crossroads* spin-off hit 'Born with a Smile on My Face'. We talk of life, love and the little-remembered episode from 1975 when Noele Gordon's wedding car was inexplicably chauffeured by Larry Grayson.

The bar thins out slowly, and our group extends to include the newly arrived Toyota TARDIS-owner Sorcha. She has arrived to take both me and it home, although at present it's debatable as to which one of us will be spending the night on the drive.

'You're early!' I hiccup, noting her frosty glare as Nathan transports the latest round of drinks from the bar. 'You said you were coming at midnight!' Somewhere in the beer-sodden muddle of my mind, it's barely half past nine and the evening is young, and filled with potential. Sorcha wordlessly taps her watch to reveal that it's actually twenty past twelve. The tension is only defused when John welcomes her warmly, and coerces her to reveal that her earliest memory of *Doctor Who* was an episode that she's convinced kicked off her life-long fear of spiders – a story in which the Time Lady Romana picks up an intergalactic coconut and inexplicably holds it to her face, cracking the fruit open and unleashing onto her cheek a giant arachnid clearly constructed from pipe cleaners and buttons. Very early in our relationship, I'd identified the story as 1980's 'Full Circle' – set in the strange alternate universe of E-Space, where physics work differently and spiders are rubbish – and dug out the video to show her in an attempt to expunge her deep-seated childhood trauma, convinced that the nature of the scene as viewed through adult eyes would be enough to reverse twenty years of spider-related anguish. Five years of therapy later, she'd just about recovered sufficiently to watch the new series of *Doctor Who* without having to glimpse it furtively through her fingers.

The conversation, in my mind, lasts ten minutes. The conversation, in the real world, lasts nearly three hours. It's 3am before she manages to persuade me, as John wobbles to the bar once more, that 'one for the space-time continuum' is really not an option she's prepared to consider. I'm dragged bodily from the bar, and Nathan – opportunistic as ever – manages to coax a lift home as well. As we pass through the High Street, a substantial fight is breaking out by the town hall, and a blockade of police cars is moving in to dispel the trouble. 'Where are the Axons when you need them?' I slur, and Nathan's unmistakable laugh ack-acks around the car. Sorcha, surprisingly, seems considerably less amused. I close my eyes and dream strange, twisted dreams of Stephanie de Sykes and Blue Riband biscuits.

BLOODY STUPID THINGS I HAVE DONE IN THE NAME OF FANDOM NUMBER ONE: BUILDING A FULL-SIZED K-9

It's February 1984, and myself and my new best friend, Doug Simpson, are entrenched in Doug's dad's garage putting the finishing touches to our full-sized model K-9. Doug's dad is a carpenter with a burgeoning rabbit-hutch business, and Doug is more adept with a hacksaw and a smoothing plane than most eleven-year-olds are with cardboard and scissors. Me included, and in recognition of my ineptness I've been relegated to cutting out the robot mutt's ears from an old Tudor crisps box found abandoned at the back of the workshop. I've probably removed a couple of fingertips already.

K-9 is our first finished project. He's solid, made of wood, and painted with grey Dulux Matt Finish from Yarm's modest hardware store, presumably part of a job lot left over from decorating the nearby Young Offenders Institute. We've constructed him on gloomy school evenings and freezing weekends amid a private tirade of ill-informed filth, Doug being Levendale Primary School's recognised amateur expert on all matters sexual. We'll be at secondary school within months, and are enjoying a last fling of innocence before puberty arrives, although Doug already has a voice deep enough to rattle crockery at twenty paces. We're obsessed with the vintage 'nuddy calendar' hidden behind a dirty overall at the back of the workshop, a long-abandoned relic displaying enough female pubic hair to carpet a modest stairwell.

Although admittedly, at this stage in our development, we wouldn't have a clue what to do with any of it. Given the opportunity, we'd probably use it to give K-9 a Frankie Goes to Hollywood hairstyle.

'Finished,' says Doug, sticking on the dog's ears with some carefully adhered Bostik. 'Look at that, what a fucking beauty.'

'What should we do with him now?' I ask, idly seizing the Bostik to reapply a severed finger.

'Photo shoot,' replies Doug, with the seasoned, sassy confidence of an eleven-year-old media whore. 'We'll have to take him to your house, though – my dad's camera's shagged.'

It's half a mile from Doug's house to mine, along the busy main road that runs straight downhill to the dreaded Yarm High Street. Safe to say the sight of two tousled-haired eleven-year-olds pushing a full-sized K-9 along a bustling suburban highway doesn't go unnoticed amongst Yarm's gentlemen motorists. This afternoon is the first time in my life I've seen anyone make a fully fledged 'wanker' sign.

Half an hour later, we trundle K-9 into my parents' drive and push him into the garden, pressing my poor, giggling mum into service as our resident David Bailey. I convince myself that our nonplussed collie, Ricky, is actually a strange, mutated, hitherto unseen Dalek, genetically modified especially by Davros to have a mane of shaggy auburn hair and an insatiable desire for intergalactic Bonios. We're finished in time for the start of *Grange Hill*, and I generously leave Doug to push K-9 home by himself. I've no doubt, two decades on, that he enthusiastically pressed into service a 'wanker' sign of his own, behind my unsuspecting back as he bade me a fond farewell. By the end of the week, K-9 is being proudly paraded in assembly before a packed Levendale Primary School hall. Our amazingly hairy headmaster, Mr Chalkley, seizes the chance to lace our project with some ill-advised educational content.

'Of course, we all know K-9 from *Doctor Who*,' he pontificates, 'but can anyone tell me why he's actually called K-9?'

The hall falls into silence. There's an excruciating stand-off that seems to last an eon before a tentative arm protrudes from the infants, a terrified-looking four-year-old girl cowering beneath her own raised hand. 'Yes!' roars Mr Chalkley, his eyes aflame with the fires of knowledge. 'Do you know the answer?'

'No,' she replies. 'What's *Doctor Who*?'

It's a salutary lesson in my formative fandom history. It's great to have a passion for your favourite films and programmes, but you have to accept that the rest of the world is unlikely to give a toss. Still, I console myself with the possibility that that innocent four-year-old girl is now a proud, intelligent twenty-six-year-old who watches the new *Doctor Who* with her own wide-eyed children, perhaps explaining to them the mysterious origins of K-9's acronymic moniker. Failing that, she's probably in a taxi queue outside a Stockton High Street nightclub, swigging Smirnoff Ice and knocking seven bells out of the woman in front.

Twenty-one years later, I abandon K-9 once again. It's ten thirty on Sunday morning, and I feel like I've been extermi-nated through a hedge backwards. I spend twenty minutes exhaling noisily in the Summer Room before reluctantly calling it a day. Onstage, David Brierley – the voice of K-9 in five stories, starting with the legendary 'Destiny of the Daleks' – is providing a drily agreeable supply of thespian anecdotes, but I'm too hungover to face it. I end up back in the bar, crumpled into an armchair like a discarded Slitheen skin suit, alternating tentative sips on a pint of tap water and a large, black coffee. As I dissolve into misery, I hear a sombre announcement echoing from the Summer Room. 'Some of our guests are running slightly late, but we'll keep you informed of their movements,' we are solemnly promised. 'We *can* tell you that Peter Davison is currently at the Chiswick Roundabout.'

I'm soon joined by a remarkably chipper-looking John, bravely glugging on a lunchtime pint, who tells me gleefully that the series of explosions that rocked the hotel at four in the morning were apparently the result of an over-enthusiastic fan setting off a firework in his room, and not a Dalek saucer attack as a small number of terrified duvet-clutching Castellans had initially feared.

The television set is still burbling merrily to itself, although the Swallow has now surrendered so completely to *Doctor Who* madness that any semblance of terrestrial programming has been replaced by a succession of fan-produced DVDs, all of which are no doubt available to buy with matching spines on a trestle table in the merchandise room. In the current offering, a succession of fake Doctors – all decked out in random combinations of scarves, frock coats and floppy-brimmed hats – seem to be battling some unspecified horror in a baffling array of showcase locations from bona fide *Doctor Who* TV adventures. It seems curiously plot-free and meaningless, but then – in my current condition – so does real life.

Peter Davison, thankfully, is in better form. As the after-noon wears on, he escapes the clutches of the dreaded Chiswick Roundabout and emerges onto the Summer Room stage to thunderous applause. His voice has dropped at least an octave since his early 1980s heyday in the TARDIS, suggesting that he's rather more fond of Marlboro Lights than the good Doctor ever was, but he's a hilarious and engaging ambassador for the show. He enthusiastically throws himself upon the mercy of the audience's questions, and Rucksack Man's hand is thrust skyward at a velocity that threatens to drag the rest of him into geostationary orbit.

'Peter, I'd just like to ask how you thought the three recent *Star Wars* prequels compared to the new series of *Doctor Who* starring Christopher Eccleston,' he asks.

'I'm not sure, to be honest,' stammers a confused-looking Davison. 'I've got to admit, I haven't actually seen any of the *Star Wars* prequels. Why, how do you think they compare?'

A dramatic pause. 'I dunno. I haven't seen them either,' comes the perfectly timed reply, greeted by a thunderous wall of laughter so overwhelming that it prompts Rucksack Man to delve into his bag and produce a luminous, four-foot lightsaber that he proceeds to wave threateningly under the Fifth Doctor's nose before spinning round in his seat and turning his attentions to the rest of the room.

It's been, in a nutshell, an entertaining and eye-opening weekend. And yet I can't help but feel that I've fallen some way short of the full convention experience. Yes, I've slouched through panels with engaging *Doctor Who* celebrities and drunk myself insensible in the company of a man who said, '. . . like . . . ask Mark about . . . Mike Read . . . TARDIS Wendy House . . .' to Mark Strickson. But while Nathan, Rucksack Man and three hundred other *Doctor Who* fans have been stampeding through the Swallow collecting autographs, buying ridiculous merchandise and paying for photos with actresses that they'll later pretend to have been married to, I've done nothing but passively observe.

I have, I decide, been the convention equivalent of the Time Lords. Fusty, pompous, stuffed shirts doomed by their endless ancient traditions never to interfere – maintaining a dry, dreary distance from the wondrous, vibrant workings of the universe. I solemnly vow to myself that, at the next convention I attend, I will throw aside my cynical inhibitions, leaving my metaphorical clothes on the beach of ordinariness like some galactic Reginald Perrin, delving naked into a sea of science-fiction madness and maybe – just maybe – summoning enough courage to put my hand up and ask a question to a panel.

In the meantime, as Davison's session draws to a rapturous close and a slightly subdued charity auction wraps up the weekend's activities, I say my farewells to Nathan and John and wander out, blinking, into the bright, white daylight of a chilly Sunday afternoon. Stockton High Street is deserted, and as I shuffle past darkened pound shops, shuttered-up bookmakers and bakeries where pasties come to wither, groan and die, I'm overtaken sporadically by fellow convention attendees, all of us being slowly absorbed back into normal society, lazily burning off our *Doctor Who* obsession like fast-falling meteorites being snuffed out in the Earth's freezing atmosphere. It seems as though the humdrum has won, that the weekend has been a dangerously insurgent irrelevance, now stamped out and frowned upon by the agents of the everyday – work and food and pound stores and pubs and things that would never, ever, in a million years, involve a fully grown man dressed in the full, elaborate regalia of a Prydonian Chapter Time Lord. Reality beckons me onwards, the mortgage statement an inevitable consequence. And now that the weekend is over, I don't want them any more. I want to go off with the Doctor, and explore the universe in a rickety old TARDIS. I want to actually *be* in *The Battle to Save Earth*.

And then I see Rucksack Man thirty yards ahead of me, disappearing round the side of Woolworths, waving his lightsaber with carefree abandon, and veering dangerously towards two men who have bought a five-foot cardboard Dalek in a *Doctor Who* charity auction and are trying to work out the best way to fit it into the back of a Ford Fiesta.

And I realise my adventures have barely begun.

THE BATTLE TO SAVE EARTH

By Robert Fischer (Aged Eight And A Third)
Saturday 28 March 1981
PART THREE

Then the leader of the Birdmen, Gortis,
shouted 'Inside this ball are the Data
tapes of the planet Davrock!' I thumped
Gortis on the back. He dropped the ball
of tapes and I caught them. 'In that
case,' I said, 'I'll take them!' 'Stop!'
the man on the platform shouted. 'Who
are you?' I asked him. 'I am klebba Obion, leader of the
Imperial robots,' he answered. I grabbed hold of my laser
rifle and started to fire at klebba. 'Guards!' klebba shouted.
'Take him!' Several guards came rushing towards me. I did a
karate chop on one's shoulder. He fell onto the floor, dead.
One of them pulled a rifle from his belt and started firing
laser bolts at me. I dodged past them and threw the tapes to
Richard. Then I shot one of the guards and threw his gun to
Richard. Richard caught the gun and also started firing
wildly. Snakemen were being shot in all directions, and Birdmen
were trying to shoot us. klebba and Zero began retreating down
a corridor. But back in the hall the battle was still going
on. klebba and Zero went racing back down the corridor. They
ran through a doorway and into the main control room. klebba
sat down in the pilot's seat. 'Put the scanner onto the great
hall,' klebba ordered. A robot pressed some switches and pulled
some levers and a picture of the hall we were fighting in
appered on the screen. In the hall the battle had not
finished yet. Control panels on walls burst into flames
from laser bolts.
Richard and I had not given up yet...

To be continued...

STAR WARS

'That's no moon ... that's a service station.'

IT'S 4.30AM ON A wincingly cold December morning. A bleak northerly wind is not so much whistling around my face as hammering out 'The Imperial March' from *The Empire Strikes Back* on my eardrums.

On the drive, in the pitch black, with nothing but a NatWest debit card to help me, I'm trying to scrape half an inch of ice from the windscreen of Sorcha's Toyota Starlet. As I do so, my mobile phone cuts through the night air with a sharp-edged bleep. It's finally registered a text message sent yesterday evening by my old school friend Brucie, currently resident in the impossibly named mining village of Penrhiwceiber, twenty minutes north of Cardiff.

'It's getting chilly down here, we might have to cut open the Tauntauns,' he warns. It's a reference to Han Solo's heroic attempt to save Luke Skywalker's life on the ice planet of Hoth by placing him inside the steaming carcass of his recently deceased galactic camel.

If Han Solo had found the ice planet of Hoth something of a threat to the Rebel Alliance's brass monkeys, he should have tried spending a winter on Teesside. Twenty-eight years after

I first heard it, I'm haunted by a prissy prediction made by C-3PO in the opening minutes of the very first *Star Wars* film. 'I'm going to regret this,' he chirps, clambering into a rickety escape pod and preparing to launch himself into oblivion. The phrase runs endlessly through my head now, superimposed over the top of 'The Imperial March' as I prepare myself for a ten-hour round-trip to the Welsh capital, and the chance to mingle with a handful of *Star Wars* celebrities.

If Threepio's squat, annoyingly perky sidekick R2-D2 had been present, he would surely, as ever, have cheerily calculated the chances of survival to be approximately 725–1. And that's without taking into consideration the medical dangers inherent in eating Ginster's Cheese and Onion pasties at half past five in the morning.

A BLUFFER'S GUIDE TO . . . STAR WARS

In the great British sci-fi family tree, *Star Wars* is the brash, flash American cousin who came to stay for a fortnight in 1977 and never bothered going home. There are three 'original' films – *Star Wars* from 1977 (later rebranded *A New Hope* by director George Lucas, whose penchant for revisionism is legendary in sci-fi circles), *The Empire Strikes Back* from 1980 and *Return of the Jedi* from 1983. They're famously set 'a long time ago, in a galaxy far, far away', and tell the story of a universe enslaved by the evil 'Empire', a brutal totalitarian regime headed by asthmatic, semi-robotic psychopath Darth Vader, a black-helmeted 'Jedi Knight' who has been seduced by the 'Dark Side' of a mystical, all-pervading energy field known to all as 'the Force'.

Over the course of the original trilogy, Vader and his sinister overlord, Emperor Palpatine, are challenged and overthrown by a gang of motley rebels headed by the feisty Princess Leia (Carrie Fisher), wise-cracking smuggler Han Solo (Harrison Ford) and Luke Skywalker (Mark Hamill), a drippy farmhand from the arid, sun-baked planet Tatooine. Skywalker learns to become a good Jedi himself, before discovering that Vader is in fact the father of both himself and Leia, thus making a generation of grotty schoolkids go 'eew' at the realisation that Luke has spent a sizeable chunk of the previous two and a half films unwittingly snogging his own sister. When he's not slipping the lips to his twin, he's endlessly placating two bickering robots – the camp C-3PO and the cheeky R2-D2 – while Solo seems to exclusively prefer the company of his sidekick Chewbacca, a seven-foot-tall ape-like creature whose two main areas of expertise appear to be chess and sudden physical violence. Oh, and there's also veteran British Oscar-winner Alec Guinness as Obi-Wan Kenobi, an elderly Jedi Knight who gets murdered by Darth Vader two-thirds of the way through the first film, before returning repeatedly as a wobbly ghost with a Ready Brek-style blue shimmer dotted around his extremities. No, really.

Between 1999 and 2005, three blockbusting 'prequels' were released. *The Phantom Menace, Attack of the Clones* and *Revenge of the Sith* – all directed, again, by Lucas – showed Luke's father, Anakin Skywalker, slowly descending into evil, the unimaginable torment of his seduction depicted by Canadian soap star Hayden Christensen as a series of increasingly complex frowns. He's accompanied by his lissom lover Queen Amidala (Natalie Portman) and a young Obi-Wan Kenobi, portrayed by Ewan McGregor, who gamefully spends six years of his life attempting a laudable, Bobby Davro-esque Alec Guinness impersonation. Oh, and there's a strange, frog-like creature called Jar Jar Binks, who seems to have wandered in from a passing Pixar movie.

Notable *Star Wars* catchphrases include 'May The Force Be With You', 'I've Got A Bad Feeling About This', 'Beep-Bop-Bloop-Biddly-Blop' and 'It's Possible He Came In Through The South Entrance'. If you want to annoy a *Star Wars* fan, tell him that you think Jar Jar Binks was a hilarious, rounded character who should be CGIed into future Lucasfilm revisions of the original trilogy. If you want to find a *Star Wars* fan at a crowded party, ping a balloon up to the kitchen ceiling and see who tries to fight it with a rolling pin while their friend sits on the melamine worktop frowning and muttering, 'Trust your feelings, Luke.'

The *Star Wars* Christmas Celebration at Cardiff's Marriott Hotel has been a late addition to my schedule. Penrhiwceiber resident Brucie had dropped it into conversation the previous week, mentioning that he'd been to a summertime *Star Wars* event at the same venue. And tantalisingly revealing that he'd had a long chat with Belfast actor Gerald Home, who – as well as playing various masked monsters and salmon-headed officers in *Return of the Jedi* – had shot to national celebrity as the pivotal figure in a long-running series of British TV commercials. There can't be many actors who can include both 'Tessek of the Mon Calamari' and 'Mr Muscle' on their résumés.

So far, barely a handful of friends have been told about my convention mission. I'm still vaguely fearful that, if word gets out, I could find myself a social pariah in the neighbourhood, with fly-by-night vigilantes daubing ROBIN OF SHERWOOD SCUM across my front-room windows in hastily applied whitewash, and concerned parents marching the streets of

Yarm with placards proclaiming DEATH TO SIE-FI PREVERTS. Sorcha knows, of course, and I've also told my old friend Matthew, an amusingly cynical late-twentysomething journalist, who only recently outed himself to me as a sci-fi fan, casually dropping a reference to 'Terror of the Zygons' into an e-mail that would otherwise have worked perfectly well without allusions to thirty-year-old *Doctor Who* adventures. He's recently departed Teesside and materialised his journalistic TARDIS in Somerset, where his proudest achievement to date is sneaking a picture of Christopher Eccleston in full Ninth Doctor regalia onto the cover of the *Bath Chronicle*'s weekly business supplement. The week after Dimensions, I'd e-mailed him and confessed all, begging for his assistance in snapping me out of this madness.

'You've got to help me,' I'd pleaded. 'I've bought a ticket to a *Robin of Sherwood* convention in Retford.'

'Great,' he'd replied. 'Can I come? I've always wanted to meet Michael Praed.'

Bugger.

By 6am the car is hurtling towards the A19 Southbound, with fellow Teesside *Star Wars* fans Smudge and Wez playing Luke and Chewie to my podgy, pasty-fuelled Han Solo. Wez – a witty Teesside skinhead with a penchant for rare jazz and chocolate cake – is wide awake and sipping coffee from a flask. Smudge – tall, bushy-haired, with a love of vintage Hammer horror films – is sprawled, half-asleep, in the back.

'Told you we'd outrun those Imperial slugs,' I tell them, as our makeshift *Millennium Falcon* hurtles past a convoy of Tesco delivery wagons just approaching the turn-off to Kepwick. It sparks off a torturous tirade of *Star Wars*-related puns, with the car inevitably becoming 'the ship that made the Kepwick run in less than twelve parsecs'. Sadly, when Smudge requests a lengthy toilet break at Trowell Services, the urge to remark that he 'dropped his cargo at the first sign of an Imperial Cruiser' proves impossible to resist.

Like most of our thirtysomething generation, *Star Wars* was a defining moment of our collective childhoods. 'Before Elvis, there was nothing,' John Lennon had once claimed, summing up the dreary mundanity of 1950s existence in one clipped, pithy soundbite. For us, the same was true of *Star Wars*. My four-year-old self in 1977 would have given up his life for a Womble or a Mr Man, but my five-year-old self in 1978 had sold his soul to the Rebel Alliance. Clutching my dad's hand on a freezing, snowswept day, I'd entered Stockton's Odeon cinema a child and come back out again a fully fledged geek.

Oddly enough, in the intervening decades, both of my parents have gone almost out of their way to disassociate themselves from my sci-fi obsession. My mum has no interest whatsoever, and my dad has always maintained that no modern sci-fi efforts have ever surpassed the films of his youth – *Forbidden Planet*, *The Thing from Another World* and *The Day the Earth Stood Still*.

Five days before I'm due to visit Cardiff, he suffers a mild heart attack while out walking the dog, and drives himself to Accident and Emergency where he's instantly admitted to the Cardiac Unit for tests. I drive to North Tees Hospital with my mind in a whirl, and expect to find myself sitting at his bedside, like Luke Skywalker comforting Darth Vader at the gripping, moving finale to *Return of the Jedi*. 'Search your feelings, Father,' I'll say. 'I know there is some sci-fi left in you.'

'It is too late for me, son,' he'll reply, in the deep, commanding tones of every pensionable Teesside male. 'But tell your girlfriend – you were right about me.' He'll then clutch my 1978 *Star Wars Annual* to his chest while I drag him up the ramp of the *Toyota Starlet Imperial Shuttle*.

He is, thankfully, absolutely fine, and tells me to go to Cardiff as planned or he'll never speak to me again. Which I do, although to be on the safe side I don't yet tell him about the other five conventions that I've already blown half my yearly credit-card allowance on.

Sorcha, meanwhile, has spurned another golden opportunity to join me in my quest, offering her usual critical appraisal of the six *Star Wars* films – a curled upper lip and a half-hearted shrug of the shoulders. Her critical appraisal of getting out of bed at four o'clock on a December morning is, surprisingly, even less enthusiastic.

By 10am, we're in Cardiff, and the car is safely ensconced on the second storey of a grey NCP car park that Smudge insists on referring to as 'Docking Bay 94', thus swiftly ending our two-hour moratorium on *Star Wars*-related puns. Turning past Toys 'R' Us into the Marriott Hotel car park, we run slap bang into a platoon of Imperial Stormtroopers marching a frozen-looking Queen Amidala towards the main reception.

These are the UK Garrison, the self-styled 'Definitive Internet Star Wars Costuming Club'. They're a troupe of intrepid volunteers who raise laudable quantities of money for deserving charities by, well . . . squeezing into Stormtrooper outfits and parading captured princesses up and down provincial car parks. The costumes are excellent, and they're posing for photos outside the hotel as we join a queue of shivering fans snaking around the car park from a glass-windowed side door. There are at least a hundred people ahead of us, and – with no sign yet of the hotel doors opening – we hear grumblings and shufflings of feet from some of the more impatient fans. 'Nothing doing,' bellows one burly Welshman into his mobile phone. 'We'll give it another ten minutes and then fuck off.' The small number of children in the queue not wearing plastic Darth Vader helmets have their ears covered up by glowering parents.

Remembering my disappointment with my own detached, lackadaisical performance at Dimensions, I realise this could be the perfect opportunity to get involved. 'Excuse me,' I holler to a passing Stormtrooper, and he stops and cocks his head at me in a disturbingly authentic manner. 'Any chance of a picture?'

'Roger.' He nods, and his voice has the chilling, muffled, resonance of a bona fide *Star Wars* Stormtrooper, a clipped, merciless, electronic bark now employed by tellers at most of the major high-street banks. I hand my camera to Smudge and step out of the queue to stand alongside my new white-uniformed escort, who wastes no time in beckoning over one of his fellow Garrison members. This second Trooper seems to instantly descend into method-acting madness, and places a gloved hand upon my shoulder with a worryingly over-zealous grip.

'On your knees,' he snaps, and I smile quizzically back. 'ON YOUR KNEES!' he repeats, somehow managing to glower through his mask.

'And put your hands on your head!' barks his oppo, as I sink to the pavement and they gleefully strike poses, pointing bulky Imperial blasters at my head for Smudge's photo. As the crowd giggles, I notice that even the burly Welshman behind us has put his fucking off on hold and is now using the mobile phone to take his own picture of the happy threesome. It's a spine-tinglingly authentic *Star Wars* scene, perhaps only slightly undermined by the middle-aged Welsh couple in ski jackets and jeans who choose that precise moment to stride happily from the hotel reception behind us, carrying two Tesco bags and grinning enthusiastically for the cameras.

As I rise to my feet, the Marriott Hotel doors judder open and the crowd slowly begins to shuffle forward. We find ourselves in a long, thin hallway whose far end is dominated by a ceiling-high print of a vintage Death Star corridor, all gun-metal grey and cylindrical lights, draped down to the floor and being used as the backdrop for punters to have 'official' pictures taken with UK Garrison troopers for five pounds a throw. As we pass through, the Garrison's own impassive Darth Vader is posing with an amateur-looking Boba Fett, whose battle-scarred crash helmet and Toys 'R' Us blaster are audaciously combined with a crimson turtle-neck jumper that's slowly riding up a huge, hairy belly – suggesting that his job description of Galactic Bounty Hunter has been recently expanded to also include Mars Bars, Twixes and Caramel Chunky Kit-Kats. He instantly earns the nickname 'Boba Fatt'.

Stretching away from the makeshift Death Star corridor, the hallway has been filled with seemingly the entire annual output of Wales's thriving nationalised trestle-table industry, each of them piled high with sufficient *Star Wars* merchandise to fund another four prequels apiece. It's like a car-boot sale at Mos Eisley Cantina. We peruse towering stacks of TIE Fighters, Sandcrawlers and Imperial Troop Transporters, all seemingly kept boxed and in mint condition since they were first swept from the shelves of deliciously poky, family-run toyshops on hundreds of high streets in the late 1970s. And then my eyes settle on an object that actually makes me feel giddy with a heady combination of nostalgia, longing and vague, nagging resentment. A neatly boxed object that, almost exactly twenty-five years earlier, was the subject of one of the most traumatic yet ultimately character-forming experiences in my long, chequered history as a science-fiction obsessive. As Han Solo himself might say, 'She may not look much, kid, but she's got it where it counts.'

It's the *Millennium Falcon*.

CRUCIAL MOMENTS IN FANDOM HISTORY NUMBER TWO: NOT GETTING THE MILLENNIUM FALCON FOR CHRISTMAS

A long time ago, in a bungalow far, far away . . .

It's Christmas morning, 25 December 1980, and I'm eight years old. I've spent Christmas Eve, as always, at my gran's house, shuffling nervously through *The All-Star Record Breakers* and *Paddington's Christmas*, dashing outside as darkness falls to meet Lisa Wheeldon from the house round the corner, wobbling on our bikes past Mr Murray's newsagent's, and talking about Rude Things around the back of the Endeavour, the strange, enticing grown-ups' pub where my youthful uncle Trevor is drinking Harp Lager, and his new wife, Rose, is tipsy on Cinzano. I'm back home in time to find my gran, my lovely, gentle gran, singing along to *Val Doonican's Very Special Christmas* and sipping from a thimble glass of Harvey's Bristol Cream. I'm allowed to take a tantalising taste, and the burning sweetness pins me to the chenille sofa for at least thirty seconds before I'm back to my usual hyperactive self.

I've barely slept all night. And, snuggled beneath a luridly floral flannelette bedspread, I'm wide awake at 7am, staring silently at the bedroom ceiling, intoxicated by an atmosphere thick with magic and suggestion and promise. It's Christmas morning. *Christmas morning!* For how many nights now have I counted down to this? The answer: 364. And, throughout those nights, only one thought has been paramount in my tiny, excitable mind. Sorry, Jesus (and Val Doonican), but for me, aged eight and a bit, Christmas *is Star Wars*. I'm already the proud owner of a merchandise collection comprehensive enough to have *The All-Star Record Breakers* sniffing around the end of my gran's drive (although she'd probably have chased off

Norris McWhirter with a carpet sweeper) and my bedroom at home is piled high with Palitoy X-Wing Fighters, collapsing TIE Fighters, cardboard Sand Crawlers and a swelling platoon of three-inch action figures that once challenged Richard Moxham's Action Men to a fight and took the eagle-eyed bastards to the cleaners.

Intelligence reports from my mum and gran's pre-Christmas shopping expeditions to Teesside's twin toyshop emporiums – Middlesbrough's exotically named Romer Parrish and Stockton's more prosaic Leslie Brown – have suggested that all kinds of further *Star Wars*-related wondrousness are heading in my direction. And, as I lie fidgeting in the early hours of Christmas morning, determined through some kind of bizarre eight-year-old pride not to be first out of bed, I know exactly what's number one on the list.

The *Millennium Falcon* is Han Solo's rickety, patched-up starship, a Corellian-class freighter capable of attaining 'point five past light speed', and a seminal piece of sci-fi iconography whose distinctive shape was reputedly based on that of a half-eaten hamburger shown to his bemused design team by George Lucas, presumably in muffled mid-chomp. Sadly, I know full well that Palitoy's failure to meet festive demand for the boxed-up toyshop version has been the cause of simmering nationwide tensions. Rumour has it that recent outbreaks of street violence in the St Paul's area of Bristol were not, as first thought, attributable to racial intimidation and a mounting feeling of social injustice, but more down to rumours of a new consignment of *Millennium Falcons* arriving at the local Argos. Six months later, the now-infamous Death Star Playset riots in Toxteth and Brixton would bring the Thatcher administration virtually to its knees. But deep in my pounding eight-year-old heart, I have faith. At this point in my childhood I'm still convinced that life is essentially a series of wonderful, soul-affirming, carefree, joyous moments, where everything works out for the best and there's always beans-on-toast for tea. It's probably telling at this stage that I'm still nine months away from attending my first ever Middlesbrough match.

It's 8.30am now, and my heart makes the jump to light speed. Someone else is moving in the bungalow. I throw back the floral bedspread and race out of the spare room to find my pottering gran and my yawning uncle Trevor switching on the ancient kettle and prodding the TV controls respectively. It's a close run thing as to which will warm up first. My eyes are ablaze as I gaze in awe at the piles of impossibly exciting presents, stacked up like luridly wrapped breeze-blocks underneath a wheezing Woolworths Christmas tree, sagging beneath the weight of the entire Teesside tinsel reserve. Within half an hour my parents have arrived, and I'm allowed to start unwrapping my goodies. *Beano* annuals are gleefully admired and tossed aside, selection boxes torn open and devoured on the only day in the calendar when it's socially acceptable to eat a Toblerone before ten o'clock in the morning. But I know which present I'm looking for, and I'm convinced it must be in there somewhere. As my parents go pale with anticipation, and *The Pink Panther Show Christmas Special* barks into life on TV, I'm left with only one solitary present left to open. It's large, it's heavy, and it's undoubtedly something in a sturdy cardboard box. This must be it. I tear away thick layers of blindingly bright wrapping paper, itching for that first glimpse of pristine black cardboard, the double silver stripe of the unmistakable *Star Wars* logo running seductively around the edges of the box. This is it . . . this is it . . . this is it . . .

It's a dartboard.

It's a fucking *dartboard*.

I'm stunned, and I can't disguise my disappointment. My mum produces from her handbag an envelope with my name on the front, and I open it sulkily to find twenty-five pounds in cash, the largest amount of money I've ever held in my tiny hands. 'We'll put it into the building society, and you can buy the *Millennium Falcon* when they've come back in the shops,' she says warmly. I nod silently, and stare daggers at the dartboard, which – let's face it – is built to handle exactly that kind of treatment. The TV burbles pointlessly at a suddenly muted front room. The Pink Panther and his wacky friends can all go and get stuffed.

I'm exaggerating, of course. It's a smashing Christmas Day, and I've plenty of other great presents to keep me going, including more than my fair share of *Star Wars*-related loveliness. And I spend the day grinning and clapping, and laughing when my dad says *Top of the Pops* is all 'prats and posers this year'. But it's the first time in my life that I haven't got what I wanted for Christmas, and maybe – just maybe – it's the start of my *Star Wars* obsession slowly beginning to wane. I only say this because by the beginning of summer 1981, I have a) the ability to complete a 501 finish with less than fifteen darts, and b) twenty-five pounds still sitting untouched in my Junior Halifax Building Society account. And I never, ever bought that coveted *Millennium Falcon*. At the start of the summer holidays, I sacked it off and spent the lot on a hand-held mini-*Space Invaders* game, £24.99 and newly arrived on Romer Parrish's groaning shelves. Well, you know, Richard Moxham had one.

And if he jumped off a cliff, then . . . Yeah, you get the picture.

Exactly twenty-four years and fifty-one weeks later, a vintage boxed-up 1980 *Millennium Falcon* is calling to me once again, surrounded by myriad equally pristine *Star Wars* antiques. I want to pull out that NatWest debit card and buy the whole lot, and somehow make it 1980 again, with my gran still alive, and my parents still young and fit, and the dogs stealing Chocolate Buttons from the Presto selection box on the coffee table that my uncle Trevor made in woodwork class.

And then I notice that the prices attached to even the tiniest pieces of vintage merchandise would have bankrupted the average early 1980s family. Back then, my beloved platoon of well-drilled three-inch action figures had cost seventy-five pence apiece from the esteemed Messrs Parrish and Brown. In 2005, the same figures – mint and boxed – are for sale on a Cardiff trestle table for fifty-five pounds each. And amazingly, they're selling in impressive quantities. I'm not sure if it's fandom as such, or just extravagant Christmas shopping.

Bustled along to the end of the corridor, we find ourselves in the main hall. Here, yet more merchandise stalls are stacked high, and there's already a noisy, marketplace hubbub around the room. Our eyes are instantly drawn to a towering figure blocking the corridor ahead, and I can already sense Smudge gingerly fingering his *Horror of Frankenstein* DVD.

It's Darth Vader himself.

Dave Prowse.

Still an imposing, muscular giant at the age of seventy, Prowse is, in every sense, the biggest star of the day. Looking fit and strong despite a much-publicised battle against arthritis, he takes his seat in a corner of the room that has become a hastily constructed shrine to Darth Vader. As we linger on the edges of his rapidly growing entourage, we can hear him chatting amiably in the delightful West Country burr that, thirty years previously, led Carrie Fisher to nickname him 'Darth Farmer'.

He's seated at the inevitable trestle table between merchandise stalls with a raft of his own signed goods laid out in front of him. I'd assumed that the artistes present today would be taking to a makeshift stage in a similar format to Dimensions, but the arrangement here is rather different. It's very much a one-to-one experience, with us punters encouraged to circulate in a loose one-way system, stopping at celebrities' tables in an orderly fashion and engaging in conversation or autograph-collecting as we wish. It's like Ikea, but with Boba Fett and Bib Fortuna replacing Hovding wardrobes and Jennylund sofas. Although in the back of my mind is a nagging suspicion that even Hovding Wardrobes began life as one of Jabba the Hut's henchmen in *Return of the Jedi*.

Prowse seems chatty and amiable enough, although we hesitantly keep our distance, lurking at back of the small semi-circle of fans gathered around his table. For a fifteen-pound fee, he's happy to scribble dedications on a glossy A4 picture of himself wearing Vader's iconic black armour, although I'm surprised to note that any punters who've brought their own books or videos to be signed are also asked to hand over ten pounds per item. Smudge notices this too, and I watch all hope of getting a free signature on his DVD drain visibly from his face.

We're distracted by the arrival of our old schoolfriend and top convention tipster Brucie, who has arrived with his girlfriend, Charlotte, and her step-dad, John, in tow – avowed *Star Wars* fans all. 'I see the big feller's here,' laughs Brucie, jabbing a jocular thumb in Prowse's direction and leafing idly through the pages of the erstwhile Dark Lord's official autobiography. The marvellously titled *Straight From the*

Force's Mouth comes in two volumes, each priced at twenty pounds and each the approximate size and weight of the average paving slab. I'm vaguely tempted to make a purchase, but only on the guarantee that Prowse himself will help us carry them back to the car. A prominent children's charity box has been pushed to the front of the table, with a note inviting curious visitors to Vader Corner to make a generous donation.

Pressing forward to within three feet of the man himself, the old actorphobia is once again rising through my veins. I'm a freezing-cold man in a hot room, with icy beads of sweat prickling my forehead. My heart is pounding faster than any 'Imperial March', my mouth is drier than a Mos Eisley patio and yet buzzing through my head is the mangled grammar of Yoda from *Return of the Jedi*. 'You must confront Vader. Then, only then, a Jedi will you be.' The full Jedi training course would never have been for me – I can't even jack up a car, let alone raise an X-Wing Fighter from a jungle swamp – but I *have* to do this.

There's a split-second lull in the conversation at the table, and – just momentarily – Prowse glances around the throng and catches my eye. It's now or never. 'Nice to meet you, Dave,' I stammer, offering a hand, which is surprisingly gently shaken. 'Do you mind posing for a few pictures if we put some money in your charity box?'

He stares back at me. The room fills with glue, and time passes at a fraction of its normal rate. Once again I'm swept back almost twenty-five years, to an Acklam bungalow now so famous that I'm expecting, any moment, a call from the National Trust . . .

BLOODY STUPID THINGS I'VE DONE IN THE NAME OF FANDOM NUMBER 2: PUTTING HAN SOLO IN THE FREEZER

'He's alive . . . and in perfect hibernation. Just behind the arctic roll and the Findus Crispy Pancakes.'

It's the summer of 1981, and Britain is baking. Well, to be fair, my gran is *always* baking. Her kitchen surfaces are permanently groaning beneath a hundredweight of fairy cakes, flapjacks, jam tarts and currant buns, the latter of which I immediately renounce mid-chomp when my dad, on his way to Blu Tack the bumper back onto his Triumph Toledo, says with devilish relish, 'Urgh, look at you, eating the cakes with all the dead flies.' But amidst this domestic bonhomie, a mini heatwave is sweeping across the country. Hemlines are rising (on Teesside, this mainly applies to boiler suits), the little white stripe on Adam Ant's nose is starting to melt, and I have a cunning plan to cool down one of my most treasured possessions.

After three years of fevered collecting, my army of *Star Wars* figures is now large enough to rival the attendances of Middlesbrough's home matches, and Snaggletooth even has the look of a man who has sipped on meat extract while watching Irving Nattrass defend a corner. They have taken over both mine and my gran's homes, and only one icy stronghold has resisted their advances.

Until now.

At the end of *The Empire Strikes Back*, Darth Vader has captured the leading lights of the Rebel Alliance and is using them as bait to lure the unsuspecting Luke Skywalker to the mining colony of Cloud City. To quell further resistance, Vader decides – somewhat surreally, in hindsight – to freeze his enemies solid. No, really. Skywalker himself is the main prize but, in order to test the complex's industrial freezing facilities, Han Solo is encased in a solid block of 'Carbonite', lips parted and hands raised in protest, before being handed over to Boba Fett and spirited away to intergalactic gangster Jabba the Hutt. In a spaceship that also looks like it's held together with Blu Tack.

I don't have access to industrial freezing facilities, but I have an empty Stork SB tub (my Gran does a lot of baking, remember), a glass of weak Robinson's orange squash ('Don't use too much, it's twenty pence a bottle' – my mum). and the tiny freezer compartment at the top of my gran's Electrolux fridge. It takes an entire day for action figure Han Solo to become fully encased in a solid block of urine-coloured ice, but I'm delighted with the results. And, once transported back to our own freezer, he stays there until the end of the school holidays, being shunted from his icy limbo only when our family's voracious fishfinger addiction needs sating.

Twenty-four years later, as I grasp Dave Prowse's hand over a Cardiff trestle table, I toy with the prospect of telling him about my attempt to re-enact one of Darth Vader's most dastardly plots, but thankfully I conclude – ahem – that there are better ways of breaking the ice.

I smile gormlessly, still gripping the former Sith Lord's hand as Smudge, Wez and Brucie take pictures, and by the end of our impromptu photo call I am incapable of coherent speech. Well, more incapable than usual, anyway. I wander along to the corner of the room and take a seat to regain my composure – which, I soon realise, has placed me slap bang next to a fully functional R2-D2 being expertly operated via remote control by a grubby-faced Welsh boy who looks only slightly younger than I was when Han Solo first took up residence alongside the entire 1981 Findus range in my Gran's fridge-freezer. I try to perform a subtle Jedi mind trick to make him leave and let me take over the controls. 'This isn't the droid you're looking for.' I murmur, narrowing my eyes and glaring. 'You can go about your business.'

Amazingly, it seems to work, and he toddles away to find his parents, leaving the clammy remote-control handset loose on the floor. I pick it up and make a considerably more hamfisted attempt at bringing Artoo to life, even managing to dislodge one of the blue panels from the top of his head as I attempt to brush a curious Cardiff fly from his sensors. Inexplicably, I can't resist looking inside, as though I expect to see a grumpy-looking Kenny Baker glaring back at me from within a nest of cables and levers. Nevertheless, I manage to build my confidence back up to a point where I'm smiling once again for Smudge and Wez's cameras, and cracking jokes for passers-by. It's a sense of well-being and euphoria that lasts at least forty seconds, before I realise that I've forgotten to put any money into Dave Prowse's charity box, and have to creep back to the table to slip a two-pound coin through the slot without him noticing.

Wandering further around the room, we take a closer look at some of the merchandise on display. There are boxes full of the brilliant, luridly coloured *Star Wars Weekly* comic that filled my childhood, arriving on musty newsagents' shelves every Wednesday morning and providing the only source of new adventures for Luke, Han, Chewie and the gang throughout the interminable three-year wait between films. And there are numerous completed sets of Topps *Star Wars* Bubble Gum cards, the promise of which might feasibly have driven my six-year-old self to actually kill a man.

I wouldn't have been alone with my murderous intentions. Back at Levendale Primary School, the mass hysteria that had accompanied the release of *Star Wars* had reached epidemic proportions virtually overnight, turning previously wide-eyed and innocent infants into grasping, green-eyed consumer culture junkies. Everybody – girls *and* boys – loved *Star Wars*. When I was wheeled into North Tees Hospital myself in 1979 to have my inflamed tonsils and adenoids removed, one bleary-eyed, bleach-smelling morning was livened up immeasurably by the arrival of thirty Get Well Soon cards handmade by my six-year-old classmates. Every single one of them had a scribbled, wax-crayon depiction of an iconic *Star Wars* scene on the front. Including one from the foul-smelling Chris Herbert who, a matter of weeks later, caused a Cuban Missile-scale crisis on the last day of term by stealing the knobbly plastic Gaffi Stick from my Tusken Raider action figure. For five whole minutes, the world held its breath. Which was always a good idea when Chris Herbert was in the room.

The initial rush of punters now seems to have subsided, and – after meeting the genuine article – I decide to follow in the footsteps of hairy-bellied Boba Fett, and pay five pounds for a picture taken with the UK Garrison's fake Darth Vader. It suddenly strikes me that this is the second time in my life I've embarked on such an adventure, and the long-buried memory of a day trip to Scarborough in summer 1979 returns to the forefront of my mind, my mum and gran and me being stopped on a blisteringly hot seafront by a man dressed in a Darth Vader costume, waving a plastic lightsaber. I'd attracted attention to myself by wearing my favourite *Star Wars* T-shirt (Han and Chewie blasting out from behind that iconic logo), and Darth and his camera-toting henchman were selling photos of grinning gap-toothed kids being menaced by an authentic North Yorkshire Lord of the Sith. My mum had dutifully handed over her pound notes, and we'd posed for the picture and left our address. And – what seemed like several lifetimes later – a pristine, glistening photograph had arrived in the post at my gran's sci-fi HQ in Acklam.

As we sneak past Jeremy Bulloch – the *real* Boba Fett, not the hairy-bellied Cardiff version – the prospect of repeating the experience is becoming irresistible. And yet, as I trudge back to the Death Star print, Garrison members, Stormtroopers and willing punters all seem noticeable only by their absence. 'I was just after a picture. Am I too late?' I ask a passing fan.

'Darth Vader's on his lunch break, and the Stormtroopers have gone for a pint,' he replies. Adventure, excitement, egg sandwiches, a Jedi seeks not these things. The Scarborough Darth Vader would never have been so sloppy, he'd have despatched his Stormtroopers to bring him chips while on the job.

I console myself by buying a signed picture from the trestle table of Brucie's old chum Gerald Home, who sells me a glossy A5 photo of himself in classic Mr Muscle pose, and scrawls above his pipe-cleaner arms the immortal dedication 'For Bob, from Gerald Home, the ORIGINAL Mr Muscle! Good luck cleaning all those awkward little nooks and crannies.'

It's hard to explain the combination of anticipation, nerves and outright terror that bundle up inside the stomach when faced with the prospect of actually meeting someone whose work has been a part of your life for so long, and the sensation of post-meeting euphoria that descends instantly following a successful encounter. One of my earliest memories is of wanting to stage a back-garden *Star Wars* theatre production, and looking strongly at the prospect of casting one of our rough collie dogs in the role of Chewbacca. From then on,

Star Wars has always been, for lesser or greater, a part of my life. My one and only playground fight – in 1983 – was a pre-*Return of the Jedi* discussion about Luke Skywalker's parentage that escalated out of control. Even in my cynical student years, *Star Wars* drinking games ('Take one drink whenever something is Luke's des-ti-ny') were a regular and popular part of university life, and when the special edition films arrived in 1997 I was sitting in my new local multiplex with an attractive brunette and an ill-advised beard, staring at the screen with a wide-eyed wonder and admiration not too far removed from the look that had crossed my face as the velvet curtains of Stockton's Odeon cinema opened up on the original film twenty years previously. It's hard to put all of this into words when faced with the prospect of opening a conversation with Darth Vader (or indeed Mr Muscle) and – as Brucie and Wez jostle me eagerly towards the exit door – I feel pretty relieved that I didn't actually try.

We emerge blinking into the Cardiff daylight, assured by the girl at the door that we can return to the Marriott later so long as we get a Rebel Alliance logo stamped on our hands, but I think we're all reconciled to the fact that we've had our fill of *Star Wars* fandom. Charlotte takes us over the road to Mulligan's pub, where I'm disappointed to discover that the UK Garrison Darth Vader and his entourage of Stormtroopers and assorted Bounty Hunters aren't propping up the bar, swigging pints of Buckley's IPA, playing darts and shouting at the horse-racing on Channel 4. Walking back through the city centre, we say our goodbyes and head back towards the NCP, and I feel a curious post-convention depression descending, knowing full well that within a few hours I'll be back in the front room on Teesside, and Sorcha's first and overriding concern will be whether we got her car back in one piece.

By the time I arrive home at 10pm, sweaty and tired and

stinking of Monster Munch, *Star Wars is* actually the last thing I want to talk about. Sorcha is sitting in front of the television wrapping Christmas presents, and I'm relieved to see that none of them are shaped anything remotely like a vintage action figure or a set of Topps Bubble Gum cards. Back in the real world I've got normal, humdrum work to finish before Christmas, and then all of the fussing and fretting that surrounds the festive period to think about as well. I phone my mum, who tells me with relief that my dad is due to return from hospital within the next forty-eight hours, in plenty of time for Christmas Day. Sorcha is heading back to her native Cornwall for Christmas, but I've decided to spend it on Teesside, with my mum and my dad and with the new dogs causing havoc, just as I did back in 1980. And there won't be a *Millennium Falcon* in sight.

I sink a large brandy and collapse into bed, and I don't think about *Star Wars* at all until a week later, on Christmas night, when – five minutes after I return from my parents' house – my friend Stuart arrives at the front door, eager to watch David Tennant's full-scale debut as the Tenth Doctor in 'The Christmas Invasion', the much-hyped hour-long special that has become – amazingly for us long-suffering fans – a cornerstone of BBC1's festive schedule. And, at the end of the episode, Stuart gives me a small, impeccably wrapped present, and I peel off the paper to discover that – for the first time in at least twenty years – I'm spending part of my Christmas Day tearing wrapping paper from a black cardboard box with that unmistakable *Star Wars* logo emblazoned across the front. And then, uncannily, the doorbell rings, and it's Smudge and Wez, and we spend an alcohol-soaked evening playing my brand-new edition of Star Wars Trivial Pursuit, finding to our astonishment that we actually know the answers to questions like 'Whose shuttle had the code designation ST-321?' (Darth Vader's, in case you were wondering, although

Stuart's initial response of 'Ted Rogers' brings an already tense encounter to the brink of drunken fisticuffs.)

Three days later, embarking on a post-Christmas cleaning and clearing out campaign, I bring a battered cardboard box down from the loft, and discover that not only does it contain a tattered pile of *Star Wars Weekly* comics and a half-completed collection of Topps Bubble Gum cards, but it also plays host to my Darth Vader photo. Yes, *that* Darth Vader photo from Scarborough in 1979, with me indeed sporting a gap-toothed grin and my favourite *Star Wars* T-shirt, although the North Yorkshire Lord of the Sith is slightly less impressive than my six-year-old self had remembered, being five foot nine if he's an inch and encased in a suit of black body armour seemingly constructed from bits of gas fire and the upholstery from a written-off Ford Cortina. I'm swept back instantly and poignantly to an era when cinemas had a maximum of two screens, sold Westler's Hot Dogs in the foyer and were pervaded by a combined odour of sweat, cigarette smoke and Denim aftershave that could comfortably melt a King Cone long before the end of the first Pearl and Deans. An era when, implausibly, *Star Wars* was merely a fun-filled two-hour film that started with some robots messing about in a spaceship and ended with a big metal globe exploding. As opposed to a sprawling fourteen-hour saga that starts with some robots messing about in a spaceship and ends with a big metal globe exploding.

So it's got me again, and – despite C-3PO's prissy prediction in the opening minutes of the very first *Star Wars* film – I don't regret it one bit. I've made a convention breakthrough, I've spoken to a couple of stars and brought home some memorabilia, and when I e-mail my sci-fi chum Matthew – journalist Matthew from the *Bath Chronicle*, who wants to come to meet Robin of Sherwood – I already feel like a hoary fandom veteran, spreading my hard-earned wisdom to a less experienced student of the Force.

And then Matthew tells me something that makes me want to kill him.

THE BATTLE TO SAVE EARTH

By Robert Fischer (Aged Eight And A Third)
Sunday 29 March 1981
PART FOUR

We were still firing away at
advancing Birdmen. Richard still
had hold of the tapes and was
still dodgeing past Snakemen and
guards. Birdmen were now flying
around the hall and firing at the
same time. I could not keep in
the battle any longer so I
grabbed hold of Richard and pulled him up the steps onto
klebba's platform. Then we went racing into the corridor and
after klebba. Then I stopped and held back Richard. 'Wait a
minute,' I said. I took the tapes off Richard and looked at
them. 'I thought so,' I said. 'These are the tapes about
planet Davrock that were stolen from N.A.S.A. last week!'
'Let's get after klebba and ask him where he got them!'
Richard said. Guards, Snakemen and Birdmen were running up
the stairs and down the corridor that Richard and I had gone
down. Laser bolts were echoing down the corridor. Richard and
I entered the control room that klebba and Zero had gone
into. But only to find it empty. I sat down on klebba's chair
and looked at various controls. Then I saw a lever marked
'panel'. I pulled it. A panel on the wall slid open. klebba
and Zero were hiding behind it. klebba stepped out and drew a
laser sword from his belt. Zero followed him and pointed a
pistol at Richard. I pulled klebba's legs from beneath him
and grabbed the laser sword. klebba picked himself up and
said 'Luckily I have a spare laser sword'. He pulled
another laser sword from his belt.

To be continued . . .

BLAKE'S 7

'Wiffle Lever to full, and reverse the polarity
of the Winky Winky Generator.'

THE BASTARD.

The bastard, the bastard, the bastard.

It's an otherwise unremarkable Monday afternoon in January, and I'm reading Matthew's e-mail through a bitter, green mist of hatred. 'You'll have to promise me it goes no further,' he babbles. 'But John Paul and I are in the new series of *Doctor Who*.'

John Paul is Matthew's friend from university. I'd met him at the *Doctor Who* convention and had a quick chat, and he'd come over as a nicely grounded and amiable chap thankfully free of the worst fan excesses. Although admittedly this was before he'd revealed that he'd brought his university thesis, *Gender Studies in* Doctor Who, to be signed by Elisabeth Sladen. Thanks to a *Bath Chronicle* colleague of Matthew's – an experienced stander-arounder signed up to a professional extras agency – the pair have managed to talk their way into a day's filming in Cardiff, expertly pottering in the blurry middle distance as, ten yards closer to camera, the Doctor and Rose explore a parallel dimension infested with the dreaded Cybermen.

The bastard.

And to compound matters even further, John Paul – like an eyelash-fluttering 1940s starlet – has been pulled from the chorus line and promoted to fully fledged stardom. 'We did a shot where Billie and David picked their way through the extras before stopping at John Paul and poking and prodding him,' Matthew tells me, and in my mind's eye I can picture the saliva dribbling onto the keyboard as he types. 'He'll be in that episode, there's no question about it. They even did an extreme close-up of his ear.'

He swears me to secrecy, insisting that John Paul has told none of his *Doctor Who*-loving friends and internet acquaintances, intending for them all to be shocked into submission when the episode finally goes out on air. 'Whatever you do,' he warns, his virtual finger wagging at me furiously through the ether, 'don't mention it at that bloody *Blake's 7* convention. They're *all* going to that and none of them have a clue.'

That bloody *Blake's 7* convention – held, oddly, in the Swallow Hotel in Stockton-on-Tees, rapidly becoming the spiritual home of British science fiction – is my next port of call. Created by Dalek supremo Terry Nation, the show was first broadcast on BBC1 in the bleak, post-punk January of 1978 – bringing gritty, downbeat space opera to a nation that was already reeling from the effects of spiralling unemployment, widespread strikes and 'Mull of Kintyre' having spent the previous five weeks at number one. As a muted Christmas faded into the realms of memory, the country was gripped by a fervour to watch the new sci-fi sensation that was already threatening to set precedents for both popularity and cultural impact. And, for those that couldn't get a ticket to see *Star Wars*, there was always *Blake's 7*.

Only joking, it's great.

No, really.

In the great British sci-fi family tree, *Blake's 7* is the snotty, spiky-haired older brother who Blu-Tacks Clash posters to his bedroom wall and sticks his fingers up at kids in the street. Set amid a far-future Earth Empire controlled by the brutal, totalitarian Federation, it stars Gareth Thomas as Roj Blake, an idealistic freedom fighter who, along with a troupe of shady, often unlikeable petty criminals, commandeers the abandoned starship *Liberator* and embarks on an epic crusade of intergalactic terrorism. His 'Seven' include Michael Keating's shambling, cowardly safe-cracker Vila, Sally Knyvette's unfeasibly glamorous smuggler Jenna and Paul Darrow's grasping, sneering computer genius Avon – who manages to inject into his scenes with Blake a crackling, sizzling tension that verges permanently on the homoerotic.

Their ultimate nemesis is the curvaceous, crop-haired Federation chief Servalan, a purring dominatrix played by the formidable Jacqueline Pearce – who turns in a performance so outrageously arch and flamboyant it makes Joan Collins look like Wally Batty. The series – whose tone veered wildly from cynical grittiness to camp without batting an immaculately mascara-swabbed eyelid – ran for four series between 1978 and 1981. At the end of the final episode virtually the entire cast seemed to be killed off – including Thomas, who hadn't appeared for almost two full series, and had his character's gory end written inextricably into his contract.

Notable *Blake's 7* catchphrases include 'Max-i-mum Pow-ah!', 'Standard By Six And Rising', 'It's A Bit Elaborate For A Toothpick' and 'When's It Coming Back On, Then?' If you want to annoy a *Blake's 7* fan, tell him you remember the theme tune, then whistle the music to *The Onedin Line* instead. If you need a subtle test to discover whether the checkout girl at your local supermarket is a *Blake's 7* fan, say 'confirmed' in a deadpan robotic voice when she asks you if you'd like any cashback.

If my seven-year-old self had seen *Star Wars* and *Doctor Who* as pure, head-rush heroin, then *Blake's 7* was, to begin with, tantamount to methadone. A science-fiction TV show without a robot dog? Madness. But, by the time Avon had commandeered the *Liberator*'s controls from the departing Gareth Thomas in early 1980, I was sold. Especially when industrial action at the BBC resulted in an unprecedented eight-month gap until the next series of *Doctor Who* was scheduled. And, given my increasing maturity (I was eight at the end of the year) the adventures of Darrow and the gang seemed to offer me a sturdier, grittier and more adult edge, far more in keeping with my own advancing years and tastes. When *Doctor Who* finally returned, it respected my increased sophistication by quickly ditching the robot dog and replacing him with an air hostess. *Blake's 7*, admirably, pressed on without either, sensibly depicting its own smart-arsed super-computer, Orac, as a winking, sentient fishtank.

So it's now an early Friday evening in March, and I'm once again walking along a deserted Stockton High Street to register at the Star One convention, named after the remote White Dwarf star at the centre of the evil Federation's control network, and bringing almost the entire main cast of *Blake's 7* to this similarly bleak and inhospitable outpost. Thankfully, in the four months since I was last in Stockton, the weather has changed considerably. Back in the middle of November, it was damp, drizzly and dark. Now, in mid-March, it's freezing cold and snowing.

Huffing up the stairs to the warm and welcome enclave of the Swallow Hotel bar, I see Dimensions veterans John – the man, lest we forget, who said, '... like ... ask Mark about ... Mike Read ... TARDIS Wendy House ...' to Mark Strickson, and Nathan – he of the well-worn Janet Ellis fanzine collection – sprawled on a crimson settee by a television set that is, once again, showing tonight's episode of *EastEnders* to a room overwhelmed by haughty sci-fi indifference. We give each other a gentle hello as I pull up an armchair to join them, and their conversation – debating the merits of Dudley Simpson's instrumental music for 'Destiny of the Daleks' – barely misses a beat.

It's been an eventful few weeks since Matthew's earth-shattering revelations. I've become the main presenter of a regular show on our local radio station, BBC Tees, with free rein afforded over my choice of guests – and so, shortly after booking my ticket for Star One, I'd dropped a speculative e-mail to splendidly named convention organiser Maureen Marrs requesting a brief phone interview with Paul Darrow. To my surprise, she agreed, and to my delight, nine days prior to the convention, I'd found myself interviewing *Blake's 7*'s erstwhile anti-hero about the enduring appeal of the show and his love for taking part in events like Star One. And he'd been captivating, charming company – telling me that he'd modelled his performances in the show on Steve McQueen's tour-de-force surliness in *Bullitt*, and then chatting about his love for Manchester City with the kind of world-weary self-deprecation that only a true, long-suffering fan can muster. I'm still really scared of meeting him in the flesh, though.

Gripping fresh pints of John Smith's bitter, Nathan, John and I troop giddily back into the Swallow Hotel's Summer Room. 'There are a lot of women here, aren't there?' exclaims a stunned John as we shamble through the door. And he's right. On the way, however, we do encounter one lone male figure, lurking in the corridor pinning a series of posters to the wall. He's tall, wiry and skinny, sporting a floor-length leather greatcoat, a black eyepatch and – only slightly incongruously – a puffed-up, chequered chef's hat. I try to work out whether the eyepatch is a tribute to *Blake's 7*'s callous, disfigured bounty hunter Travis, or whether he actually has an authentic medical need to keep his left eye covered up. He isn't, I'm pretty much convinced, a genuine chef.

On a subsequent trip to the bar, I examine the posters at close quarters. He seems to be a member of a strange secret society called the Jedi Chefs, an underground organisation devoted to, well, dressing up as *Star Wars* Jedis and inexplicably sporting chef's hats. One poster is filled with photographs of the dozen or so Jedi Chef Masters, each – including Eyepatch Man – sporting the regulation uniform of flowing brown robe, dark glasses, aggressively clasped lightsaber and chequered chef's *chapeau*. The other poster is a roster of 'Celebrity Jedi Chefs' and features passport-sized pictures of a selection of US sci-fi stars – including seemingly the entire cast of *Firefly* and *Stargate SG-1* – wearing the same bizarre uniform. Our hero has clearly come here this weekend to entice Paul Darrow and Jacqueline Pearce into the Jedi Chef fraternity, and I make a mental note to keep an eye out for him during the remainder of the weekend.

So to speak.

CRUCIAL MOMENTS IN FANDOM HISTORY NUMBER THREE: WATCHING THE FINAL EPISODE OF BLAKE'S 7

'Whhaaat?'

It's Monday 21 December 1981, and something staggering is taking place before my eyes. I'm at home, sprawled in front of a crackling open fire while my giggling dad extinguishes the splinter of sizzling wood that has spat through the fireguard onto our impervious dog's hind quarters, and my mum coats the Christmas cake in a layer of marzipan thick enough to withstand a small thermonuclear explosion.

I'm watching *Blake's 7*. It's the final episode, although I'm not really aware of this at the time. My stomach is bubbling and bursting with tension, and only half of this is down to the almost certain knowledge that in less than eighty-four hours' time I'll be the proud owner of a junior table football and the latest *Star Wars Annual*. What's really making my heart race at 'Standard By Six And Rising' is the final confrontation between Darrow's Avon – as buttock-clenchingly nasty as ever – and Gareth Thomas's Blake, making his swansong appearance in the series after an absence of almost two years. Avon – convinced that Blake has betrayed him to the dreaded Federation – shoots his former compatriot squarely in the guts, resulting in a ferocious explosion of stage blood almost powerful enough to make an indentation in my mum's impregnable marzipan. It's followed swiftly by a systematic massacre of Avon's crew by a newly arrived platoon of gas mask-clad Federation troops, leaving Darrow alone upright amongst the broken bodies of his fallen comrades, with a dozen fizzling laser weapons pointing at his sneering face. Cut to end credits, silent save for a hail of gunfire before the familiar theme tune fades in. And that's it. Everyone is dead, and *Blake's 7* has finished for ever. My dad grins and merrily whistles the music from *The Onedin Line*.

I'm stunned. It's quite the bleakest slab of existential grimness I've ever seen, and surely the most disturbing slice of melodrama ever broadcast on early evening BBC1. With the possible exception of *Terry and June*. It's terrible, but brilliant at the same time, and I realise with a jolt that my favourite science-fiction things needn't always be fantasy and fun and escapism, they can be downbeat and dirty and depressing as well. *Doctor Who* – where our heroes always escape unscathed and head back to the TARDIS in time for tea and jelly babies – is never like this. And the only person who died in *Star Wars* was Obi-Wan Kenobi, and he came back transparent and blue, and could walk around the ice planet Hoth without needing his jumper on. My eight-year-old self is given to flights of outrageous fancy (as those who have read *The Battle to Save Earth* will no doubt testify) but even at this impressionable age, I'm pretty sure that Avon isn't coming back as a friendly, flickery ghost. And, twenty-five years later, when I finally meet Paul Darrow in the flesh, he is indeed wearing a big woolly jumper.

The next morning, I arrive in the bar bright and early. Too early in fact, discovering that the day's activities begin an hour later than I'd actually thought, at 10am. I've only just begun to sift through the seemingly incomprehensible timetable of events when John and his friends Damon, Neil and Sean stride purposefully from the lifts, narrowly trailing future *Doctor Who* ear artiste John Paul. 'We've been to Woolworths and bought boxes full of crap,' grins John. 'I even got a ten-inch action figure of Christopher Eccleston. It's almost exactly the same size as an erect penis.'

'He hasn't got it in his pocket, though – he's just pleased to see you,' quips Damon.

As we wander into the Summer Room, Paul Darrow is on stage, holding court and mercilessly sending up his latter-day *Blake's 7* co-star Steven Pacey. Drafted into the show following Gareth Thomas's departure at the end of series two, the impressively permed Pacey played intergalactic mercenary Del Tarrant, referred to repeatedly by Nathan as 'Fake Blake'. They goad each other into a gentle flow of *Blake's 7* anecdotes, with Pacey revealing that he was incapable of remembering the baffling flood of technobabble in the show's scripts, and would pepper rehearsal takes with vague substitutions of his own devising: 'Wiffle Lever to full!' and 'Reverse the polarity of the Winky Winky Generator!'

'There are a lot of women here, aren't there?' ponders Neil.

'That's what we said,' whispers John.

Right on cue, heads are turned by the arrival through a side entrance of Star One's first dresser-uppers, two attractive brunettes clad alluringly in the flowing robes and veils of the female assassins from the episode 'City at the Edge of the World'. As they take their seats, they are accompanied by the sound of a piercing ambulance siren speeding past below the steamed-up Summer Room windows. 'I see Gareth Thomas has arrived,' deadpans Darrow, and the room erupts into mayhem.

Jacqueline Pearce enters proceedings. As Blake's curvaceous, close-cropped nemesis Servalan, Pearce became – seemingly to her own delight – a primal sexual fantasy figure for a generation of British teenagers who suddenly felt powerful hormones raging beneath their duffel coats for the first time as Servalan's insatiable lust for power seemed to swell her bosom far beyond the boundaries of a succession of tight-fitting satin bodices. For the last twenty-five years, I'd envisaged her as an imposing, six-foot seductress, and am somewhat taken aback by the petite, silver-haired lady who elegantly picks her way to the stage. And yet, taking to the microphone, she's every inch the larger-than-life thespian, commanding the room with more power than the crappy Federation could ever muster, and filling joyous, bitchy monologues with enough theatrical 'Dahlings' to make Danny la Rue give up the ghost, shake his head in resignation, and sign up for manual labour on the nearest industrial building site.

'I made friends with my illness,' she tells a rapt and suddenly serious-looking audience. 'I called her Carol Cancer. And when I went bald, I've never had so many men trying to pick me up.' This is Jacqueline's first major convention appearance since her battle against breast cancer – about which I had no idea – and she's typically frank and contrary in her account, describing the disease as 'the best thing that ever happened to me'.

'It completely removed my fear of death,' she grins. 'And I now fully believe in reincarnation, and would like to come back as a tree or a rose bush.' She claims to have spent the winter 'hibernating' in her remote Cornish cottage, passing the brutal months in bed accompanied only by a roaring coal fire and her cat, Caspar. A small flurry of hands are raised when she appeals to the crowd for questions. 'Was there much of a down-side to having cancer?' asks one hapless punter, which seems to amuse her greatly.

She also reveals – to a smattering of spontaneous applause – that, in three weeks' time, she'll be flying to Johannesburg, then riding a bus 400 miles into the jungle to spend eight weeks under canvas caring for orphaned and injured monkeys. She makes an impassioned and emotional speech about animal cruelty and the exploitative nature of the human race, under-mined only slightly by a loud ringtone at the back of the Summer Room that interrupts her oration with a bleepy version of the chase music from *The Benny Hill Show*.

She's utterly captivating and inspiring, and part of me wishes I could spend endless nights alongside her in the teeming Transvaal clearings, swigging copiously from a bottle of Dom Pérignon and drunkenly discussing life's foibles beneath a star-strewn African sky. Instead, I venture into Colin Baker's genealogy seminar. The erstwhile Sixth Doctor, Colin's *Blake's 7* role came in the episode 'City at the Edge of the World', as a tattooed, leather-clad, heavily pierced psychopath called – brace yourself – Bayban the Butcher. Now cutting an avuncular figure, sporting half-moon spectacles and a mane of silver hair, Baker takes his seat and casts a twinkling eye around the room. 'There are a lot of women here, aren't there?' he ponders. 'It's like *Doctor Who*, but with girls.'

'That's what we said,' whispers Neil. 'You can smell the hormone patches from here.'

Crowded into a small function space already over-filled with an impressive display of vintage *Blake's 7* props and costumes, a dozen of us trusty disciples assemble plastic chairs around a Formica table, with the friendly Sixth Doctor himself generously helping to rearrange the furniture, and apologising for leaving his glowing mobile phone primed for action on the table-top. 'I've asked my daughter to update me with all the action from Wycombe Wanderers,' he smiles. 'We're at home to Shrewsbury Town today, and it might just be a tricky one.'

I'm completely starstruck. It feels heart-poundingly surreal to be sitting at a table with *the Doctor*, and I spend most of the session hiding behind a man with a ponytail so vast and unkempt that the only horse I can imagine it adorning is the one that belonged to Steptoe and Son. The rest of the group, annoyingly, seem to be much more capable of warm, informal conversation. Colin reveals that he's spent the previous eighteen months diligently researching his family tree, planning visits to various church registers and local records offices around his touring plays, and so far managing to track back sixteen generations of assorted Baker branches. Several of the punters present have been doing likewise, with varying degrees of success. 'Has anybody here uncovered any black sheep in the family?' asks Colin, mischievously. 'Yes,' pipes up a bespectacled fan in a snugly fitting Michael Keating T-shirt. 'I've recently discovered that I'm a distant relative of Fred and Rosemary West.'

Colin's face freezes into such an expression of mortified

horror that I wonder if he's about to call it quits on this mortal coil once again and regenerate into Sylvester McCoy.

As the afternoon sky begins to bruise, traditional convention boozing commences in the bar, and memories blur into one as a sea of John Smith's rises around our brains, leaving a tidemark of beery froth clinging to our neural pathways. Somewhere in the muddled mess we pose for photos with Federation phaser guns that contain enough home-made, sticky-backed plastic charm to be genuine BBC props, although that doesn't stop us throwing them around the table with all the delicate, reverential respect of a seventh birthday party. A weary-looking Neil and Sean depart for bed at midnight, just missing the dramatic arrival of Eyepatch Man, now sporting full Jedi Chef regalia and waving a humming, glowing lightsaber with reckless abandon around the busy bar. He strikes a pose for a passing Jacqueline Pearce, who shrieks with laughter, and then appears to coerce two previously dignified female attendees to lie face up on the carpeted floor while he performs a strange and dangerous lightsaber dance around their extremities.

It's 1.30am. 'Have you spoken to those girls yet?' grins Damon. 'The ones in the assassins' costumes?'

'I haven't seen them for hours,' slurs Nathan. 'They've probably been kidnapped by the Jedi Chefs.'

'No they haven't,' pipes up John. 'They're over there, dancing to Erasure.'

We crane our necks around the edge of the snug to see that a modest collection of disco lights and speakers have been arranged around the TV set, and the two shapely veiled assassins are indeed shaking their legs to one of Vince Clarke's floor-fillers while simultaneously attempting to drag unwilling sci-fi fans, hitherto happily content to while away the small hours spilling bitter onto their Servalan T-shirts, away from their velour armchairs and onto a makeshift dancefloor.

'Oh, shit,' blurts John, his face a mask of frozen terror, 'they've seen us!'

We scramble back into our secluded corner like guilty schoolboys caught scribbling obscenities in the biology textbooks, but it's too late. The assassins have hitched up their flowing silk robes and made a breathtakingly speedy beeline for our table.

'Come and dance with us,' pleads the more gregarious of the two, a pretty, wavy-haired brunette with the bubbly, magnetic persona of a 1970s *Carry On* girl. 'Nobody else will dance, and they're going to stop the disco if there's not enough people up there.'

'Not a hope in hell,' mutters John. 'Bob'll dance with you, though, won't you, Bob?'

'No,' I reply, fixing her with a steely stare. 'You must be joking. Sorry, but wild horses and Jedi Chefs combined wouldn't get me on that dancefloor tonight.'

Forty seconds later, I'm swirling my corduroy jacket around my head to the strains of Wham!'s 'I'm Your Man' as two female assassins in robes and modesty veils strike *Saturday Night Fever* poses in front of a TV on which BBC2's 'Sign Language Zone' is currently in full swing. I notice with surprise that billowing clouds of smoke are beginning to swirl about my flailing legs, and look around for the unlikely owner of the dry-ice machine, until I realise that the source seems to be the entire main cast of *Blake's 7* bemusedly observing our Terpsichorean efforts from within a fug of cigarette smoke thick enough to put half of the BBC's special effects department out of a job for ever.

It's all a long way from Christmas 1981, and my dad whistling the theme tune to *The Onedin Line* to annoy me. I'm fond of telling unsuspecting strangers that I didn't actually speak to a girl until I was twenty-one years old, and it's only a slightly exaggerated version of the truth. While many of my school contemporaries were enthusiastically practising their snogging techniques on each other long before the end of third year Juniors, I was lurking in the corner of Levendale Primary School, my head stuck inside the latest *Doctor Who* paperback or my fingers meticulously working out a detailed cross-section of the *Liberator* on the back of a piece of perforated computer paper. A childhood love of science fiction is generally not a great portent for future notches on the teenage bedpost, and the number of fresh-faced schoolgirls in 1980s Teesside who were attracted to me for my winning way with a ZX Spectrum Machine Code Assembler or my knowledge of the Third Law of Thermodynamics was, unsurprisingly, staggeringly close to zero. And yet here I am twenty years later, dancing with a gaggle of attractive, female thirtysomething *Blake's 7* fans to school-disco classics that would, back then, have had me backing piti-fully into a corner and hiding nervously beneath a pile of *Doctor Who Weeklies*. Where were all these sci-fi loving sirens back in 1987 when I needed them? Presumably hiding in their own bedrooms, convinced that no fresh-faced schoolboy on Teesside or elsewhere would be attracted to their winning ways with a Sally Knyvette action figure or their knowledge of the Star One Strategic Defence Zone. At least they're making up for it now, I think to myself, narrowly avoiding demolishing a passing trestle table with my flailing left leg.

By this stage I'm so drunk that I barely register the bleep of my mobile, and it takes the opening bars of Bananarama's 'Venus' to drive me from the dancefloor and discover a text from Sorcha – who, cannily, has this time opted against entering the Swallow Hotel and being engaged in several hours worth of discussion about the physics of E-Space, and is waiting in the car outside, having brought the family dog with her as an added insurance policy against me keeping her waiting for hours in the snow.

I give both robed assassins a chaste peck on the cheek before flouncing out of the bar in a swirl of corduroy, giving John,

Damon and Nathan a theatrical wink and a wave on my way out, a dramatic exit only slightly undermined by the fact that thirty seconds later I have to reappear to collect my holdall, still propped up on the seat where I'd left it five hours, seven pints and two double whiskies earlier.

Hurrying downstairs, I mentally prepare myself for Sorcha's inevitable furious frown, and an angry *Blake's 7*-related argument. It won't be my first . . .

BLOODY STUPID THINGS I HAVE DONE IN THE NAME OF FANDOM NUMBER THREE: STARTING A YOGHURT FIGHT WITH IAN MACDONALD

'They did!'
  'No, they didn't!'
  'Yes, they did!'
  'They flippin' didn't!'
  'THEY DID!!!!'
  Splodge.

In the critical cultural melting pot of early 1980s Levendale Primary School, *Blake's 7* didn't enjoy either the widespread mass hysteria afforded to *Star Wars* or even the widespread mild interest afforded to *Doctor Who*. But it did gain a select cult following, largely amongst the kind of boys who inexplicably brought packed lunches to school, and actually bothered to fasten up the waist cord on their navy blue, fur-lined parkas. My *Blake's 7* companion was the languid, pale Ian MacDonald, and we enjoyed endless, lurid lunchtime conversations about Blake's crusade and the brutality of Servalan's oppressive totalitarian regime, all conducted over Mother's Pride egg sandwiches so brilliantly white that our lunchboxes, when opened, bathed our faces in a stark, unearthly glow. They're like Samuel

L. Jackson's briefcase in *Pulp Fiction*, although ours probably contained more Hula Hoops than his did.

But we did fall out once over *Blake's 7*, and this is it. We're in the school dinner hall, snuffling into our packed lunches, and the whiffy Chris Herbert is opposite, looking concerned as this testing sci-fi diplomatic incident escalates. It's January 1982, we've not long returned to school after the Christmas holidays, and – after breathlessly debating that brutal last-ever episode – our conversation has turned angrily to the wider issues of life.

'I'm telling you, the Daleks were in *Blake's 7*!' bellows Ian, showering the table with a flurry of eggy mush. 'They were in an early episode and they tried to exterminate Jenna.'

'Bog off, they weren't,' I reply. It's strong stuff for a nine-year-old, but I'm angry. I'm not used to having my sci-fi authority challenged, especially when I know my opponent is talking out of his asymmetrical thrust computer.

Ian is undaunted. 'You don't know what you're talking about because you haven't been watching it as long as I have,' he snorts, shaking his head and peeling the wrapper from an Orange Club. Jamie Oliver would have a field day with our spiralling daily tartrazine intake.

That's it for me. Ian's unlucky enough to have snapped my normally boundless reserves of patience just as I'm about to shovel a teaspoon of quivering Strawberry Ski yoghurt into my mouth. The red mist (or rather the pink slurry) descends, and instead of taking a mouthful, I fling the spoon and its lurid, sticky contents all over his new acrylic tank top. The yoghurt splatters like a lumpy, thick snowball, and bits of it drip onto his bottle-green corduroys.

'And what do you think you're doing, Mr Fischer?'

The subsequent bollocking I receive from the impassive Mrs Gallon, yellow-coated enforcer of the school's feared

Dinner Nanny brigade, leaves me ear-ringingly acquiescing to a series of pointedly escalating accusations. Not only have I let myself down, I've also let down Ian MacDonald, my parents, Levendale Primary School, the town of Yarm, the county of Cleveland, the Queen and quite possibly – at a push – Bucks Fizz, currently enjoying a third week at the top of the charts with their second Number One single 'The Land of Make Believe'.

Still, it's all a long time ago. And twenty-four years and a Persil Automatic boil wash later, I'm still good friends with Ian. I'd even e-mailed him prior to the convention asking if he'd care to join me, although he'd replied in the negative, claiming that his new girlfriend 'might just tolerate me doing *Doctor Who* things, but she'd draw the line at *Blake's 7*'. Reading between the lines, I'm convinced that my deadly accuracy with a globule of Ski yoghurt and an R2-D2 teaspoon was the real reason he was reluctant to attend.

Splodge.

On Sunday morning, having learned nothing from my experiences at Dimensions, I'm once again slumped in a plastic chair in the Summer Room watching the first panel of the day and feeling like several important areas of my head have been occupied by Federation Forces. Outside, it's snowing more heavily than ever, although curiously none of the flakes seem willing to spend much time on the pavement, instead retreating to the gutters and forming thick, slippery piles of freezing, grey slush. I'm inclined, at this stage, to join them.

Gareth 'Blake' Thomas is onstage, gazing with a wince at the flurries of snow passing outside the Summer Room window.

'Good God,' he laughs, with a wheeze. 'Forty years in the business, and this is where I end up.'

He's clearly an experienced convention guest, and reels off a string of splendid acting anecdotes and witticisms, all the while smoking furiously in the now-traditional *Blake's 7* manner. He bemoans the lack of challenging parts for older actors, confessing his tendency to take what he describes, rather wearily, as 'bottle-of-whisky-a-day' roles. 'I really like the different weapons you used in *Blake's 7*' says a small boy at the front, his voice trembling with terror and anticipation. 'Which one was your favourite?'

'The cheque,' smiles Thomas, and lights up another cigarette.

Afterwards, I decide to gather what remaining nerves I have and make my way to the professional photo studio, where Gareth is heading to pose for pictures with paying fans. I troop up the hotel's back stairs to a tiny utility room at the entrance to an endless corridor of guest bedrooms, and – peering nervously around the doorway – I hear a muted thespian discussion from within. 'Seems to be a bit of a lull,' intones a vaguely familiar voice. 'Should we nip downstairs for a coffee and a cake?' I anxiously decide to take the plunge, and step forward with a gentle clearing of the throat. 'Oh, sorry!' comes the response. 'Hang on, we've got some business!'

It's Michael Keating. In the twenty-five years since Vila was cowering his way around the galaxy in a haze of lock-picking and shame-faced retreating, he's barely changed, and now greets me smiling at the doorway, resplendent in slacks and fluffy jumper. Gareth Thomas is lurking behind, and he too flashes a welcoming grin. 'Sorry if I look rough,' I stammer. 'I'm afraid I'm a little bit delicate this morning.'

'So am I, but I find this helps!' he roars, glugging heartily from a glass of white wine so enormous that it should, by rights, come supplied with a lifebelt and a yellow flag. 'The hair of a particularly vicious dog,' he beams.

Malcolm the photographer places us before a sky-grey vinyl background rolled down against the far wall, and the two actors squeeze either side of me, making me the willing meat in a Keating and Thomas sandwich. I jut out my jaw and grin inanely as the flash goes off. 'We need to do that again, you've got a strange expression on your face,' mutters Malcolm.

'He's always got a strange expression on his face,' laughs Thomas.

The flash fills the room once more.

'Nope, you had your eyes shut that time,' comes the response. 'Close your eyes, I'll start counting and on the count of three open them as wide as you can and smile.'

I follow Malcolm's instructions to the letter.

'Perfect,' he exclaims, examining this third attempt, and I shake hands warmly with the two actors, thanking them for their time and patience. When I collect the resulting picture thirty minutes later, it's clear I've thrown myself into the situation a little too enthusiastically, and have the wide-eyed, startled expression of a man with a thespian's hand freshly inserted up his anus. Which obviously didn't happen – I'm just not that kind of convention attendee. Besides which, I'm saving myself for *Robin of Sherwood*.

Even at lunchtime, the weekend seems to be very much winding to a close, and – bolstered by my photographic experiences – I decide to forgo the afternoon's panels and join the Star One autograph queues. I've brought with me no less than two well-worn DVD box sets of *Blake's 7*'s first series, one of which is my own, and the other – implausibly – is owned by Sorcha's mother.

There has been, against all the odds, a recent thawing in Sorcha's long-term state of sci-fi denial. At Christmas and on birthdays and during various scattered 'saying sorry' escapades, I've recently taken to buying her the DVDs of her teenage sci-fi favourite *Red Dwarf*. And she's taken to watching them voraciously, and – amazingly – when I brought up again the prospect of that weekend in the Peterborough Holiday Inn with Craig Charles and Danny John-Jules, she didn't attempt to perform rectal surgery on me with my sharp-edged Dalek bubble-bath dispenser.

Things had taken an even more dramatic turn a matter of weeks ago, when a short visit from the Cornish in-laws took on surreal proportions. Performing a ritualistic dusting of the front room within thirty seconds of walking through the door, Sorcha's mum had found her eyes alighting with delight on my collection of *Blake's 7* DVD box sets. '*Blake's 7*!' she'd cooed. 'We shall watch those, when the room becomes habitable.' Sorcha and her mother had then proceeded to spend two days solid in front of our television gripped beyond comprehension by the early exploits of Blake, Avon, Vila and the rest of the motley rabble. 'I'm going to a *Blake's 7* convention next month if either of you want to come,' I'd babbled, in a passing moment of ill-considered madness.

'No,' they'd both instantly retorted, with a synchronised, withering female firmness that would have had Servalan cowering into her BacoFoil bodice. A sense of cool, graceful relief had washed over me. Nevertheless, in a rare display of forward planning, I've already bought Sorcha's mum the series one box set for Christmas, and I've decided the phrase 'One for me and one for the mother-in-law' should be enough to elicit a smile from even the scariest autograph-giver.

Blake and Avon are doing the honours. And before Messrs Thomas and Darrow have even taken their seats, the queue for their signatures is already stretching out of the signing room and through into the hotel bar.

Gareth arrives first, still sloshing a precariously full glass of white wine in his hand. He sits at a vacant trestle table and begins signing, the queue moving frustratingly slowly as he laudably takes the time to chat at length with each admiring punter. Half an hour later, the queue has barely moved when Paul Darrow arrives in a blaze of noise and sets up stall at an adjacent table. 'Release the geese!' he proclaims, lighting up another cigarette and throwing his arms into the air. 'Paul has to leave at four o'clock on the dot, or we're all in trouble,' I hear one stony-faced steward tell his colleague. I take a surreptitious glance at my mobile phone to see that it's now 2.45pm. The chances of procuring 'One for me and one for the mother-in-law' from both actors are receding fast.

Half an hour later, I find myself, for the second time in a day, being gripped tightly by Gareth Thomas as we pose for a picture, my DVD box sets both flamboyantly signed.

'How's the wine going down?' I enquire with a knowing nod.

'Rather too well, actually,' he grins, and squeezes my shoulder. I shuffle away to join Darrow's queue. 'Last one here, Maureen!' says the steward, dramatically waving his arm behind me and indicating to a fraught-looking Maureen Marrs that no more punters will be allowed to join the queue behind me. I feel like the Indiana Jones of the autograph world, narrowly sliding underneath a closing tomb door and just reaching back in time to grasp my trusty permanent marker pen.

The following forty-five minutes are riddled with such anxiety and cinematic tension that even Alfred Hitchcock, in the unlikely event that his silhouette had ever peered through a frosted hotel window in Stockton-on-Tees, would have had to take a break from proceedings and go for a nice sit down and a biscuit. With the dreaded four o'clock racing towards me like the *Liberator* on Standard By Ten (which is pretty much, as Servalan would no doubt proclaim, 'Max-i-mum Po-wah!'), the queue has reached a virtual standstill. I can feel my blood pressure rising by the second, driving the remains of last night's alcohol out of my beleaguered brain for ever. At one minute to four, the brace of women in front of me – having treated Darrow to a ten-minute potted history of their upbringing in Leicestershire – wander away, and I find myself face to face with the scourge of the Federation, clumsily hankering after my usual dual auto-graph attack.

'One for mother, and one for the me-in-law,' I stammer, predictably, as he offers me a beaming smile. 'And by the way, I'm Bob from BBC Tees. I spoke to you on the phone last week.'

He laughs warmly and shakes my hand with a titanic grip. We chat for at least forty seconds about life, love, sex, death and Manchester City's last-minute 2–1 defeat at Portsmouth the previous afternoon. I can see the steward casting despairing glances at a worried Maureen as the town hall clock chimes four times with ominous significance.

And then it's back to the Summer Room, where a glamorous closing ceremony has been arranged. Neil, John, Sean, John Paul and Damon are already in their seats. 'You look rough,' says Neil, with a demonic smile. 'Remember, if you've been affected by any of the issues raised at the Star One convention, then please contact the *Blake's 7* support line on this number . . .'

Darrow is joined onstage by Thomas, Keating and Peter Tuddenham, the octogenarian actor who provided the voices of the programme's assorted sentient computers. Keating modestly accepts a round of applause when Darrow reveals that he's recently become married to 'a wonderful woman who's upstairs, cleaning his dirty underwear'. But it's Tuddenham who brings the house down, launching into a dazzling and oddly moving medley of his various *Blake's 7* voices. 'We've had a lovely time here in Stockport.' he says, in the servile voice of the team's latter-day master computer, Slave.

'You can't even get the name right,' snaps pithy, cynical Orac. 'It's Stockton-on-Tees, you stupid computer.'

'Confirmed,' intones Zen solemnly, to thunderous applause.

I look around the room and swear I can see a single salty tear running gently down the contour of Neil's left cheek. I also spy Eyepatch Man cradling impressive official photographs of Gareth Thomas and Michael Keating in full Jedi Chef regalia.

Five minutes later, I'm shambling contemplatively past the shuttered-up pine furniture showrooms of Stockton's Bridge Road, as the last flurries of snow flutter around my feet, still resolutely refusing to spread themselves on the pavement. Which is more than can be said for some of last night's revellers. And, for the first time at the close of a convention, I'm filled with a reasonable sense of achievement and well-being. I still haven't asked a question to a celebrity panel, but I feel much more as though I've been a willing participant in the weekend. I've chatted with the stars, queued for autographs, posed for photos, danced to Wham! with women dressed as dangerous, veiled assassins and – most importantly of all – I haven't breathed a word to anyone about John Paul and Matthew's forthcoming appearance in *Doctor Who* (the bastards). I climb into the car, reverse the polarity of the winky winky generator, and drive into an early evening Teesside sunset safe in the knowledge that I've made more advances in my own personal quest than Blake and the gang ever did against the dreaded Federation.

'Did you have a good time?' asks Sorcha, as I troop, exhausted, into the front room, throwing the two fully autographed box sets into an armchair. 'Confirmed,' I reply, in a deadpan robotic voice. Standard By Six and Rising upstairs to bed.

THE BATTLE TO SAVE EARTH

By Robert Fischer (Aged Eight And Five Twelfths)
Wednesday 22 April 1981
PART FIVE

I switched my laser sword on and tried to cut klebba's arm off. But klebba hit my laser sword with his laser sword and forced me back. I slashed at klebba's arm. My laser sword sunk into his shoulder. klebba fell back in agony. Then Richard fired at Zero. The laser bolt hit Zero in his chest and stunned him.

We both ran out of a doorway. We both ran out of it. We were on a long ramp above a thirty metre high drop. Prison cells were attached to a wall. Suddenly I heard a voice coming from one of the cells. 'Hear that?' I said to Richard. 'You bet,' Richard answered. The voice seemed to be coming from cell no. 12086. I got my gun and shot the cell door down. When the smoke had cleared I saw another boy dressed in a green uniform, a green cape and black boots. 'Who are you?' I asked him. 'I am Dirk Obion, son of klebba Obion,' the boy replied. 'What are you doing here?' Richard asked him. 'I tried to escape from this evil planet but the guards caught me and put me in this cell . . .' said Dirk. 'Well now that you're free could you please help us escape back to Earth?' I asked Dirk. 'I can try,' Dirk answered. 'By the way,' I said, 'I'm Robert Fischer and this is my best friend, Richard Moxham'. I had just finished when a whole army of robots and guards came rushing onto the ramp. A group of Birdmen and Snakemen followed them.

To be continued . . .

JAMES BOND

HER MAJESTY'S FINEST SIGNING SESSION
INFINITELY BETTER STORE, SWINDON
THURSDAY 29 JUNE – SATURDAY 1 JULY

'Miss Ekland? She's in the left-hand corner, 🪐
just under Ian Botham.'

'THE NAME'S FISCHER, Bob Fischer.'

Hurtling recklessly along a wide expanse of empty motorway, I repeat this suave mantra to myself, slipping into arguably the most unlikely Roger Moore impersonation since Eddie Large hung up his revolving bowtie. I daringly raise a cocked eyebrow in the rear-view mirror, attempting to infuse my body with the kind of effortlessly debonair sophistication that once lured a string of leggy lovelies – usually with a talent for some implausible martial art and a name containing at least three double entendres – to a succession of exotic, satin-draped bedrooms. All, I hasten to add, belonging to Roger Moore rather than Eddie Large. It isn't an easy act to pull off when you're driving a mud-caked Toyota Starlet whose glove compartment is so overflowing with empty Monster Munch packets and Kit-Kat wrappers that they're beginning to cascade onto the passenger seat below, but I try my best.

I have to. For, like Rod Stewart and Peter Sellers before me, I have a date with Britt Ekland.

Admittedly it's hard to imagine that either of those seasoned lotharios ever arranged to meet the Swedish sex kitten of their dreams on the first floor of a deserted shopping arcade in Swindon. Although it's a claim I can make with less certainty about her most recent husband, Slim Jim Phantom, a lanky rockabilly revivalist with the look of a man who's spent much of his life hanging around windswept malls waiting for the winklepicker to come back into fashion. Nevertheless, my mission – handed to me in a coded e-mail by undercover *Bath Chronicle* agent and celebrated *Doctor Who* background artiste Matthew – is to infiltrate the Brunel Shopping Centre and confront the woman who, thirty-two years previously, played unlikely British Intelligence officer Mary (wait for it) Goodnight opposite the triple-nippled Christopher Lee in *The Man with the Golden Gun*. Expertly performing her undercover duties in the inconspicuous, handkerchief-sized bikini that was presumably standard MI6 issue for all female agents throughout the 1970s.

A BLUFFER'S GUIDE TO . . . JAMES BOND

It's inconceivable that much of a bluffer's guide to Bond is required – unless, of course, you've spent the last forty-five years marooned on an alien planet. Or, more appropriately, tied to a slab in a secret underground lair beneath a dormant volcano while an evil genius called Maximus Nastinuss (duelling scar, Nehru jacket, vaguely Germanic accent) tells you in minute detail about his plans to destroy the world by bouncing ultra-gamma infra-violet radiation from the space shuttle wing mirrors, then leaves you to die at the mercy of an elaborate threshing machine with the 'off' button handily within throwing distance of the telescopic bowie knife hidden inside the fake filling on your upper maxillary third molar. In the British sci-fi family tree, James Bond is the aloof, womanising uncle who claims not to like science-fiction at all, but occasionally gets discovered watching *Battlestar Galactica* with his trousers round his ankles.

James Bond was originally introduced in a series of novels by former World War II naval commander Ian Lancaster Fleming, who stole the name from a famous American birdwatcher and gave many of his own lifelong passions – coffee, jetsetting, scrambled egg, shagging – to his fictional hero. Bond himself is a secret agent working for MI6, and boasts the elite Intelligence Service code number '007', the '00' being representative of his 'licence to kill' during the course of his duty. He's suave, well dressed, occasionally callous and capable of consuming staggering quantities of vodka Martini without ever dribbling down the front of his virtually omnipresent tuxedo.

Since 1962, there have been twenty-two official Bond films, with six actors having stepped into the role. In order: Sean Connery (the rugged, hairy, Scottish one), George Lazenby (the short-lived Australian one), Roger Moore (the debonair one with the eyebrows), Timothy Dalton (the 1980s one in the leather jacket), Pierce Brosnan (the Irish one with the twinkly eyes) and Daniel Craig (the 'blond Bond' with the scary stare). Although all of them are arguably still living in the shadow of one of the first actors to step into the role – future *Blockbusters* presenter Bob Holness, who took the honours in a 1956 South African radio adaptation. The plots inevitably involve a twisted foreign madman with designs to destroy 'ze vurrrld', a succession of scantily clad women with implausible names, lots of exotic, sun-drenched foreign locations (populated entirely by scantily clad women with implausible names. In bikinis) and a car chase. Or a helicopter chase. Or a space-shuttle chase. Or all three. At once.

Notable Bond catchphrases include 'The Name's Bond, James Bond', 'Shaken Not Stirred', 'No, Mr Bond, I Expect You To Die' and 'Is This The One Where They Paint The Girl Gold, Or Is That The Other One?' If you want to annoy a James Bond fan, tell him that Bob Holness is the best actor to have played the role. If you want to emulate James Bond and live the life of a debonair, globe-trotting spy, then get as drunk as humanly possible, have anonymous casual sex with a stranger, and drive an expensive car dangerously fast around a built-up urban area with the narrowest streets you can find. Middlesbrough is filled with these budding secret agents.

It's been, for me, a traumatic few weeks. The new series of *Doctor Who* has punched another TARDIS-sized hole in BBC1's Saturday-night schedules, with David Tennant's hyperactive Tenth Doctor showing no sign of losing his grip on the imagination of eight million viewers. Least of all Sorcha, who – four weeks previously – had leapt from the settee in an explosion of excitement during a seemingly innocuous scene. 'There he is! I'd know that walk anywhere!' she'd shrieked, jabbing a finger at the TV screen as the Doctor and Rose Tyler paced the streets of a parallel-universe London, the imminent threat of a violent Cyberman invasion – spear-headed, naturally, by Trigger from *Only Fools and Horses* – hanging perilously over their heads. And she was right. Lurking behind David Tennant's left shoulder, clearly concentrating intently on not tripping over the kerb and ruining the umpteenth take of the day, was a vaguely familiar figure. It's Matthew, gaining his moment of sci-fi immortality by stealing a good half-second of screen time from the good Doctor and his lissom companion.

Five minutes later, our heroes had stopped perplexed as a busy street of pedestrians halted silently in their tracks at the command of their sinister Bluetooth headsets. One of them, a stoic-looking man in a navy blue suit, had his earpiece inspected at close quarters by the Doctor, manfully resisting the temptation to blink even with a pouting Billie Piper whispering delicately around his earhole. Yes, it's John Paul – last spotted playing the proverbial silly buggers with a *Blake's 7* phaser gun in Stockton-on-Tees, but now preserved on celluloid for ever as 'Man in Street' in the brand-new *Doctor Who* episode 'Rise of the Cybermen.'

It's hard to put into the words the conflicting emotions that raced through my mind at this point. For the last thirty years, *Doctor Who* has been my favourite sci-fi refuge, an enclave of all-encompassing fiction that submerges me completely in its warm, enveloping universe. Bubble-wrap monsters, cardboard sets and spacecraft made from egg boxes have never taken me out of the drama, but the illusion is punctured completely by the sight of Matthew and John Paul striding purposefully through this episode, strange and incongruous interlopers from my boring, everyday existence. I imagine I'd have felt the same if the crucial confrontation scene between Luke Skywalker and Darth Vader in *The Empire Strikes Back* had been suddenly interrupted by my dad, sporting his favourite gardening sweater and nonchalantly walking his Staffordshire bull terrier across the Cloud City gantries, a copy of the *Mail On Sunday* tucked neatly underneath his arm. Although admittedly it's a scene that might have livened up *The Phantom Menace*.

I do, of course, contact Matthew immediately and congratulate him on his performance. And – in one of the greatest efforts of willpower I've ever been able to summon – I even resist adding the phrase 'It should have been me' to the end of my text. And we swap excited e-mails during the week afterwards, during which he casually drops into conversation the fact that a gaggle of Bond girls are preparing to descend onto Swindon's celebrated film memorabilia store Infinitely Better for two days of signing, chatting, hand-shaking and posing for shaky photographs with sweaty, ruddy-faced, breathless fans. I can't resist – even though the prospect of spending two nights in Matthew's spare room in Bath places me right at the frontline of a potential torrent of sickeningly first-hand *Doctor Who* production anecdotes.

4.15pm. The Brunel Shopping Centre dominates Swindon's central skyline like a giant, plastic-coated spider, digging its fangs into small, vulnerable high-street stores and drawing them into its sinister web of retail. It's a stiflingly hot Thursday afternoon, and I've made the mistake of slipping into my corduroy jacket before tramping up an out-of-order escalator to the first floor. By the time I arrive at the top, salty goo is pouring so heavily from my forehead that I can barely make out the Infinitely Better shop twenty yards in front of me, and the small gathering of fans who are patiently queuing outside – most of them reclining languidly on an array of portable garden furniture so impressive that I wonder if the manager of the local Wyevale Garden Centre is already halfway to Barbados carrying a suitcase stuffed full of crumpled banknotes.

I'd expected to find James Bond fandom attracting an array of chisel-jawed lotharios in sports jackets with dangerously bulging pockets, gently sipping bourbon from titanium flasks that also double as tear-gas canisters should SMERSH agents make a last-ditch attempt to infiltrate the Brunel Shopping Centre and kidnap Britt Ekland. I'm disappointed to discover that the only element of my fantasy that seems remotely close to the truth is the flasks, although they're geared more towards PG Tips and Robinson's Orange Squash than Kentucky Four Roses. I quickly find myself sandwiched between a gangly, sandy-haired fan with an unruly moustache, and an admittedly *slightly* suave silver-haired gent whose immaculate tweed attire is only vaguely compromised by an intriguing sticking plaster on his upper lip, which I convince myself is the result of a recent duelling match with a leather-clad fencing seductress called Thiza Kimbo. Moustache Man tells me enthusiastically that he's priced up the cost of getting all of the autographs he requires this weekend to complete his Bond Girl collection, and it comes to an entirely reasonable £160. He then embarks on a passionate verbal assault on Swindon Town's newly appointed manager, Dennis Wise, who he seems to consider as much a threat to global security as SPECTRE's evil-genius frontman Ernst Stavro Blofeld. I mentally drift away from the conversation, unable to stop myself picturing a grinning Wise spinning round menacingly on a swivel chair in his County Ground office, clutching a white Persian cat to his Nehru jacket and drawing up sinister plans to offer Jerel 'the Beast' Ifil a one-year extension to his contract.

I'm only dragged out of this reverie when the queue starts to shuffle forward, and I find myself being caught in a pincer movement between three T-shirted Infinitely Better employees, whose combination of eager enthusiasm and courageous facial hair experiments remind me a little of the Lone Gunmen, the trio of conspiracy theory obsessives so beloved of Agent Mulder in *The X Files*. 'Where can I find Britt?' I ask as I shamble through the shop doorway, eager not to cause embarrassment by rambling on about *The Wicker Man* and Rod Stewart to a confused-looking Maud Adams.

'Miss Eckland?' comes the laudably straight-faced reply. 'She's in the left-hand corner, just under Ian Botham.'

The shop itself is a stunningly impressive shrine to film and celebrity memorabilia, and jostling for space on every wall are delightfully incongruous collections of signed and framed publicity photographs. An autographed shot of Kevin Spacey in full Lex Luthor regalia is available for a modest seventy-five pounds, positioned directly above an identically priced homage to *Brookside*'s Jennifer Ellison. Various Bond-related celebs have been stationed at trestle tables around the edges of the main shop floor, including a so-far-unconfused-looking Maud Adams, last spotted in the title role of 1983's *Octopussy* as the proprietor of a travelling circus consisting entirely of luscious, athletic women with blue-ringed octopuses tattooed on their arses. But it's Britt who I'm keen to meet, and I scan the walls nervously for the giveaway picture of English cricket's finest all-rounder of the 1980s.

And there she is. Tucked in the corner of the room, indeed situated directly beneath a signed photo of Ian Botham, Britt Ekland is seated at a trestle table, cradling a tiny teacup Chihuahua that seems entranced by a nearby publicity shot of former Spurs midfielder Glenn Hoddle. As I approach, the suave gentleman with the lip plaster moves away, and she looks up at me with the same startlingly hypnotic blue eyes that have driven a succession of dashing millionaire playboys (and Slim Jim Phantom) wild with desire.

It's time for a confession.

CRUCIAL MOMENTS IN FANDOM HISTORY NUMBER FOUR: FANCYING BRITT EKLAND IN THE MAN WITH THE GOLDEN GUN

It's Christmas Day afternoon, 25 December 1984. I'm twelve now; scruffy, cheeky, considerably less innocent and no longer spending my Christmases at my gran's bungalow in Acklam. Instead, my gran comes over to our house, and I idle away Christmas Eve watching *Only Fools and Horses* and *Cagney and Lacey* instead of *Paddington* and *The All-Star Record Breakers* (although we still find time for *Val Doonican's Very Special Christmas*). I'm not even at Levendale Primary School any more – I'm now a uniformed first year 'Foggy' at Conyers, Yarm's sprawling local comprehensive, and have picked up a small smattering of French and a slightly larger smattering of filth from Doug Simpson's increasingly impressive knowledge of all matters carnal.

I still haven't quite got the hang of fancying people, though, and with the benefit of hindsight I'm convinced that 1970s and 1980s science fiction is largely to blame for this strange, worrying oversight. There's just not a lot of pulchritude to choose from. Princess Leia had a certain wholesome charm, but I don't recall ever thinking of her as anything more than Luke Skywalker in a long dress, with a Belgian bun stuck firmly to each ear. Servalan wasn't fanciable, she was just terrifying – a point of view that now, at the age of thirty-three, I'm still inclined to defend. And *Doctor Who*'s myriad female companions seemed to be eternally the kind of well-heeled, toffee-nosed girls I imagined owning ponies and reading Charlotte Brontë novels – which didn't do a lot for me as a grubby, snotty, twelve-year-old oik. Although admittedly it drives me crazy as a grown-up.

All that changes at ten past three on Christmas Day afternoon. I've had five solid hours of hogging the TV with my brand-new ZX Spectrum, and am already suffering from a condition that a generation of 1980s paediatricians came to know wearily as '*Jet Set Willy* Thumb'. As my parents, my gran, my uncle Trevor and his wife, Rose, and their kids prepare for Christmas dinner, I'm reluctantly forced to unplug the computer and switch to Tyne Tees for the traditional festive Bond film.

As a spaceship-loving child of the 1970s sci-fi revolution, the only Bond movie that has ever really caught my eye so far is 1979's *Moonraker*, a film that somehow managed to bridge the cultural gap between *2001: A Space Odyssey* and *Carry On at Your Convenience*. It's hard to hear lines like 'He's about to attempt re-entry' without imagining Sidney James lurking at the back of Mission Control, puffing heartily on a woodbine and yak-yak-yakking his trilby into geostationary orbit. And even then I don't think I've ever seen the whole film in one session. But today, with a face full of sage stuffing and my dad's vinegary home-made wine, I'm about to undergo a Road to Damascus moment. ITV's afternoon film is *The Man with the Golden Gun*. And I've never seen anything quite like Britt Ekland, especially when she slips into *that* microscopic bikini.

I'm convinced to this day that the experience kickstarts my idling hormones into puberty, and by the time the *Give Us a Clue Christmas Special* comes on at half past five (Bernie Winters in devastating form), I've got skin like half-popped bubble wrap and a voice that's deeper than Barry White's. It's probably not true, although I'm sure there's a certain young adult maturity to my actions later that evening, when I storm upstairs following a blazing row with my dad, who forbids me to press on with *Jet Set Willy* in favour of watching the *Just Good Friends* Christmas special.

I'm a man now, and it's all downhill from here.

Back in tropical Swindon, Britt is still holding my gaze. 'Hello!' she says, in a voice that still betrays a hint of that erotic Swedish accent. 'I'm Britt, nice to meet you!'

'I'm Bob,' I reply, and shake her hand limply. I'm terrified, and I want to play *Jet Set Willy*. 'Can I trouble you for a photograph, please?'

'Yes, of course!' she replies, with admirable enthusiasm, and climbs from behind her table, releasing the terrified-looking Chihuahua from her grasp and letting it skitter nervously around our feet.

'What's he called?' I ask.

'Tequila,' she beams.

'Does he make you happy?' I grin, making a valiant attempt to engage one of the greatest sex symbols in cinematic history with small-talk centred entirely around lyrics by Bradford's mid-1990s pop-metal sensation Terrorvision. She smiles back politely and silently, and I console myself with the knowledge that she's probably more of a Tygers of Pan Tang fan.

The official Infinitely Better photographer, a man the height and width of the average Mendip, is beckoned hurriedly from the back room, and Britt and I huddle together for a picture. She's surprisingly petite, and looks vaguely aghast at the fact that, even in the stifling heat of the crowded shop, I'm still wearing enough clothing to attempt a modest Arctic expedition. 'Come on, take your jacket off,' she snaps, halting the photographer in his tracks and placing her hands theatrically upon her hips.

'Sorry,' I reply. 'It was actually quite chilly when I left home this morning.'

'Chilly?' she shrieks, with a look of shocked indignation. 'Where are you from, the North Pole!?'

'Close,' I reply, reluctantly removing my jacket to reveal a checked shirt slightly more damp and considerably less fragrant than the average dishcloth. 'I'm from Middlesbrough, in the North-East.'

'Oh well,' she pouts. 'I was nearly right.'

Twin thoughts race simultaneously through my reeling mind. Firstly, does Britt Ekland *really* know where Middlesbrough is? And secondly, isn't it a bit rich to have the climate of my home town brought into question by a woman who was born and raised in Stockholm, where the average annual temperature – according to the BBC Weather Centre – is a bone-chilling 3.66 degrees Celsius?

I also fleetingly wonder how many other men have, when sternly instructed to remove items of clothing by an eyelash-fluttering Britt Ekland, reacted by pondering churlishly on international climate statistics. I instantly rule out Rod Stewart and Peter Sellers, but – again – I'm not sure about Slim Jim Phantom. We pose for the picture, and she smiles charmingly and returns to her trestle table, where a small queue of autograph-hunters – including Moustache Man – are now gathering. I say my thanks and slip back into my jacket, bending down to give Tequila a gentle scratch, and sending the terrified creature scattering wide-eyed towards the shelter of Maud Adams's ankles.

Thirty seconds and twenty pounds later, the photo arrives, and I look every bit as unsavoury as I'd expected. I'm fat, hot and sweaty, and the heat seems to have turned my recently trimmed hair into a bizarre, lolloping quiff. I console myself with the fact that I probably remind Britt of a young Peter Sellers.

A muggy Swindon afternoon gives way to a beautiful Bath

evening and, two hours later, I'm sitting beneath a parasol sipping gin and tonic with Matthew and his fiancée, Tara. The cares of a stressful day are soon flooding away beneath a calming blanket of early evening sunlight, which settles like freshly poured honey over the garden of their impressive Bath townhouse. Tara, a willowy, witty blonde who rolls her eyes and dives for the Bombay Sapphire every time Matthew and I head into sci-fi-related ramblings, suggests that we sample the weekly Thursday-night quiz in their favourite city-centre pub, the St James Wine Vaults. 'You'll love it,' she grins. 'It's Johnny Depp's new local, and he's always in for the quiz.'

'What?' I splutter, almost spitting the last mouthful of gin over Matthew's carefully distressed Tenth Doctor tribute red Converse All-Star trainers. 'Apparently he's bought a house in Bath city centre and is drinking in the local pubs,' nods Matthew. 'We're getting sightings reported to the paper on an almost daily basis. Vanessa Paradis goes shopping here on a Sunday.'

I clumsily text Sorcha to tell her of this latest development as we amble through the gorgeous, rustling haven of the Royal Victoria Park. On the way, Matthew and Tara ask me if I've any other fandom events lined up in their area, and I mention – perfectly reasonably – that I've heard talk of a *Hitch Hiker's Guide to the Galaxy* vs *Blake's 7* water-pistol fight taking place in a Dorset quarry in the middle of August. They insist that I break my journey in Bath on the way down, and – terrifyingly – that I bring Sorcha with me this time. Five minutes later, we crash, semi-drunkenly, through the doors of the St James Wine Vaults. We're just in time to register for the quiz.

My eyes dart nervously around the packed oak-panelled pub in search of Johnny Depp, and my stomach lurches with giddy excitement when I spy, propped languidly against the window, a whippet-thin figure whose tangles of dark hair brush elegantly against cheekbones sharp enough to open a packet of pork scratchings at twenty paces. I'm convinced that, for the second time in one day, I've met an international celluloid sex symbol in the most unlikely of locations. My heart is pounding hot, gin-riddled blood into my throbbing head as Matthew, Tara and I settle at the adjacent table and order a round of Butcombe bitter as the answer sheets are passed around.

'What are we calling our team?' asks Tara.

'"The Three Doctors",' chips in Matthew, effortlessly referencing the 1972 adventure in which erstwhile TARDIS incumbent Jon Pertwee is joined in his quest against the renegade Time Lord Omega by his irksome predecessors Patrick Troughton and William Hartnell.

At this, Johnny Depp sparks into life, and shifts around to face us with a theatrical deliberateness that sets my heart racing. '"The Three Doctors"?' he asks. 'Don't tell me you're *all* in the medical profession?' Sadly, the question is posed in an accent that owes far more to the Somerset Levels than Beverly Hills. My heart stops racing, bends double, and proceeds to blow through its cheeks with its hands on its knees while staring blankly into the middle distance. Johnny Depp he is not.

'Erm, no . . .' blushes Matthew. 'It's . . . actually an old *Doctor Who* episode.'

'Oh, *really*?' asks Non-Johnny Depp, suddenly sparking into animated excitement and glugging heartily from an enormous glass of red wine. 'I always liked *Doctor Who*, but I'm much more of a *Blake's 7* fan. Paul Darrow was my childhood hero!' I grudgingly begin to wonder whether there's anyone left in the country who hasn't emerged from the sci-fi fandom closet in the sixteen months since *Doctor Who* returned to our screens, and begin to feel as if some of my exclusive right to geeky cult-TV self-absorption is being unceremoniously chipped away.

He introduces himself as Will, and amiably shakes our hands. 'I went to a *Blake's 7* convention a couple of months ago,' I authoritatively intone, desperately trying to reclaim the higher sci-fi moral ground.

'Were there lots of women there?' asks Will, draining the dregs from his Merlot. 'That's what I've always heard.' He proceeds to undermine me even further by telling me that, at the age of nine, he'd attended the legendary 1983 *Doctor Who* convention at nearby Longleat House, the grandaddy of all chaotic UK sci-fi events, when almost fifty thousand fans turned up to an occasion that organisers had anticipated would attract no more than a couple of thousand. The situation hadn't been helped when Mark 'Turlough' Strickson, on the now-legendary '... TARDIS Wendy House' edition of *Saturday Superstore*, had urged *Doctor Who* lovers to come along even if they *didn't* have a ticket. The resulting humanitarian crisis was reportedly given a cursory glance by several passing United Nations relief organisations, who promptly shook their heads, took sharp intakes of breath and decided to press on to the Sri Lankan Civil War instead.

Sadly these crucial revelations are of no use to us whatsoever when it comes to tackling the quiz, so it's as much of a surprise to us as anyone else in the pub when it transpires, through a drunken mist, that we've actually won the bloody thing.

'What did he say?' barks Matthew, cocking his ear at the question master like a freshly awoken border collie.

'He said, "Tonight's winners are the Three Doctors"!' cries an utterly astonished Tara, and sends me up to collect the prize money. As the question master presses two crisp twenty pound notes into my hand, I'm frogmarched to the bar and made to buy a round of drinks generous enough to keep all four of us talking celebratory shite until almost 2am. At which point we bid our farewells to Will and shamble home via Bath's historic and exclusive Royal Crescent, no doubt managing to wake up a sizeable percentage of Somerset's multi-millionaires with an enthusiastic rendition of the theme to *Robin of Sherwood*.

'Johnny Depp would have won that if he'd turned up,' slurs Matthew.

'Bollocks!' I shout defiantly, as bedroom lights begin to flicker into activity all around the Royal Crescent's exclusive upper storeys. I convince myself that one of them belongs to Depp himself, shamelessly eavesdropping on our drunken ramblings and cursing Vanessa Paradis for making him stay in to watch *Holby City* instead.

I spend a muggy, sticky Somerset night unconscious in Matthew and Tara's spare room, the sash window jammed wide open to allow the occasional breeze to waft beer fumes around the ceiling. By the time I stumble downstairs at 11.45am, Matthew has long since departed on the five-minute walk to the *Bath Chronicle*'s HQ, and – according to a remarkably chatty Tara – was 'looking rather pale'.

There are no more Bond signings at Infinitely Better until tomorrow lunchtime, and as a result I've a full afternoon to fill by myself, let loose amidst the Somerset and Wiltshire country-side. I dimly remember Matthew's recommendation that I indulge my *Doctor Who* fan genes and make a spiritual pilgrimage to Nine Elms, the sleepy rural idyll that played host to Billie Piper's formative years before pop sensation, Chris Evans and the lure of the TARDIS time rotor pulled her away from Swindon for ever. I shove the thought discreetly to the back of my mind, not entirely able to convince myself that this activity doesn't count as stalking, even if the object of my interest is almost certainly eighty miles away in an expensive London apartment.

Instead, I cross the M4 and find myself passing through myriad exquisitely picturesque hamlets and villages. Slowing to a snail's pace, I daringly wind down both car windows and drink in the sun-drenched thatched-roofed beauty of Minety and Lydiard Millicent, making a vague promise to spend the remainder of the afternoon searching for a cold drink, an ice cream and – just possibly – a location to watch some of today's crunch World Cup quarter final between Germany and Argentina.

As I meander through the bumbling country lanes, my mind drifts back once again to Levendale Primary School, and I try to dredge up memories of James Bond's influence on our budding, impressionable young lives. The undisputed king of Bond trivia at school had been the imposing David Samson, a hilarious, larger-than-life figure sporting a sensational Vegas-era Elvis haircut. David could quote virtually any Bond film word for word, and, the last I'd heard, had put this childhood obsession with hi-tech gadgetry and daring military escapades to good use, as a flight lieutenant in the RAF, completing recent tours of service in Kosovo and Iraq. I wonder to what degree these formative influences play a part in shaping our adult lives, and contemplate whether – as a childhood *Doctor Who* obsessive – I was always predestined to wind up an irritating, badly dressed twat travelling aimlessly in an increasingly unreliable blue box. The Doctor's blue box was made by the Time Lords of Gallifrey, mine was made by Toyota. There's very little difference in the great, cosmic scheme of things.

It's difficult to say whether it's providence, fate or some strange, sci-fi bubblings in my subconscious that are responsible, but, emerging from this nostalgia-soaked reverie, I chug unwittingly into the tiny village of Nine Elms.

I leave the TARDIS on a grass verge and step out into the

very dictionary definition of an English summer's day. The air is thick and syrupy with heat, and great white whales of clouds are loping aimlessly in an endless azure sky. I trail my hand along a hedgerow that's alive and teeming with a million tiny, buzzy things. Across a bleached pavement, a dappled brown horse is munching lazily in a shimmering, silent paddock. I feel suddenly elated, as though every glorious summer afternoon of my childhood has been rolled into one sweet, sticky mess and drop-kicked idly into the centre of the Wiltshire countryside. So often those that succeed in the entertainment business seem driven by a desire to escape the often bleak and unforgiving dreariness of their backgrounds. If, like Billie, I'd been brought up in this rural paradise, it's hard to imagine I'd have ever left the back garden. I'd still be there now, thirty-three years old, acting out scenes from *Star Wars* with my action figures in the paddling pool.

My shirt sticking relentlessly to my chest, I cross a winding, pebble-strewn track and make for the Nine Elms pub. For a split second, as I push open the wooden door, I wonder how I'd react if Billie herself was propping up the bar, sinking a cheeky shandy and digging in for the afternoon's football. But all I find are a handful of local men, slouched amiably in the corner of a traditional oak-beamed snug, leisurely sinking daytime pints, watching the match on a quivering big screen and arguing genially about whether the natural tongue of Manchester United's Argentinian full-back Gabriel Heinze is, in fact, Welsh. Which, I'm amazed to discover on my return home, it is – hailing as he does from an area of Patagonia colonised by several hundred Cambrian settlers in July 1865. I buy a pint of Diet Coke and a copy of the *Purton Parish Magazine*, which contains a timely warning for local drivers to beware of increasing numbers of buzzards on the roads.

I vow to be on my guard.

That night, Matthew and I find ourselves once again drawn to the St James Wine Vaults. There's no sign of Johnny Depp, or even his Somerset doppelgänger Will, but we fill ourselves once again with Butcombe bitter and discuss my plan of action for tomorrow. Arriving at Infinitely Better in the morning are another flurry of Bond-related celebrities, including legendary British model and actress Caroline Munro.

In the 1970s, Caroline gained a reputation for wholesome, girl-next-door sex appeal; her pout and raven-black hair making her one of the faces of the decade, and giving her a delightfully incongruous doubled-edged career – she spent ten years as the face of an advertising campaign for Lamb's Navy Rum, while simultaneously becoming the only actress ever signed to a long-term deal by Hammer Films, strutting her sensual stuff in the likes of *Dracula AD 1972* and *Captain Kronos: Vampire Hunter.* I'm terrified at the prospect of meeting her – even more so when Matthew makes me drunkenly promise that I'll make a trip to Morrison's in the morning and buy a 700-millilitre bottle of Lamb's Navy Rum for her to sign.

In 1977, Caroline appeared in *The Spy Who Loved Me*, a gleefully overblown Bond escapade in which Roger Moore predictably 'keeps the British end up' in a film whose outrageous arch Englishness seems to have been deliberately calculated to coincide with Jubilee year. She played the part of Naomi, an unlikely helicopter pilot in the pay of silver-haired madman Karl Stromberg. Commandeering her chopper aided by nothing more than a ludicrously tight white blouson and a succession of cheeky winks, Naomi chases Bond along the sun-dappled coastal roads of Sardinia, before the sneaky secret agent transforms his speeding Lotus into a mini-submarine and destroys her from the sea with a surface-to-air missile. Caroline has also recently popped up in a Big Finish *Doctor*

Who audio, playing – bizarrely – the misguided fiancée of *The Three Doctors* renegade Time Lord, Omega.

My loyalties are predictably divided.

BLOODY STUPID THINGS I HAVE DONE IN THE NAME OF FANDOM NUMBER FOUR: TRYING TO MAKE MY NIPPLES GO 'HARD WITH DESIRE'

It's a few months AB (Anno Britt) now, sometime in early 1985, and I'm lying on my bed in the late evening, having only recently been disconnected from the ZX Spectrum that's now become such an integral part of my day-to-day existence that my dad calls it my 'life-support machine'. There's a dim light shining from the *Doctor Who* lampshade onto the *Star Wars* wallpaper that's now been present just a *few* too many years to be strictly healthy, and I'm reading a book. It's a well-thumbed paperback that I've bought on a recent foray to the secondhand book stall at the centre of Stockton Market, a grubby 1960s-style thriller with the price tag of '3'6' still unclipped at the bottom of the cover. It's Ian Fleming's *From Russia With Love*. And I am, to be perfectly frank, playing with myself.

No, behave. Not like *that*. I'm just intrigued by a scene midway through the book, where Bond returns, exhausted after a busy day's secret agenting, to his Ankara hotel room, only to find – predictably – a beautiful young KGB agent named Tatiana Romanova languishing in his bed, wearing nothing but black stockings and a ribbon round her neck. During their inevitable coupling, Bond cups her breasts in his hands and, intriguingly, feels her nipples 'harden with desire'.

I'm baffled by this. Is that really what happens? I've passionately desired many things in my short life (Palitoy *Millennium*

*Falcon*s, early exits from Middlesbrough matches, Britt Ekland) but none of them have ever made my nipples stiffen. I've simply never heard of the phenomenon. I put the book down and try to conduct a biological experiment, wiggling my fingers over my own pale pigeon chest to see if it elicits any response. Princess Leia looks down disapprovingly from the wallpaper. There's nothing doing, so I wonder if external stimulation is the answer and tentatively recruit two three-inch *Star Wars* action figures from the bedside table to act as humble assistants. At which point my dad barges through the bedroom door to tell me it's time to settle down to sleep, only to discover his twelve-year-old son lying topless on a *Star Wars* bedspread with a grimacing Imperial Stormtrooper clasped firmly to each nipple. I can tell from the look on his face that he's already assumed Darth Vader is practising his dark arts somewhere in my pyjama bottoms.

The *Star Wars* wallpaper, curtains, bedspread and pillowcases are removed by mutual consent a matter of weeks later. I am, mercifully, allowed to finish the book, although I should report now in the name of research that my nipples remain unmoved throughout.

It's Saturday morning. With Matthew alongside me for moral support, I'm less nervous this time, and although the Brunel Shopping Centre is arguably hotter and certainly busier than it was two days previously, I feel cool and relaxed as we take our place in another small but perfectly formed queue. As we shuffle into position, the morning's celebrities file out of the shop doorway and pose in a smiling, orderly line in front of the main window, as a photographer from the *Swindon*

Advertiser snaps away. Caroline Munro is unmistakable in the line-up, still sporting her trademark raven-black tresses, now augmented by the occasional blonde highlight, and gathering an elegant blue shawl around her impeccably suntanned shoulders.

The queue moves quickly, and – as we all amble into the shop – Matthew finds the signed picture of Jennifer Ellison a little too conspicuously hilarious. Caroline is clearly intrigued, and throws a gleaming smile in our direction as another happy punter vacates her trestle table.

I'm shaking, and I see a slightly worried look cross her brow as I start rummaging around in my holdall. 'You probably get asked this all the time,' I stammer nervously, 'but I couldn't resist bringing this for you to sign.' Narrowly avoiding producing the packet of soggy Wagon Wheels that I'd bought for the journey on Thursday morning, I produce a pristine bottle of Lamb's Navy Rum. Matthew and I have had a gentlemen's wager on how frequently Caroline is presented with the same item by eager autograph-hunters, keen to stand out from the queuing masses. He reckons 'not at all'; my metaphorical money is firmly placed on 'every single bloody time'.

'Oh, how sweet!' shrieks Caroline. 'Do you know, no one has ever asked me to sign one of these before!'

Matthew gives me a smug 'told you so' look as Caroline nudges Martine Beswick – last spotted as Caribbean beauty Paula Kaplan in *Thunderball,* and now apparently running a successful removals business in London – and gleefully shows her the bottle, which Martine finds hilarious. 'Do you actually like the stuff?' She grins, proudly displaying an exotic accent and an attitude to British rum entirely becoming of a former Miss Jamaica.

'Yes,' I stammer. 'Lovely with a drop of Coke.'

'Even nicer with coffee,' beams Caroline, with a knowing look that suggests the crates of complimentary booze she surely received throughout the 1970s from a grateful Lamb's marketing department didn't go entirely to waste. She gleefully writes 'To Bob, you're the first!' around the label's iconic Union Jack logo, and treats me to two hand-drawn kisses (or 'dink dinks', as she calls them) around the forty per cent proof declaration. My legs, by this point, have turned to blancmange. I'm like a schoolboy on his first date, blushing bright red and failing miserably to finish my sentences. Matthew is acting as official photographer, and Caroline jumps from her seat to pose for a picture, oozing photogenic star quality as we clasp the Lamb's Navy Rum between us. I'm euphoric, even more so when I realise that this is probably the first time these two iconic British symbols (Caroline and the rum, not Caroline and me) have been photographed together since 1979. I vaguely wonder which other household items I can bring to be signed at future conventions, and it strikes me that, in order to accommodate the vast array of domestic products advertised by Chris Barrie, I'd need to back a fleet of Tesco delivery wagons into the Peterborough Holiday Inn well ahead of September's *Red Dwarf* weekend.

The whole experience passes, just like all my celebrity encounters so far, in a state of strange hyper-reality. I feel like I'm in the opening pre-credit sequence of *The Spy Who Loved Me* myself – an adrenaline-pumping, white-knuckle ride down a terrifying conversational ski-slope, dodging the fizzing bullets of social faux pas and only feeling the cold relief of freedom when Matthew and I bid Caroline our farewells and leave the shop, my metaphorical Union Jack parachute billowing wide through the Infinitely Better doorway and guiding me to the safety of the Brunel Shopping Centre. Outside, Matthew and I laugh and both make breathless comments as to how nice Caroline had been, and we begin to troop down the escalator, slapping each other's backs. Thirty seconds later, I realise I've left the bottle of Lamb's Navy Rum at the side of her trestle table, and have to shamefacedly retrace my steps to retrieve it. 'The last thing you want to do is lose your bottle,' she winks, as I mumble my apology and slink back out of the shop. My legs this time have gone beyond blancmange and have all the consistency of weak orange squash. I bid farewell to Matthew, and – ten miles north of Swindon city centre – I pass a dead buzzard at the side of the A419.

I arrive back on Teesside just as England's crunch quarter-final match against Portugal reaches half-time, and troop wearily through the door of Smudge's new house in Darlington, bearing the carefully pressed DVD sleeves (*The Wicker Man* and *Captain Kronos: Vampire Hunter*) that he'd given me to be autographed by my new chums Britt and Caroline, and proudly displaying the Lamb's Navy Rum bottle to a gathered football-loving throng that includes a grinning Sorcha. 'Did you meet Johnny Depp, then?' she asks, with just a hint of malevolent evil in her voice. 'And when am I coming down there to look for him?'

'Five weeks' time,' I sigh, resigned to my fate. 'We're both invited. Did I mention the *Hitch Hiker's Guide to the Galaxy* vs *Blake's 7* water-pistol fight?' At this point, the room falls silent. I look around to see if the very mention of this brilliantly ludicrous escapade has been enough to turn a roomful of friends previously sympathetic to my cause into hostile, geek-baiting macho men, but realise to my instant relief that the cause for their disquiet is merely a red card being waved before the slack-jawed face of Wayne Rooney.

'No, you didn't,' she smiles. 'But I'm definitely up for that! And by the way, can I come to *Red Dwarf* as well?'

I gaze longingly at the signed bottle of Lamb's Navy Rum

now sitting idly on the front-room floor, manfully resisting the temptation to lose myself in its charms.

It's going to be a long, hard summer.

THE BATTLE TO SAVE EARTH

By Robert Fischer (Aged Eight And Five Twelfths)
Wednesday 22 April 1981
PART SIX

Dirk jumped onto the ramp and started running towards another doorway at the opposite side of the ramp. Richard and I followed him. We ran into another room. It contained a group of private escape ships. I did not go near the ships, but instead, stood by the doorway we had just come through. I had only been there a few seconds when the guards and robots came charging through the doorway. As soon as I saw the first robot come through, I shot him to pieces with my rifle. Then I ran to join Richard and Dirk at the private ship. Dirk kicked open the door and jumped into the pilots seat. Richard and I got into the co-pilots seats. Dirk flicked some switches and pulled a lever and there was a roar of engines. A panel in the wall opened and revealed the darkness of space. The spaceship sped through and disappeared into space. Suddenly a hatch opened on the side of the planet that we had just escaped from. A laser cannon started firing beams at our ship. But Dirk had been a pilot nearly all his life. He was weaving the ship through all the lasers. 'What was that planet?' I asked. 'The planet Davrock,' Dirk answered. Then an explosion rocked the ship. Richard fell off his chair. I looked out of the window and saw a patrol of Imperial fighters. I told Dirk. 'Get to the rear laser,' Dirk said. I climbed over Dirk's chair to a huge gun at the back of the ship. . .

To be continued . . .

STAR TREK

YORK MAZE
TOM PEARCY'S FARM, YORK
MONDAY 31 JULY

'You mean Captain Kirk and Mr Spock *shag* each other?'

A STRIDENT MIDDLESBROUGH ACCENT ricochets around the classroom. 'Mr Fischer,' it announces as the room falls silent. 'Captain Kirk does not scratch his backside with his protractor!'

It's late 1984, and I've just turned twelve. It's a few months now since I arrived at Conyers, Yarm's sprawling, modern, glass and concrete comprehensive, and I'm starting to find my feet. And, it seems, the itchiest part of my left buttock with the edge of a half-moon protractor. I whirl round to find Mr Harrison – our thirtysomething drama teacher, pure Teesside and able to pull a devastating Les Dawson gurn at the drop of a Stanislavski textbook – grinning at me. 'Get on with it,' he drawls, as I coyly smile and mumble at my feet. With teenage life less than a year away, I've become something of an expert mumbler when the mood strikes, and am slowly working my way towards full-scale surly grunting.

Our drama class has been split into several groups, and given twenty minutes to devise a short comedy sketch. My team has been handed the task of producing an amusing *Star Trek* spoof, with Mr Harrison asking me to step into the ample puffed trousers of Captain James T. Kirk, and the droll, lanky Simon

Bentley to be Mr Spock, a casting decision perhaps wholly inspired by Simon's almost entirely square black haircut, the corners of which seem to bisect his temples at an angle of exactly ninety degrees. I'd have checked with more precision if I hadn't had my protractor up my arse.

But – and this is the key – he doesn't want us to be Kirk and Spock in their youthful, vigorous prime. No – what we've been asked to do is to spoof *Star Trek* as it's seen *now*, in the mid-1980s – with the valiant crew of the *Enterprise* doddering around the bridge on Zimmer frames and Stannah stairlifts.

'Phwattt?' I stammer in a creaky old man's voice, deafly cupping a hand to my ear and wobbling into a gum-stained chair. 'Phwattt's that Uhururura, Phhhwarp Factor PHWATTT?!' It's cruel, but there's an element of truth here. It's now fifteen years since the cancellation of the original *Star Trek* TV series, and the franchise has only recently been revived as a series of successful big-screen blockbusters. Yet it hasn't gone unnoticed – not least by Mr Harrison – that several of the main characters are being played by veteran actors boldly venturing well into their fifties (stand up, Kirk and Spock, if you can). And that the likes of James 'Scotty' Doohan and DeForest 'Bones' Kelley are at least a decade older than that.

Which had shocked me a little bit when I'd seen the first film. I just hadn't bargained on the fact that my sci-fi heroes could ever grow old. After all, *Star Wars* was a saga virtually characterised by the youthful energy of its principal actors, and *Doctor Who* was a show in which the main protagonist made a habit of regenerating into a younger man every three or four years. *Star Trek*, the original TV series that is, lasted for a mere three years in the late 1960s, but a seemingly endless loop of BBC repeats throughout my childhood had rendered the cast practically ageless – they just didn't seem to change at all, despite the fact that their legendary 'five-year mission' – rolling around indefinitely in BBC1 repeat seasons – never showed any signs of ending. Subsequently, when *Star Trek: the Motion Picture* gave me my first glimpse of an updated *Enterprise* crew in 1979, the sight of a wrinkled, slightly paunchy Kirk and a sixty-year-old Scotty sporting silver hair and moustache had been a huge culture shock for my seven-year-old self. I actually found the whole concept slightly frightening, the weight of mortality and human frailty being brought home to me with sledgehammer brutality. And it didn't even have the proper theme tune at the start.

A BLUFFER'S GUIDE TO . . . STAR TREK

Star Trek was conceived in the mid-1960s by former World War II fighter pilot Gene Roddenberry, an all-American aviation expert who later served with the Los Angeles Police Department – alongside a Lieutenant Wilbur Clingan, whose surname he would adapt to adorn his most celebrated race of TV baddies. In the 1950s, however, he found his vocation as a scriptwriter for the hit TV western *Have Gun, Will Travel*. And, inspired by the success of *Flash Gordon* and *Buck Rogers*, *Star Trek* – his '*Wagon Train* to the stars' – debuted on 8 September 1966, introducing American viewers to the crew of the twenty-third century starship *Enterprise*, shot into deep space by the 'United Federation of Planets' to . . . well (clears throat, parts legs), 'explore strange new worlds, to seek out new life and new civilisations, to boldly go where no man has gone before'. And, in the process, to create perhaps the most famous split infinitive in the history of human civilisation.

The key crew members have entered into the pantheon of cultural legend. There's Captain James T. Kirk (William Shatner)

– solid, determined, not averse to snogging brightly coloured women from other planets; medical officer 'Bones' McCoy (DeForest Kelley) – old-fashioned, prickly, given to exclaiming 'Dammit, Jim, I'm a doctor, not a [insert random non-doctorly occupation here]' to his captain when asked to think outside the box; engineer Montgomery 'Scotty' Scott (James Doohan) – creative, put-upon, not entirely convincingly Scottish; helmsman Mr Sulu (George Takei) – thoughtful, gentle, rather too interested in sword-fencing; and communications officer Lieutenant Uhura (Nichelle Nichols) – professionally flirty, with enormous earrings and an unfeasibly short skirt. Persistent rumour has it that Nichols considered leaving the show at the end of the first series, but was persuaded to stay on by Martin Luther King, who considered her the perfect TV role model for the young African-American disenfranchised. King, in a presumably entirely unrelated incident, was assassinated a mere six days after the second series ended, thus robbing him of the opportunity to convince Patrick Troughton to stick around for a fourth series of *Doctor Who*.

Our heroes were joined in the second series by Lieutenant Chekov, (Walter Koenig) – twitchy, naïve and with a tendency to credit his beloved 'Mother Russia' for the invention of anything from Scotch whisky to, erm, communism.

However, all of these characters are mere striplings compared to the mighty sci-fi oak who bestrides the *Enterprise*'s desk like a squinting, square-haired colossus. Leonard Nimoy's Mr Spock has, over the course of the last forty years, become one of most iconic figures in global popular culture. A pointy-eared half-human, half-Vulcan, he's responsible for countless generations of playground heroes doing brilliant slitty-fingered salutes to their dinner nannies and crippling weaker, packed-lunch-eating nancies with excruciating 'Vulcan death grips' to the shoulder. And all of this while playing folk songs on a Vulcan lyre. He's cool, taciturn, ultra-logical and capable of dismissing any brazen example of rash human emotion with a single withering glare. He is, in a nutshell, the Vulcan Alan Hansen.

The show ran for three series, before dwindling ratings led to its seemingly permanent demise in 1969. A brief animated version followed in the mid-1970s, before the original cast reunited in 1979 for a big-screen revival, the success of which has led to ten cinema sequels to date. In September 1987, the franchise returned to TV as *Star Trek: the Next Generation*, starring fruity-voiced Yorkshire character actor Patrick Stewart as Captain Jean-Luc Picard, arguably popular fiction's least convincing Frenchman since the gendarme from *'Allo 'Allo!* Further spin-offs have included *Star Trek: Deep Space Nine*, *Star Trek: Voyager* and, most recently, the ill-fated *Star Trek: Enterprise*. And the original series, to distinguish itself from the various offshoots, is now known universally as just that: *The Original Series*, or 'TOS', to the amusement of overgrown schoolboys everywhere.

Notable *Star Trek* catchphrases include 'Beam Me Up, Scotty' (which was never actually said), 'Highly Illogical' (which Nimoy turned into a brilliantly whimsical pop song during his late 1960s recording career), 'Ye Cannae Break The Laws Of Physics, Jim' and 'I Bet The One In The Red Shirt Dies First'. If you want to annoy a *Star Trek* fan, call him a 'Trekkie' rather than the infinitely more politically correct term 'Trekker', and if you want to shatter his dreams completely, go on national television and tell him to get a life, kiss some girls and move out of his mother's basement. William Shatner famously did, and the fallout wasn't pretty.

'I bet the one in the red shirt dies first,' says Wez. He's looking at me and grinning evilly as we budge along the back seat of the *Toyota Starlet Enterprise*. He's referring to *Star Trek*'s notorious 'Red Shirt Phenomenon' – the theory being that if a hitherto unknown crew member wearing a red shirt accompanies Captain Kirk to an alien planet at the start of an episode, he'll be dead before his ankle boots have touched the polystyrene rocks. I look down disparagingly at my own bright crimson apparel as Wez and his fellow *Star Wars* comrade Smudge laugh demonically. Sorcha is driving, and Stuart – he who brought the *Star Wars* Trivial Pursuit round on Christmas Day – is also with us. He's a towering skinhead whose intimidating appearance is only slightly compromised by a pair of baggy khaki shorts and a rather camp-looking cricketing hat. He looks like the meaner, taller brother of 'Lofty' Sugden from *It Ain't Half Hot Mum*. We're going to the York Maze. Or, to put it slightly more accurately, the York Maize Maze.

It's a staggering local phenomenon. Every summer since 2002, ambitious farmer Tom Pearcy has drawn thousands of tourists to his sprawling land by transforming a thirty-two-acre crop field into the largest maze in the world – using computer technology to cut increasingly complex designs into the maize, producing patterns that, from the surrounding hillsides, look like a brilliantly bloody-minded Yorkshire version of the Nazca Sand Drawings in Peru. This year Tom, an avowed science-fiction fan, has chosen to commemorate the fortieth anniversary of *Star Trek*'s TV debut by producing a maze of breathtakingly beautiful complexity – its narrow, winding pathways fusing together to create a montage of scenes from the franchise. A perfect starship *Enterprise* cruises into orbit round a ringed planet, firing an industrial-strength phaser beam at an evil Borg Cube as Mr Spock and Jean-Luc Picard look on, in profile. In a sheltered corner of a quiet pub in York's labyrinthine Shambles quarter, a group of scantily clad Nazca warriors are sitting in silence, shaking their heads and weeping into their Stonewall bitter.

I haven't heard anything about the maze until a week previously, when it had been mentioned in hushed, reverential tones on the car radio as I'd driven along Yarm High Street. In a frenzy of illogicality that would make Mr Spock trash his lyre, we'd all booked a day off work to investigate. With the car bursting at the rivets on a staggeringly hot, sunny morning, and even our amiable collie Allie panting and rummaging in the boot, we set off heartily down the A19.

I've come out of the closet recently. Most of my friends are now aware that I've thrown my summer over to pure sci-fi indulgence, and I've finally managed to tell my parents about the quest too, after my mum – ever the amiable nosy parker – kept badgering me to reveal where Sorcha and I were spending our holidays this year. 'Peterborough,' I'd eventually mumbled, over a cup of coffee in our kitchen. 'We're going to a *Red Dwarf* convention.'

'And Leicester,' Sorcha had chipped in. 'You promised I could come to Discworld too.'

Thankfully both my parents had found the prospect hilarious. Three days later, my mum had arrived at the house with a mysterious-looking laundry bag in tow. Inside I'd found, to my utter childish delight, my old *Star Wars* bedspread and pillowcases, last spotted being bundled into the loft twenty years and at least three family homes previously. I'm still intending to put them on the spare bed in the box room, but – six months on – I haven't quite got round to washing them yet. Well, I've been busy.

The weeks ahead are metamorphosing into a backbreaking national tour gruelling enough to make the Rolling Stones take a sharp intake of breath. Or, indeed, anything else they might have to hand. The convention whirlwind is taking over my life, and running up a series of overdrafts and credit-card debts so impressive that I'm tempted to approach Bob Geldof to stage a series of benefit gigs for me sometime in the autumn (not 23 September, though, we'll be away in Peterborough with Danny John-Jules). I'm in genuine financial trouble, but – in the immortal words of Freddie Mercury, who'll be there in spirit at the Fischer Aid Relief Concert – don't stop me now, I'm having such a good time. And, although I'm not quite travelling at the speed of light, we are doing almost seventy-five miles per hour in the outside lane of the A19.

On the journey down, I tell Sorcha, Stuart, Wez and Smudge about some recent delvings into online fandom oddness. I've discovered, with a mixture of incredulity, hilarity and slight arousal, the phenomenon of 'slash fiction'. This, I recount through a fit of shameful schoolboy giggles, is a sub-genre of fan-written fiction focusing on romantic physical encounters between male sci-fi characters. It's thought to have originated when female *Star Trek* fans in the late 1970s decided that the TV relationship between Mr Spock and Captain Kirk was somewhat less intimate than the one they'd like to read about. I find a site that dedicates itself to *Enterprise*-based gay romantic poetry – some of which is actually really good, and rather touching in a way I find it very hard to explain. My favourite being Clopton Stanhope's marvellous 'Amok Time in Iambic Tetrameter':

> *The time of fire in blood and heart*
> *Did nearly tear poor Spock apart,*
> *But once he fought and hurt his Jim,*
> *He knew that was the man for him.*

It's best if you read it in a Leonard Nimoy voice.

There's also, more wholesomely, the phenomenon of 'shipping'. 'Shippers', I discover, are more interested in the sentimental side of science fiction, and write florid reams of romantic prose in which Captain Kirk and Lieutenant Uhura decide to knock all that Klingon-baiting nonsense on the head for a week or two, and enjoy long, romantic walks in the countryside with the occasional chaste snog beneath the fourth moon of Omega IV. The term, I discover, derives from the word 'relationship'. I find the concept really charming and heart-warming.

All of this is lost on Sorcha. 'You mean Captain Kirk and Mr Spock *shag* each other?' she gasps, before breaking into hysterical laughter. Forty minutes and one lengthy poo-stop later (the dog this time, rather than Smudge), we're pulling into the car park of the York Maize Maize.

It's the beginning of the school summer holidays, and the place is crawling with enough grubby-faced kids to take down a Klingon warship, disarming their Disruptor guns and D'K Tahg knives with a combination of junk food, snot and relentless, piercing screaming. We wander towards the ticket booth, set up in the window of what looks like a customised ice-cream van, and I'm slightly relieved to find that we've missed the inaugural York Maze naturist night, held two days previously on a balmy Saturday evening. There's probably a fascinating and insightful academic text to be written about the sociological crossover between science-fiction fans and nudists, but it's hard to imagine anyone being keen enough to do the research. There are *some* final frontiers that no one wants to examine too closely.

We pay our five-pound entrance fees, and shamble through, with dog on lead, to the main entrance to the maze, a narrow chipboard tunnel from which life-size cardboard cutouts of the principal *Enterprise* crew in their late 1960s pomp gaze down on us with haughty disdain. Stuart and I pose for a picture with a glowering Captain Kirk, who seems to be staring at me with a look that falls somewhere between accusatory hatred and withering disapproval. And I've a terrible, guilty feeling that I know the reason why.

CRUCIAL MOMENTS IN FANDOM HISTORY NUMBER FIVE: WALKING OUT OF STAR TREK: THE MOTION PICTURE

It's late 1979, I'm seven, and I'm walking back from Mr Murray's newsagent's, past Shipman's bakery where mutant cream slices grow to dangerously outlandish sizes, round the corner where the low-rent emporium of Hinton's supermarket smells permanently of baked beans and cats, and back to my gran's bungalow in Acklam. I'm entirely resistant to any of these enticing retail opportunities, because I'm reading *Doctor Who Weekly*. It's a recently launched title boasting exciting comic strips and fascinating behind-the-scenes stories, and I've bought it since the first issue. The edition I'm currently perusing is undoubtedly number ten, and if I'm at my gran's house then it must be a weekend, and I wouldn't have waited till the Sunday, so amazingly I can pin the date down to Saturday 15 December 1979. Detective work, eh? Give me a deerstalker and a long, bendy pipe and I'll have that Jack the Ripper nonsense sorted out in two shakes. And, amazingly, I'm not even reading about *Doctor Who*. No, what's actually caught my eye is the advertisement on the back of the comic. It's a full-page, rainbow-coloured poster for *Star Trek: the Motion Picture*.

Now I like *Star Trek*; I watch it on telly with my dad. And he peppers our viewing experiences with snippets of fascinating trivia that are still lodged inside my tangled, overgrown brain two and a half decades later – like the fact that Bones is called Bones because ships' doctors in long-gone seafaring days were pejoratively nicknamed 'Sawbones', and the *Enterprise* takes all of its lingo from maritime rather than aviation history. And I thank him for enriching my childhood and stimulating my ever-developing sense of cultural awareness in this way by rolling my eyes and saying, 'Shurrup, Dad, the man with the pointy ears is on.'

Everyone at school watches it as well. I suppose it might seem odd, in this fast-moving, multimedia age, that a generation of seven-year-olds could be intimately familiar with a programme first broadcast almost twice their little lifetimes ago, but back in 1979, it really, honestly wasn't. It's probably worth reiterating at this point 'for our younger viewers', the shape of the TV landscape back in the late 1970s. The UK had a grand total of three TV channels – BBC1, BBC2 and a regional variation of ITV, of which ours in North-East England was Tyne Tees Television. There was no breakfast television. At all. If you tried watching any of your TV channels before nine thirty in the morning, you would see a static, patterned test card accompanied by some light orchestral music. Then you might see some brief news, and a few educational programmes for schools and colleges, followed by children's shows (*Rainbow*, *Play School*, *Bod*) around lunchtime. Then, more than likely, the musical test card again, as there were frequently no afternoon shows to speak of. The children's schedules would kick in again at about 3.30pm, and would run into the evening primetime. All three channels closed down around midnight, at which point a tired-sounding continuity announcer would remind us to unplug our TV sets, wish us a restful good night, and play a snippet from the national anthem. No, really. Then they'd bung the test card on for the best part of another ten hours. All this was, of course, dependent on there being any TV at all – for, in a decade dominated by trade-union unrest, the television industry was often both willing volunteer and unwitting victim. In early August 1979, just as I was getting into my *Star Trek* and *Doctor Who* stride, ITV went on strike completely, replacing all of its programming with a simple blue caption apologising for the lack of service. That caption stayed there, uninterrupted, for – wait for it – almost three months, until the end of October. During which time BBC bosses drank Eddie Large's weight in champagne whenever their weekly viewing figures arrived.

The possibility for autonomy when it came to watching TV was virtually non-existent. On the lovely, regular occasions when my gran would join us to goggle at the box, the recurring mantra she invoked at the end of every programme now seems almost heart-breaking in its simple, innocent charm. 'What do we get now?' she would say, as the closing credits rolled on *The Dick Emery Show* or *When the Boat Comes In*. Not 'What shall we watch now?' but '*What do we get now?*' For my gran and her generation, *and* for my parents, and for *me* – until my teenage years at least – TV was an entirely passive experience, a domestic version of the theatre or cinema. We sat in our armchairs and the TV people – whoever they were – showed us what they wanted, in the order they decreed. We were even, at this stage, several years away from the arrival of the home video recorder – making this an age when 'appointment viewing' meant exactly that. If we wanted to watch our favourite programmes, we had no option but to sit there and wait for them to come on. And if we missed them . . . well, we *had* missed them. Probably for ever.

There were no satellite or cable channels, no Freeview boxes, no red buttons and other assorted interactive guff, no games consoles or home computers, no DVD players or recorders, no internet or e-mail, no digital radios, no mobile phones; in fact at this stage in my life I didn't know anyone with an answering machine for their phone; in fact I *even* knew a few people who didn't have a landline at all. Blackberries were something that my gran made into lovely crumbles, and if my dad had seen a mouse in the house, he'd have hit it with a bloody big spade. So we didn't have this modern-day welter of technological overload, but we made up for it with a sense of communal cultural experience that's been almost completely eradicated now. Quality TV programmes became seismic, news-worthy events, and ordinary TV shows were still universally watched. It still sends a shiver down to my spine to think that *The Morecambe and Wise Christmas Show* in 1977 attracted over twenty-eight million viewers – around half the population of the UK at that time. And Lord only knows what the other half were doing. But even more standard, weekly fayre – *Blankety Blank* or *Sale of the Century* – commanded viewing figures of up to twenty million. So yes, in a nutshell, all the kids watched *Star Trek*. There was, to put it bluntly, fuck all else to do.

Anyway, I quite fancy the film. Up until this point, I've only been to see six films at the cinema. In order: *The Jungle Book*, *Star Wars* (twice), *The Rescuers*, *Pete's Dragon* and *Superman: the Movie*. I'm keen to add to my portfolio, so I submit an official verbal cinema request to my parents ('Pleeeeeeeeeeeeeeeease') and – yay! – a matter of days later, my mum – my poor, overtired mum who would surely rather be curled up with the latest Jilly Cooper or watching *To the Manor Born* – takes me back to Stockton's Odeon and we claim our seats at the back of the theatre.

What I'm expecting is everything I love from *Star Trek* – fast spaceships, scary monsters, phaser guns and Captain Kirk being dead, dead brave. Unfortunately, within twenty minutes, I'm shuffling uncomfortably in my seat and yawning. There's been a load of stuff about the *Enterprise* having a refit – which, however impressively you dress it up, amounts to little more than watching the twenty-third century equivalent of an MOT – and the main baddie is a cloud. That's right – a *cloud*. Not a gang of big, veiny, dome-headed nutters like the Talosians; not a band of white, violent apes with horny heads like the Mugatos; not even a plague of fluffy, purring pests like the Tribbles. No – a *cloud*.

This, I decide, isn't what I came to see. I can see clouds anywhere. There are loads of them above Middlesbrough, especially in December. And they're not exactly in short supply at the height of summer, either. There are, however, no Talosians on Teesside (although Boro striker Billy Ashcroft looks a bit like a Mugato) and that's a huge part of the science-fiction experience for me at this age – the ability to remove myself from the ordinary, the everyday and the humdrum, and to immerse myself in this incredible universe, to let it power my imagination and fuel my playtimes.

'It's a bit boring this, isn't it?' I whisper to my mum.

'Do you want to go home?' she whispers back, with – I can tell – a fair degree of hope in her voice.

'Yeah,' I reply with barely a moment's thought.

It remains the only cinema screening that I've ever walked out of before the final credits. And I don't watch the full movie until ten years later, when I pass a dull Sunday afternoon as a callow sixth-former sprawled languidly across my parents' settee, unable to summon up the energy to change channels when the film pops up on TV.

And this time, to my immense surprise, I love it. Yes, it's slow and ponderous, but it has an elegance, a depth and an intelligence that's utterly laudable and almost entirely unnecessary for a mainstream, blockbusting adaptation of a cheesy old 1960s sci-fi show. And the return of Kirk and Spock and the gang is handled with the utmost sensitivity – they're not fifty-year-old actors squeezing into corsets and pretending to be thirty; their characters have grown with them, and the sight of a wrinkled Kirk stepping out of retirement, gazing mistily down the *Enterprise* corridors and earning the respect of younger colleagues who had previously found him fusty and outmoded, is a joy to watch. It's no surprise that my seven-year-old self didn't like it, because it owes less to *Star Wars* than to *2001: A Space Odyssey*. And I'd hated that as a kid as well, finding it equally slow and ponderous, and failing to understand why Rigsby from *Rising Damp* would lower himself to such lesser fayre. But, with the passage of time, I've taken lessons from the dignified maturity of the *Enterprise* crew, and realised that *Star Trek: The Motion Picture* has far more to offer than just glitzy effects and whizz-bang set-pieces.

Although *Star Trek II: The Wrath of Khan* is better, obviously. It has big explosions, a proper baddie and wiggly worms that crawl in people's ears.

We're in the maize maze, and I'm part unnerved and part entranced. Unnerved because it has never occurred to me in the thirty-three years that I've been on the planet what a scary prospect it might actually be to get trapped in a field of maize. These crops aren't nice, floaty, wavy crops, rippling in a delicate breeze and inviting wanton lovers to lose themselves in their charms; they're big bloody spiky things – densely packed, over eight feet tall and with huge, nasty, grabby, pointy leaves. You'd be hard pressed to ripple these buggers with a bulldozer. The maze's claustrophobic, winding thoroughfares are barely six feet across, and it's impossible to see anything but the immediate pathways before and behind us. There are no wanton lovers here, and if there were, they'd have weals on their backsides. I start to feel a pang of sympathy for the nudists. And *there's* a Rolling Stones song if ever I heard one.

Entranced because, at heart, I love woods and wildernesses and wild places in general. As a small boy, the scattered woodlands and copses and farmers' fields around Yarm's outskirts were brilliant, magical places – filled with the fairies and fawns of my favourite childhood fables. The passing of the years has never robbed me of these childhood fantasies, and even now I can happily while away an afternoon wrapped in the roots of a sessile oak. I wouldn't take any chances with a downy birch, though – even on a first date, they're all twigs and branches.

We begin to tramp our away around the labyrinth, encountering petrified-looking kids, determined-looking dads and the occasional timber vantage post that elevates us just high enough to give a tantalising glimpse of the full *Star Trek* picture. It's vast, and it's brilliant – and I really do feel as though Scotty has beamed us down to some strange, surreal, spiky alien netherworld. It's like spending the afternoon in a page from *Where the Wild Things Are*. It's a sense of delirious otherworldliness only consolidated when Sorcha points out that we make a reasonable facsimile of the gang from *The Wizard of Oz*. She's cast herself as Dorothy, of course (I was robbed); with huge, gentle Stuart the cowardly Lion; bald, mechanically minded Wez the Tin Man; and me – scruffy, haphazard, a bit dopey – as the Scarecrow. We've even got the dog. Smudge, we decide, will have to stand behind a curtain in a frock coat and pretend to be the Wizard himself, and is dutifully despatched to take a photo of the rest of us, arms linked, dancing through a corridor of maize chanting 'Tribbles and Klingons and Borg! Oh my!'

We don't get out much.

The afternoon whiles away, shadows begin to lengthen, and – ominously – dark, grumbling storm clouds begin to gather in intimidating numbers in the skies above us. As the first spots of rain appear, we decide to shake our fists defiantly at the weather gods, and buy a round of ice creams from an incongruous cheerful-looking van plonked unceremoniously in a small clearing in the centre of the *Enterprise*'s exhaust vent. We're now almost completely lost, seeing fewer and fewer fellow maze-explorers on our travels, and keep blundering into clearings in which huge twenty-foot chainsaw sculptures by Lincolnshire artist Mick Burns loom over us with sinister intent. They're terrifying, lolloping tree men with jagged, pointed limbs and blankly baleful faces. They rise out of the crops like a terrifying mish-mash of random childhood nightmares – twisted, elongated versions of Raggety the Twigman, Rupert the Bear's disturbingly spiky chum. They're great.

And then the rain arrives in earnest, and we realise for the first time that all five of us are clad in skimpy summer clothing, lost in an open-air maze with no idea of how to return to shelter. It starts to hammer down – not a light, revitalising summer shower, but a full-blooded dirty, blattering downpour that stings our milky legs and puffs the dusty pathways into billowing clouds of muck. The giant maize crops steam and rustle and grumble as we run. I'm back in the Land of Oz again, and half expect the nastier plants to pluck off their cobs with spindly green arms, taking vicious potshots at the dog as we pass. I glance down at my sopping red shirt, now clinging unpleasantly to my stomach, and wonder whether I'll be first to get picked off.

After twenty minutes of frantic dashing, and some expert mental cartography from Wez, we arrive back at the main entrance, retreat to the car, and attempt to dry ourselves off with empty packets of Flamin' Hot Monster Munch.

Happy days.

BLOODY STUPID THINGS I HAVE DONE IN THE NAME OF FANDOM NUMBER FIVE: ATTEMPING TO USE LEONARD NIMOY LYRICS AS A BLUEPRINT FOR HAPPINESS

It's September 1994, and I'm lying face down on Ian MacDonald's parents' front-room carpet. Yes, *that* Ian MacDonald, the one who had strawberry yoghurt flicked over him thirteen years earlier as the result of a furious *Blake's 7* dispute. I'm twenty-one years old, and I'm very, very depressed.

And I'm drinking too much. Not in a roister-doistering, painting the town red, arms around your mates way, but in a sad, lonely, rather pathetic manner. If I go to the pub – which I do, three or four times a week – I can never remember getting home. If I don't go to the pub, then I go to someone's house, and drink a bottle of wine. Or, to be more accurate, two bottles of wine. Or vodka. I like vodka a little bit too much as well. Don't worry, this isn't where the story turns unremittingly bleak – it's only a brief spell in my life, it all blows over within a few weeks, and there's no huge, soul-destroying blackness at the heart of my misery. I'm just struggling to come to terms a bit with the changes in my life. I've just graduated from university, moved back to my parents' house after three years away, and started full-time work for the first time in my life. I'm worried about my skin, my weight, my student debts, my string of abject failures with women and Middlesbrough's current form. I am, to be frank, in a bit of a state.

So, on a rainy Friday night when Ian's parents are away, a handful of us shamble over to the house, with clanking, bottle-filled carrier bags in tow. The garden backs on to Levendale Primary School, a place I've recently taken to visiting secretly at nights – staring wistfully into the playground, desperately attempting to rekindle the carefree spirit of my childhood. 'A man's work is nothing but this slow trek to rediscover through the detours of art those two or three great and simple images in whose presence his heart first opened,' I mumble to myself, slobbering drunkenly into the front-room carpet. It's a quote from Albert Camus. I've just finished a degree in philosophy, and am full of stuff like this – although, if plied with enough Cabernet Sauvignon, I'll probably admit I got that particular quote from the back of an old Scott Walker LP.

It's not Scott Walker I'm listening to now, though.

Oh no.

It's Leonard Nimoy.

Yes, Mr Spock himself. Between 1967 and 1970, Nimoy recorded five studio albums – interspersing straight covers of light pop classics like *Everybody's Talkin'* with bizarre, sci-fi themed monologues, often in character as the deadpan Mr Spock. His singing voice is tremulous, fragile and, actually, pretty good, and his spoken voice is laced with authority and gravitas. The CD I've brought with me tonight, and placed amazingly unchallenged on Ian MacDonald's stereo, is a compilation called *Highly Illogical*, released – slightly incongruously – on Rev-Ola Records, a subsidiary of Alan McGee's legendary Creation label. It's difficult to resist speculating that the nineteen million-strong sales of *(What's the Story) Morning Glory?* funded a string of mid-1990s Leonard Nimoy re-releases, and it's a shame that the 1960s-obsessed Gallagher brothers never returned the favour by taking future inspiration from brilliantly bonkers tracks like 'Amphibious Assault' (in which an interstellar military attack on an alien coastline is combined with a swinging cocktail party on a 'vermilion fleece rug') and 'The Ballad of Bilbo Baggins', a touching tribute – of course – to the 'bravest little hobbit of them all'.

Be Here Now, my arse.

But it's the earnest spoken-word homilies that are really tugging at my heartstrings. In particular a track called 'Spock Thoughts' in which, over syrupy strings and gloopy keyboards, Nimoy sagely recites the old, inspirational prose poem *Desiderata*, much beloved of earnest religious types and love bead-draped hippies alike. 'Go placidly amid the noise and the haste, and remember what peace there may be in silence,' he mutters, with a solemnity and biblical reverence that would have Charlton Heston's Moses choking on his tablets. 'Do not distress yourself with imaginings. Many fears are born of fatigue and loneliness.'

I can listen to the album now, and it's cheesy and fun and hugely enjoyable, but in 1994, in my delicate, desperate, drink-sodden state, it's nothing short of inspirational. I've felt, for the past few months, as though my happy childhood and teenage years have crumbled around me, and left me utterly exposed to a filthy storm of adult trauma. But I have, as Leonard gently points out, been through a fair old bit of fatigue and loneliness recently. Mainly because I've been staying up drinking until 4am and snatching three hours' sleep before getting up for work. Perhaps it is time to stop distressing myself with imaginings, and to go placidly amid the noise and haste. Taking care not to fall into any ditches on the way home.

As I lie there on the floor, with half a bottle of cheap vodka bubbling in my guts, two lungfuls of Silk Cut smoke and the imprint of Ian's parents' own vermilion fleece rug imprinted in dappled pink blobs on my left cheek, my eyes start to moisten. I let the CD finish, throw my empty cigarette packet into the kitchen bin, then bid my friends goodbye and begin the half-hour walk back home alone. And I don't touch another drop of alcohol for the best part of two months, by which time I've got the whole sorry business out of my system.

So thanks, Mr Spock, and Warp Factor Ten to the rest of my

life. Oh, and by the way – the cover to *A Touch of Leonard Nimoy* (1969) is one of the funniest things I've ever seen in my life.

After ten minutes basking in the artificial heat of the *Toyota Enterprise*'s rudimentary air-conditioning system, we take the Grimston Bar Park-and-Ride to York city centre, and eat fish and chips on a bench in Whip-Ma-Whop-Ma-Gate. And yes, it is named after York's proud history of public flagellation, being the site of a sixteenth-century pillory constructed for the painful flogging of petty criminals and traitors to the city. Which seems almost appropriate, as I'm not sure I haven't committed my own particular brand of treacherous sci-fi betrayal. Put it this way: *Doctor Who* has pacifism, tolerance, unity, compassion and the celebration of all varieties of existence as the cornerstones of its moral universe. So, in effect, does *Star Trek*. Yet when fans of each series get together, they're duty bound to knock seven bells out of each other to settle, once and for all, which of them is the *more* peaceful and compassionate. Nathan – *Doctor Who* Nathan, he of the Janet Ellis fanzines – has told me of the time one brave foot-soldier turned up to a previous Swallow Hotel convention in full *Star Trek* Starfleet regalia. The sharp intakes of breath from two hundred *Doctor Who* fans in assorted scarves, frock coats and cricketing whites had been enough to suck the carpet up the walls.

In short, there's rivalry. *Doctor Who* fans think *Star Trek* is boring. Limited plots rehashed weekly on a dreary, clichéd space-ship set, and every episode condescendingly moral, their points driven home with sledgehammer subtlety. And *Star Trek* fans think *Doctor Who* is childish – rubber monsters, jelly babies, wobbly sets and silliness – disposable escapism for fans who deserve nothing more.

I wonder what that makes me, if I like both? Am I the sci-fi equivalent of Mr Barraclough from *Porridge* – wavering, indecisive, good-naturedly trying to see both sides but ultimately ending up weak and ineffectual? Or is it more sinister than that – am I the convention circuit's own Lord Haw-Haw, the British World War II traitor who broadcast Nazi propaganda to an incredulous, seething public? I decide, after considering the matter dutifully over a mouthful of mushy peas, that I'll continue to follow the example of the *Enterprise* crew's dignified maturity, and not give a toss either way.

When we arrive home, I browse the York Maze website and discover, to my immense disappointment, that – in a matter of weeks – it's playing host to a mini-*Star Trek* convention, equipping hardy fans with replica phaser guns and setting them loose in the labyrinth to obtain hidden dilithium crystals from staff disguised as deadly Borg warriors. The website promises free entry for anyone arriving in a home-made Starfleet uniform, and I find myself secretly hoping that one brave soul will turn up in a full Tom Baker hat and scarf ensemble, and generate enough *Star Trek*-related breath intake to suck the cobs off the crops.

The reason for my disappointment, by the way, is entirely honourable. I can't go. The convention is on Saturday 19 August, a day on which I'll be in the Hinckley Island Hotel in Leicestershire, swopping Thieves' Guild bullet points with eight hundred fellow Terry Pratchett fans at the world's largest Discworld convention. And I'll have Sorcha with me, no doubt faffing around endlessly with her shoes and hair before we arrive late for a seminar on the Unseen University's contribution to particle physics research. Or something.

The convention trek, boldly going where – well, frankly, lots of men have gone before, although I suspect not so many women have ever bothered – is beginning to eat increasingly into my working days. I've found myself spending long, arduous afternoons checking room reservations and ticket availabilities, locating willing dog-sitters, printing out reams of AA Route Finder pages and looking for obscure hotel locations on Multimap webpages so dangerous and labyrinthine-looking that no one in a red shirt would touch them with a dilithium crystal. Sorcha is now determined to accompany me on the expedition to Dorset for the *Hitch Hiker's* water-pistol fight and I've also persuaded her to make a weekend of it and drive, the following day, to the Welsh coast to visit the surreal purpose-built folly of Portmeirion, known to a generation of cult TV fans as 'The Village' from Patrick McGoohan's bizarre 1960s drama *The Prisoner.* The show's dedicated 'Unmutual' fan club are holding a day-long convention there, and it looks like too good an opportunity to miss. Meanwhile Matthew has gratefully received his *Robin of Sherwood* ticket, and – as the official hotel is long since booked up – negotiated beds for us at his parents' house in nearby Attenborough. And Wez's Glasgow-based brother, Paul, alerted to my quest, has offered us rooms in his new house in Wishaw if we want to make a weekend of Doune Castle's annual Monty Python celebration in September. I feel like one of the Four Yorkshiremen in Monty Python's own legendary sketch: 'When I were a lad, I had to get up in the morning at ten o'clock at night, half an hour before I went to bed, drink a cup of Dalek blood, spend twenty-nine hours a day at a science-fiction convention, pay Terry Pratchett for permission to read his books, and when we got home our dad and our mother would kill us and dance about on our graves singing the theme from *The Onedin Line.'*

And you try telling that to the young people of today, they won't believe you.

Oh, and just in the interests of research, and to take a break from the administrative madness I seem to have suddenly landed myself in, I buy *Star Trek: The Motion Picture* and watch it for only the second (and a half) time in twenty-five years. And it's still good, but I do fall asleep just before the forty-five-minute mark – not as a result of juvenile boredom this time, more down to the fact that I was awake until 3am the previous night trying to calculate the quickest route from Bath to Dorset at half past nine on a Saturday morning to meet a handful of water-pistol-brandishing *Hitch Hiker's Guide to the Galaxy* fans in the car park of Wareham Railway Station.

To coin a phrase . . . don't panic.

Yet.

THE BATTLE TO SAVE EARTH

By Robert Fischer (Aged Eight And A Half)
Sunday 10 May 1981
PART SEVEN

I looked through a screen and got the fighters in range. Then I pulled a lever. A blue beam of light shot out from the gun. One of the fighter ships exploded into millions of peices. 'Good shot,' Dirk said. Suddenly there was a big crash. 'What happened?' Richard asked Dirk. 'We've landed,' Dirk answered. 'On Earth?' Richard asked. 'No,' Dirk said. 'We've landed on a planet called Swamp-world, and it looks like this planet lives up to its name because we've landed in a swamp!' Dirk pushed open the ship door and looked out. We were surrounded by dirty green water. Beyond the swamp was a thick jungle that was almost made invisible by a strange green mist. Dirk jumped into the swamp. The dirty water came up to his knees. Richard and I jumped in after him. Suddenly something moved past my leg. I was pulled underneath the water. Dirk whirled round and drew his gun, but all he saw were a few bubbles on top of the water. 'Something's pulled Robert under,' Richard said, drawing his gun. Underneath the water I was struggling with a sort of shark. It had fins on each side of its body and evil red eyes. I grabbed my gun from my belt and shot it. I got back up to the surface of the water. 'What was it?' Richard asked me. 'I don't know,' I answered. We climbed onto the mud by the swamp. Our ship was slowly sinking in the swamp.

To be continued . . .

THE HITCH HIKER'S GUIDE TO THE GALAXY

ZZ9 PLURAL Z ALPHA ANNUAL WATER-PISTOL FIGHT
WINSPIT QUARRY, DORSET
SATURDAY 12 AUGUST

'Behold . . . the Sponge of Doom!'

IT'S EARLY FRIDAY AFTERNOON. I'm hot, flustered and bad-tempered, and am pacing around the hallway at the bottom of the stairs.

'Hurry up!' I shout.

'Fuck off!' comes the reply.

'I said we'd be there by six!'

'Go by yourself, then!'

A fluffy pair of slippers are suddenly hurled from the top of the landing and strike me firmly in the small of the back.

If I was a character in a Looney Tunes cartoon, there would now be steam whistling from both of my ears, and throbbing red vines of blood vessels strangling the pupils in my bulging, pounding eyes. I've been attempting, for the last hour, to set off for the *Hitch Hiker's Guide to the Galaxy* versus *Blake's 7* water-pistol fight in Dorset. We've arranged to meet at noon tomorrow at Wareham Railway Station, and are breaking the journey tonight in Bath, staying once again in Matthew and Tara's rambling terraced townhouse. It had taken me ten minutes to pack a bag and print out a few directions for my previous visit to Somerset. This time round, Sorcha's month-long preparations for the

149

weekend's activities have made the average space shuttle launch look like an impromptu charabanc trip to the seaside. And still we're running late.

A BLUFFER'S GUIDE TO . . . THE HITCH HIKER'S GUIDE TO THE GALAXY

In the great British sci-fi family tree, *The Hitch Hiker's Guide to the Galaxy* is the high-IQ older brother who likes *Doctor Who* and *Blake's 7*, but only so long as he can poke fun at them, spending his workdays writing spoof fan fiction in which the Doctor is attacked by giant jelly babies, come to avenge the centuries of abuse their heartily consumed brethren have endured at his hands. And publishing it on one of the twenty-seven websites he runs from his parents' basement. Probably wearing thick-rimmed spectacles and a novelty K-9 tie.

Hitch Hiker's (as it's universally known to the fans) was written by former bodyguard and chicken-shed-cleaner Douglas Adams, a Cambridge University graduate who had passed the time between odd jobs with the occasional Monty Python collaboration, before winding up as script editor on *Doctor Who*. The *Hitch Hiker's* phenomenon began its long, meandering lifespan as a little-publicised radio serial, originally broadcast at 10.30pm on BBC Radio 4, on a wet Wednesday night in March 1978. It introduced bemused listeners to the slightly grumpy 'everyman' figure Arthur Dent, who wakes up one morning to discover his house being unexpectedly knocked down by the local council. He's immediately rescued from this situation by his impish friend Ford Prefect, who quickly reveals himself to be not – as Arthur had always believed – from Guildford, but from a small, previously unknown planet somewhere in the vicinity of Betelgeuse. Ford is a field researcher for an intergalactic electronic travel book called *The Hitch Hiker's Guide to the Galaxy*, and – with the book safely stashed in his satchel – he transports himself and Arthur away from Earth and onto an orbiting spaceship commandeered by a *very* grumpy Vogon captain. The Vogons, ironically enough, are demolishing the entire Earth to make way for a hyper-spatial bypass, and Arthur and Ford have escaped in precisely the nick of time. Later, they meet roguish two-headed, three-armed Galactic President Zaphod Beeblebrox, and his girlfriend, Trillian (née Tricia McMillan), an attractive astrophysicist whom Arthur once singularly failed to impress at a long-ago party in Islington. There's also Marvin – the notoriously miserable 'paranoid android' who complains constantly about the 'pain in all the diodes down his left-hand side' – and Slartibartfast, a whiskery, mythical planetary designer who won an award for his work on the 'lovely crinkly bits' dotted around the coast of the now-demolished Norway.

The original radio series was popular enough to warrant a follow-up the following year, by which time Adams's much-delayed novelisation of the *first* series (submitted only when the author was succinctly told by his publishers to 'finish the page you're on' – which he did) had become a sensational bestseller, followed – over the course of the next thirteen years – by four other equally bestselling sequels, and converted into a successful six-part TV series in 1981. The character of Arthur Dent was based on and portrayed by Adams's old university friend Simon Jones, whose winning combination of typically English befuddlement and an excitingly stained dressing gown proved perfect for the role. And the whole story is pithily narrated by *The Hitch Hiker's Guide to the Galaxy* itself, the voice of the book on both radio and TV being supplied by former *Rag Trade* actor Peter Jones, who famously claimed on several occasions to be completely bewildered by the whole strange phenomenon.

The books, which are both hilarious and intelligent, bravely delve into complex areas of philosophy and theology without ever losing their sense of fun. They simultaneously pay tribute to and mercilessly send up several generations worth of serious (and not so serious) science fiction, and Adams was attempting to revive a long-awaited movie adaptation of the series when he died suddenly, aged forty-nine, during a vigorous workout session in a Californian gym in May 2001. The film, extensively rewritten by American screenwriter Karey Kirkpatrick, was finally released in May 2005, to decidedly mixed reviews. Not least from Sorcha and myself, but more of that a little later.

Notable *Hitch Hiker's* catchphrases include 'Don't Panic' (written in large, friendly letters on the cover of the book itself), 'Forty-Two' (notoriously the answer to Life, The Universe And Everything), 'I Thought Some Of The Metaphysical Imagery Was Particularly Effective' (said by Arthur as a response to the Vogon captain's poetry) and 'Why Stop Now, Just When I'm Hating It?' (quintessential Marvin). If you want to spot a *Hitch Hiker's Guide to the Galaxy* fan at a pub table, he's the one in the novelty K-9 tie who requests a Pan Galactic Gargle Blaster when you order a round of drinks. If you want to annoy a *Hitch Hiker's Guide to the Galaxy* fan, turn up ten minutes late for a midday rendezvous at Wareham Railway Station for their annual water-pistol fight against *Blake's 7* fans.

The fight has been organised by ZZ9 Plural Z Alpha – *The Hitch Hiker's Guide to the Galaxy* Appreciation Society, formed in 1980 and still going strong with a modest, homely internet presence. The event seems to be an annual fixture in their calendar, and over the course of the last few weeks I've swapped friendly e-mails with meetings organiser Doug and *Blake's 7* fan Judith to check on details and locations. I'm determined to organise this excursion meticulously, recognising full well Sorcha's staggering ability to make any seemingly water-tight schedule start leaking profusely at the joints. She'll not only be late for her own funeral, she'll still be barking instructions at the undertaker a fortnight later, having returned to the funeral parlour three times to change into a better pair of shoes, remove a smudge from her pashmina, and ask repeatedly if her hair 'looks funny at the back'.

A week earlier, I'd made a foray into Stockton High Street for the first time since *Star One,* storming into Woolworths accompanied by Stuart, the gentle six-foot Teesside skinhead, he of the *Star Wars* Trivial Pursuit and amusing shorts and cricketing hat ensemble. 'Excuse me, mate, we're looking for a decent set of water pistols,' I'd mumbled to the sullen acne-ridden youth dripped slowly into a Woolworths uniform and hung out to dry on the edge of a modest-looking toy department.

'Follow me,' he'd muttered back, 'they're over here. What are they for, a stag weekend?'

'No,' I'd replied. 'I'm a *Hitch Hiker's Guide to the Galaxy* fan, and I'm driving three hundred miles to a quarry in Dorset to spend an afternoon shooting jets of cold water at a bunch of *Blake's 7* lovers in a desperate attempt to recapture the free-wheeling spirit of my childhood, and to form some kind of all-encompassing theory as to the nature of cult and sci-fi fandom.'

I hadn't really. What I'd actually said was, 'Yes.'

Aided by Stuart, I'd bought two impressive-looking Super Soaker 3000 water pistols for £12.99, passing on the way to the checkout a shelf stacked entirely with twelve-inch-high David Tennant action toys, all complete with miniature sonic screwdrivers. The urge to buy one had been greater than any temptation I'd encountered since I'd given up smoking four summers previously. Thankfully I'd managed to resist, and had cursed the absence on the open market of sci-fi addiction patches: perforated adhesive squares that attach to the shoulder of cult TV fans and release a slow-burning formula of common sense into the bloodstream, gently decreasing the ever-present temptation to bring an assortment of brightly coloured cash-in merchandise through the front door.

Anyway, they're not toys, they're collectable figurines.

I'm armed, tooled, primed and ready for action.

CRUCIAL MOMENTS IN FANDOM HISTORY NUMBER SIX: RECORDING THE HITCH HIKER'S GUIDE TO THE GALAXY SOUNDTRACK OFF THE TELLY

It's 1987, I'm fourteen, and I'm enjoying one of the strangest summers of my life. I'm spending virtually every day in the company of my new best friend, Chris Selden, a shy Yorkshire youth who had arrived at Conyers School a handful of months previously amidst a flurry of tousled, sandy-coloured hair. Peering out from behind grey-rimmed glasses and sporting a surgically attached blue and tan ski jacket on even the hottest of summer's days, Chris is the proud owner of a Commodore 64 – the yin to my Spectrum-obsessed yang – and he plays the cornet in his local Salvation Army band. And, from the minute we're thrown together on a two-man table in Mrs Bush's form class, it quickly becomes apparent that we share a mutual obsession. In May 1987, for the first time in five years, *The Hitch Hiker's Guide to the Galaxy* is repeated on BBC2. And we watch it. And we love it. And we quote it to each other. Not just now and again, but all the time. *All the bloody time.* To the point where an exasperated Mrs Bush has to ask us to stop, just for the sake of her own fragile sanity.

It's hardly surprising. For the first time in my TV-watching life, I have research tools at my disposal.

My family are one of the last in the Western world not yet to have acquired a video recorder of any description, and in the summer of 1987 we're still watching TV programmes as and when they're broadcast, seemingly oblivious to the fact that the primitive Jarawa tribes of the Andaman Islands are merrily taping *Moonlighting* on BBC2 every Monday night while they go hunting for turtles off the coast of Dugong Creek. But – in an early example of my obsessive desire to collect and archive my favourite TV shows – I'm making audio recordings of the *Hitch Hiker's* TV episodes.

I have a small Matsui portable cassette recorder that spends most of its miserable existence chained like a remand prisoner to my ZX Spectrum, its musical soul being slowly chipped away by the endless, excruciating loading noises for *Jet Set Willy* and *Atic Atac*. Boooooo-bip. Booooooo-biddlybiddlybiddly-biddly. But every Friday night it gets liberated from home computing duties, fed with a brand-new blank C-60, and balanced precariously on a wobbly three-legged telephone table, just the right height to be pushed up against our old TV set's tinny loudspeaker. Despite the fact that I now own a pristine new DVD edition of the entire series, packed with extras and other sundry goodies, I still have these battered, distorted audio cassettes, muffled reminders of an innocent, pre-digital age. On one episode, as Zaphod Beeblebrox's spanking new *Heart of Gold* spaceship engages its Infinite Improbability Drive and passes simultaneously through every point in the universe, my mum is clearly audible, saying, 'Turn it down a bit, we can hear that in the bedroom.'

As a result, my fourteen-year-old self is spending considerably more time learning the complex monologues of 'The Book' than he's ever devoting to preparing for his forthcoming career as a GCSE student, and – it transpires – Chris is doing the same. By the time the summer holidays roll round, we're conducting entire conversations in fluent Douglas Adams. The very mention of even the tiniest phrase from the books or TV shows is enough to send us spiralling into hours' worth of *Hitch Hiker's*-based recitals that must driven our parents, friends, relatives and even the primitive Jarawa tribes of the Andaman Islands to consider whether it might be kinder, for the greater good of humanity, just to have us both humanely destroyed in our sleep. At the end of the summer, Chris and his family move suddenly to Morecambe amidst mutterings about his father's job, but I often wonder if they'd taken a cruel but ultimately necessary decision to take him away from my unhealthy influence. We never saw or contacted each other again, but his legacy lives on – I still find it hard to say the words 'car park' without doing it in the voice of Marvin the Paranoid Android.

Sorcha and I survive the drive to Bath without further attempts to kill each other, and – lost amidst the labyrinthine one-way system – I hit my own Infinite Improbability Drive (driving randomly around the town centre, turning left whenever possible) and, amazingly, we quickly pull up outside Matthew and Tara's front door with only a brief volley of swearing and a minor map-throwing incident for our troubles. After the regulation bellyful of Butcombe bitter in the St James Wine Vaults (Johnny Depp enjoying a quiet night in again), Sorcha and I spend a restful night slumbering beneath the watchful eye of the talking Darth Vader helmet in Matthew's spare room, before the alarm wakes us at 8am, and we leave our hosts in bed to clamber sleepily back into the Starlet.

It's seventy-five miles to Wareham, through Somerset and Dorset's winding tangle of A-roads, and at 10.30am we're gridlocked barely halfway there, swearing profusely under our breaths and checking the map for alternate routes. It's a baking, sun-drenched summer's morning, but it's not a pleasant, bumbling sunshine – all laughs and japes and frolics under garden showers – it's a nasty, sticky, sweaty sunshine. The sunshine of headaches, dripping armpits and foul, bad-tempered tantrums. We're still hot, tired, lost and decidedly unhappy when, at nine minutes past twelve, Wareham Railway Station seems to swim into view from a misty haze, in a location we swear we've driven past at least four times already. Perhaps it's the Brigadoon of the transport network, a mystical, magical hideaway that only exists for one afternoon each year, winking into existence at noon every 12 August to play host to a celebration of eccentric sci-fi fandom. Or perhaps we were holding the roadmap upside down.

We pull sharply into the only free space available in the car park (and yes, I *do* say it in a Marvin voice), narrowly avoiding the toes of a large, bearded man with a rucksack on his back. As I shamble around to the boot of the car to retrieve our brace of Super Soaker 3000s, I notice the slogan on his black and silver T-shirt. It says, 'Life . . . Don't Talk to Me About Life.' Another downbeat, careworn catchphrase of Marvin the Paranoid Android.

We've arrived.

We get out of the car and shake hands warmly. The man with the beard is Doug, ZZ9's genial meetings organiser, and Judith – the *Blake's 7* correspondent, resplendent in a *Liberator* T-shirt – is here as well. She's tall and slim with a warmly academic air, and she gives us both an unexpected but entirely welcome hug. Doug is friendly and softly spoken, and shakes his shoulders when he laughs, which is often. They're all intrigued by Sorcha's name, and ask if she has Celtic ancestry. Doug in particular notes her 'Irish hair', a colour Sorcha has always defiantly described as 'strawberry blonde', proudly maintaining a noble tradition passed down through generations of equally misguided souls with Ginger Bloody Hair. During this conversation I also notice that – in the spirit of sisterly, sci-fi conciliation – Judith is wearing a pair of *Hitch Hiker's Guide to the Galaxy* Babel Fish earrings. And it strikes me that this whole madcap event might just be the heart-warming, cross-fandom equivalent of trench-footed German and British soldiers swapping chocolates on Christmas Day 1914. Although it's worth warning our fellow fandom affiliates that if anyone attempts to remove the Double Decker secreted in Sorcha's rucksack pocket, open warfare will be resumed faster than you can say 'informal armistice and cessation of hostilities'. Which, admittedly, isn't very fast.

They're like that, are strawberry blondes.

We're also introduced to Daniel and Nic – two young sci-fi fans, both bespectacled and endearingly shy – and fellow twenty-something Kelvin, who's tall and enviably skinny with a long, dark ponytail. The plan, we're told, is to set off in convoy to the tiny Dorset hamlet of Worth Matravers, where we'll be able to park the car and make the ten-minute downhill ramble to the mystical Winspit Quarry. Sorcha offers to drive, and Judith volunteers Kelvin to be our in-flight navigator. He looks vaguely worried about the prospect, clearly recognising the maniacal gleam in the eye of a woman permanently prepared to commit genocide for seventy-two grammes of cereal, chocolate and nougatine paste.

I clamber into the back of the car, leaving Kelvin and Sorcha in the front, and sprawl across the back seat as we trundle slowly through the Dorset countryside. Before long, rolling hillsides shuffle sheepishly to the lower horizon, and a stunning, glistening English Channel rises up in the distance. We turn a treacherous corner and sidle into a gravel-strewn car park.

We're at Worth Matravers. We're introduced to Richard – chatty, fifty-ish, fruity-voiced, with a mane of ginger hair and a fabulous bushy beard. He reminds me a little of my hero Vivian Stanshall, the celebrated British eccentric and frontman with the Bonzo Dog Doo-Dah Band. There's also Henry – tall, wiry, early twenties-ish – also sporting a bushy ginger ponytail and cradling, quite terrifyingly, the largest water pistol I've ever seen in my life. It's the size of the average Shetland pony, and just as capable of squirting out nasty liquids at high velocity. He produces another similarly-sized weapon from the back of his car, and hands it to Kelvin – who sparks into life as they strike up a brilliant 'Hail, fellow, well met!'-style rapport. It suddenly strikes me that they're brothers and Richard and Judith are their parents. I follow them down to a brick-built gentlemen's toilets at the bottom of the car park, where they proceed to fill up empty lemonade bottles from a wheezing, groaning tap. Clutching this enormous, watery arsenal, and both now sporting backpacks the size of family saloons, they look like maverick English members of the *Ghostbusters* team (Affiliated Dorset Branch). 'Don't cross the streams!' I shout, as they test their pistols in the porcelain basin. Two burly ramblers, busy at the urinal behind us, glance over their shoulders at me with violently startled glares. Ten minutes later, I realise that they thought I was talking to them.

We begin the walk down to Winspit Quarry, and I can't stop smiling – I feel fantastic. Our numbers seem to swell by the minute – we're like sci-fi pied pipers, attracting a legion of ponytailed pistol-packers as we march inexorably down towards the glistening sea. And they're *lovely* people. As we pass the Square and Compass pub – where cheery, midday drinkers raise their glasses under parasols and await the arrival of the village's annual stone-carving festival – Henry and Kelvin break into a song I vaguely recognise. Clambering over a rickety style, I realise exactly where I know it from – it's J. R. R. Tolkien's 'Ent's Marching Song' from the second book of *The Lord of the Rings*. *'We come, we come with roll of drum: ta-runda runda runda rom!'*

I'm in heaven. A feeling only compounded when we emerge from a meadow of swaying purple foxgloves onto the brink of Winspit Quarry.

I've never been to a quarry before, but it's fair to say my mental image has always been somewhat less than positive. I'd have said 'ugly'. I'd have said 'slate-grey'. If I was really on a roll, I'd have whistled up 'a desolate far-flung outpost of human endeavour with all the aesthetic qualities of a landfill'. But if Winspit Quarry is at all representative of their oeuvre, then whoever is in charge of the UK's Quarry Marketing Board (I'm picturing a Ronnie Barker-esque spokesman with a grey pencil moustache and hair coated in rock dust that flies up into a cloud whenever he gets excited) needs to seriously buck up their ideas.

It's gorgeous.

The quarry itself hasn't produced any stone since before World War II, during which time it was converted into a Naval and Air Defence site. It's an amphitheatre of sun-bleached rocks – a semi-circle of towering limestone riddled with exciting caves and boltholes, stacked around the edges with impossibly high columns of boulders, and the crumbling, moss-covered ruins of man-made brick shelters and old, rusting gun emplacements. The whole thrilling kaboodle looks out over an infinite stretch of sparkling English Channel, and – as we group in Judith's self-declared 'Safe Zone' in the centre of the quarry and unpack our sandwiches – seagulls whoop and circle ahead. I'm vaguely reminded of the setting to 'Destiny of the Daleks' – The First

Doctor Who Story I Watched Without Being Scared, remember – and the windswept, excitingly sculpted landscape that so inspired me as a six-year-old boy. Judith tells me that the water-pistol fight is in at least its thirteenth year, and that – fantastically – no one involved has any recollection whatsoever of how it actually started. It's become its own special sci-fi legend, origins lost in the swirling mists of time. And probably a fair old bit of real ale as well.

Our group has swelled to about twenty fans now, and the sandy ground at our feet begins to accumulate a pile of terrifying-looking weaponary on a scale probably unseen in these parts since May 1945. Henry and Kelvin's Shetland pony-sized water pistols seem to be par for the course, and our Super Soaker 3000s, so deadly and impressive when I cradled them in Woolworths, now look like comparative tiddlers in a sea of pump-action great white sharks. 'So who are the *Hitch Hiker's* fans and who are *Blake's 7*?' I ask Judith casually.

'Oh, that doesn't really matter,' she smiles. 'It's everyone for themselves, really.'

As she speaks, I see Henry catch an unsuspecting Kelvin with a gentle, surreptitious jet of water that threatens to dislodge the tahini sandwich from his hand. 'A cowardly drenching, sir, and one which shall be avenged!' he bellows, good-naturedly. It's going to be a fun afternoon.

Kelvin volunteers to take Sorcha and me – the only newcomers to the group so far – for a brief reconnaissance mission around the terrain. He guides us into a pitch-black cave in the far quarry wall, a terrifyingly dark cavern that stretches at least a hundred feet into the limestone. We shuffle blindly around in the darkness, stumbling over fallen rocks and walking into walls. The cavern is riddled with nooks, crannies, towering columns and hidey-holes. 'This is the arena of main engagement,' he pipes up cheerily. Like the rocks, we're petrified.

On the way back, in the sunshine, I notice a fifty-foot pile of rock-fallen boulders stacked up against the quarry wall – at the bottom of which is a huge, flat, dusty stone table, propping up the rest like a doughty limestone Atlas. 'That looks quite familiar,' I mumble. 'Have I seen it on TV somewhere?'

'It's where the TARDIS lands in "Destiny of the Daleks", replies Kelvin. 'But you'll have to ask the others about it – I'm not a big *Doctor Who* fan.'

My head goes all swimmy, and I have to sit down. On the TARDIS rock itself, it takes me thirty seconds to realise. Twenty-seven years ago, I used to dream about this location. Quite literally. My infant head would fill up during night-time sleep with the exhilarating, feature-length adventures of myself and Richard Moxham dodging Daleks and Imperial Stormtroopers on the dusty, windswept planet of Skaro. I now have a grin on my face bigger than any Shetland pony, and force Sorcha to take endless photos of me sprawled on the rock itself, gurning with my best Tom Baker expression and wishing beyond all hope that I'd brought a scarf and hat to pose in. Meanwhile, Henry and Kelvin scale the rock stacks above us with effortless, Gollum-like ease, looking for a 'secret top entrance' to the cave system, one which 'requires the maximum agility'. I last see them forty feet above us, both clinging casually to an overhanging rock with one hand, before they vanish completely into the crags. The Daleks couldn't have caught them for toffee. Although Sorcha would probably do it for a bite of Double Decker.

By the time we arrive back at the Safe Zone, more intrepid pistol-packers have arrived, and we're ready to play. Guns filled to the brim with water, Richard gives a whistled signal and we pelt, en masse, into the pitch-black caverns. A natural coward, I feel my way to a groove in the cavern wall and crouch down on my haunches, hearing the blatter of industrial-strength water jets hitting the rocks around me. Screams, laughter and obscure sci-fi war cries reverberate around in the darkness. Kelvin and Richard – veteran campaigners both – have immediately darted in the inky blackness to the very back of the cavern, and secreted themselves amid damp, dank hollows to pick off less experienced interlopers. Judith has taken Sorcha under her wing, and I can see them in silhouette at the opposite end of the cavern, flattened against the black rock wall before a window of stark white daylight. The rest of us, with scant regard for such impressive tactics, are just squirting the hell out of each other. Henry, now sporting a huge double-barrelled water machine gun with an ammunition silo the size of a septic tank, passes within three feet of me in the darkness, and fails to spot me lurking at his feet. I catch him full in the midriff with a blast from my modest Super Soaker 3000. 'You, sir, have signed a death warrant!' he exclaims, and drenches me with the kind of aquatic assault normally reserved for rioting football fans.

Again and again we plunge back into the caverns, secreting ourselves in darkened nooks and jumping out Banzai-style to launch surprise explosive assaults on each other. Occasionally, a party of passing tourists or day-trippers peer nervously into the darkness, hear the screams, and gingerly back out again, muttering to themselves. Although one female member of our party, back at the Safe Zone, relates through giggles how, as she was silently crouching in the murk at the back of the cave, an unsuspecting holidaymaker wandered in, unzipped his fly and let loose with a powerful stream of wee less than six feet from her hidey-hole.

'Can you show me the secret entrance?' I ask Henry, as we trot back to the caverns. He gives a daredevil grin and guides me back to the TARDIS rock, telling me to keep clambering as high as I can. Forty feet up the boulder pile with Henry shouting directions from below, I find myself peering into a pitch-black crack that I'm not convinced affords the thirty-six-inch gap required to accommodate my expansive waistline. Noticing that my cheap supermarket trainers now have their soles hanging loose like panting dogs' tongues, I cautiously dangle my feet into the darkness. My bare legs are immediately caught in the cross-fire of at least four stinging, hissing jets of water. My fingertips lose their grip on the ledge outside, and that thirty-six-inch waist plummets through the crevice, scraping curly rivulets of pale Teesside skin on the edge as it falls. The drop is much deeper than I thought – maybe six or seven feet, and as I clatter clumsily to the ground my footing slips completely, sending me sprawling helplessly on the cavern floor in the pitch blackness. My right hand smashes into a jagged rock, and my pistol scatters across the ground. My own carefully selected sci-fi war cry ('Ayyafuckingtwattingfuck') deflates somewhat the air of genial family-oriented playfulness we've been cultivating carefully all day.

But within seconds of me falling, I'm suddenly being helped to my feet by at least two pairs of hands, asked in concerned, sympathetic voices if I'm OK, and having my thankfully unscathed Super Soaker 3000 pressed back into my trembling palm. I seem to have fallen to the very back of the cavern, and I think it's Kelvin and Richard who help me, breaking cover from their hide-outs to make sure that I'm not too badly hurt. I'm fine, and they guide me gently back into the half-light of the cave entrance for me to make my way back to the distant Safe Zone. Blinking back into the sunlight, I notice a jagged, bloody graze on my right wrist, the skin gently peeling away like a long curl of planed hardwood. 'Brilliant, you've got a sci-fi scar!' laughs Sorcha, throwing her arms round me as I flop, grinning, onto a mossy stone wall. And she's right – a year later, as I write this, there's a silver streak of badly healed skin joining two moles at the base of my palm. We're having, for the first real time on this voyage of discovery, an utterly fantastic time together. *The Hitch Hiker's Guide to the Galaxy* has, well . . . guided us towards happier times. But as we laugh at each other in the now-hazy sunlight, I remind myself that this hasn't always been the case . . .

BLOODY STUPID THINGS I HAVE DONE IN THE NAME OF FANDOM NUMBER SIX: ARGUING WITH SORCHA ABOUT THE HITCH HIKER'S GUIDE TO THE GALAXY MOVIE

'Why do you have to be such a twat? Whenever I say I like something, you rip it to pieces, you tosser.'

It's Thursday 28 April 2005, around two o'clock in the afternoon, and we're stuck in a traffic jam trying to join the busy A66. We've just been to see the brand-new movie adaptation of *The Hitch Hiker's Guide to the Galaxy*, unleashed like a panting dog into our local Showcase Multiplex this morning, and – as they used to say on *Winner Takes All* – we have a difference of opinion here.

'I'm not ripping it to pieces, I just didn't think it was great.'

I'll get her a Double Decker on the way home, and everything should be all right.

The process of adapting *The Hitch Hiker's Guide to the Galaxy* for the big screen has been one of the most laboured, frustrating sagas in recent celluloid history. The idea had been mooted as early as 1982, when former Python Terry Jones had been interested, before Adams moved the project to Hollywood and began working on a screenplay for Columbia Pictures. Ten years later, a workable version had still yet to materialise, and the project was linked to James Cameron before Adams bought the rights back at considerable expense and began working on a new adaptation with former Monkee Michael Nesmith as producer. In 1997, in the wake of the success of *Men in Black*, he sold the rights to Disney, keen to capitalise on another sci-fi comedy, but still struggled to produce a script that pleased the cigar-chomping moguls. The Hollywood process, Adams declared at the time, was like 'trying to grill a steak by having a succession of people coming into the room and breathing on it'. He'd moved to California in 1999 to be closer to negotiations, and was working out his frustrations in the gym in 2001 when his own Infinite Improbability Drive finally gave out for the last time.

But in 2005, the movie has finally arrived. With a script completed by American writer Karey Kirkpatrick, whose previous screen credits include Nick Park's *Chicken Run* and *Honey, We Shrunk Ourselves*, the film assembles an impressive if oddball ensemble. It stars Martin '*The Office*' Freeman as Arthur Dent, American rapper Mos Def as Ford Prefect and quirky British flavour-of-the-month Bill Nighy as Slartibartfast. And Stephen Fry – a close friend of Adams, seemingly partially down to their shared devotion to the Apple Mac computer – steps into the breach perfectly as the voice of the Book.

Settling into our seats in the Showcase Cinema, I'm filled with anticipation. It's been a good summer for sci-fi already. I've blubbed and cheered my way through the first revival series of *Doctor Who*, during the final moments of which – as Christopher Eccleston regenerated into David Tennant – Sorcha, resting her head on my chest, actually asked if I was feeling all right, as my heart was racing so far out of control. I've also enjoyed the third and final *Star Wars* instalment, *Revenge of the Sith*, whose ending tied neatly into the beginning of the original 1977 instalment by decking the entire cast in blowdried bouffants and sideburns for the final twenty minutes of the film.

So I'm hoping for similar fun from *Hitch Hiker's*, and things start brightly, with Fry's pithy narration a delight. But it's not long before things start to go missing. Important things like dialogue. And plot. And my attention.

After twenty minutes, I'm starting to gently seethe. Loads of my favourite dialogue – Adams's absolute forte, his genius, his unique selling point, y'know – stuff he's really good at – has been chopped, changed, dropped and buggered about with. Hilarious scenes from previous versions are lost completely, and replaced with dismal knockabout comedy that puts me in mind of . . . well, *Honey, We Shrunk Ourselves*. As the final credits roll, I rise from my seat a broken man. Sorcha, who – on our first proper date – told me she loved *Hitch Hiker's* nearly as much as she loved Terry Pratchett, and that she loved Terry Pratchett even more than she loved Double Deckers – turns to face me. I can only imagine the disappointment she's feeling as she slips into her overcoat. I turn to face her, expecting the tearful worst.

'That was brilliant!' she beams. 'Can we watch it again?'

The ensuing hostilities on the way home almost threaten to buffet the car into the crash barriers of the A66. And since then, *The Hitch Hiker's Guide to the Galaxy* movie has become the great unmentionable in our house. Amazingly for two inveterate hoarders, neither of us has bought it on DVD, and the subject – like the redecoration of the bathroom ceiling and my night with Julie Halliwell in 1996 – is now tacitly and silently out of bounds for us both.

Thankfully, so far, there's been no sign of a sequel – my cardiovascular system might be able to survive a run-of-the-mill *Doctor Who* regeneration, but I reckon a similarly divisive visit to The Restaurant At The End Of The Universe might be just too much for my fragile sci-fi constitution.

'Behold . . . the Sponge of Doom!'

It's five o'clock in Winspit Quarry, and the temperature is starting to plummet. Our plethora of cavernous water containers are down to the last few inches of sloshing, tepid ammunition, but the sun has vanished behind some ominous-looking storm clouds, and our sopping clothes are no longer drying in the baking, midday heat. We're all grazed, tired, hungry and increasingly cold and wet. Sorcha is pale and visibly shivering, and pulls a baseball cap over her face as she nestles into my shoulder. Richard and Doug, however, have one final, daredevil mission in mind.

'I'm going to give my son a good drenching!' declares Richard, defiantly grabbing the largest, nastiest-looking gun he can find, and seizing one last filled-up water barrel with the other hand. Kelvin, it seems, has holed himself up right at the back of the cavern, a renegade warrior, like *Apocalypse Now*'s Colonel Kurtz, hell-bent on destruction and driven half-mad by the futility of warfare. Richard and Doug, like Martin Sheen before them, are set to terminate his command with extreme prejudice. Oh, and a big, soppy, waterlogged sponge.

Yes, Doug has unveiled his secret weapon. A squishy purple and blue water grenade that actually sits in a secure canopy on the underside of his gun. It is, he whispers in a sinister sotto voce, 'the feared Sponge of Doom'. There's a ripple of awed reverence amongst the tired fans now slumped around his feet, and even the skies seem to grumble with a dark, foreboding respect. Doug, meanwhile, now has a maniacal, distinctly un-Marvin-like gleam in his eye, and he and Richard give each other a curt nod before striding manfully back towards the cavern entrance.

We hear the sound of muffled shouts, crashes and splashes from deep within the caves, and I half expect to see a cartoon cloud of dust billowing from the gloomy entrance, and a single, buckled bicycle wheel wobbling out from the darkness within. Instead, two minutes later, Doug and Richard emerge victorious with a dripping, grinning Kelvin following closely behind. The Sponge of Doom has been deployed to full effect.

With spots of rain starting to fleck the quarry walls, we pack up and begin the walk back to Worth Matravers. On the way, Judith tells us enthusiastically about the gargantuan labour-of-love *Blake's 7* website she runs, and some of the fan fiction she's written, including one inspired by 'Blake's Lock on the Avon Canal'. She also introduces us to the seasoned fandom practice of 'filking', which – we're relieved to hear – isn't as rude as it sounds. It's the phenomenon of writing sci-fi-inspired lyrics to famous tunes, her proudest achievement being her and fellow fan Kathryn Andersen's belting 'The Curse of the Fatal Death', sung to the tune of 'An English Country Garden':

How many different ways are there to die,
In a science-fiction story?
I'll tell you now of some that I know,
For all the rest are rather gory.
Viruses are all the rage,
Here's a new bacteriophage
In my laboratory.
We've a new disease that kills thousands with a sneeze,
In a science-fiction story.

The word 'filk', she tells me, derives from a misprint of the word 'folk' in a long-forgotten convention programme.

Back up in the car park (Marvin voice again), we give hugs and shake hands with Richard and Judith and they reveal – brilliantly – that next weekend they'll be making their traditional family outing to the Terry Pratchett Discworld convention in Leicestershire, and they promise to find us there. Doug, meanwhile, asks me if I'd be interested in writing a short report about the day's activities for ZZ9 Plural Z Alpha's regular newsletter 'Mostly Harmless' (named after *The Hitch Hiker's Guide to the Galaxy*'s succinct description of the entire planet Earth), and I'm delighted to accept, finding it difficult to refuse the advances of a man who has, by now, changed into a T-shirt featuring a melting Dalek, in a delightful pastiche of Salvador Dalí's famous *Persistence of Memory* painting. The caption underneath reads, inevitably, 'Salvador Dalek.'

By eight o'clock we're back with Matthew and Tara in Bath, and they're eager to know of our exploits. We ramble excitedly about TARDIS rocks and Sponges of Doom, noting with amusement the worried look that momentarily crosses their faces when we introduce the word 'filking' into proceedings. And we decide, with impressive adult maturity, to have an early night after dinner, knowing full well that Sorcha and I need to be awake at five to make the long drive to the Welsh coast and Portmeirion. It's an impressive display of willpower that we manage to maintain all the way up to 1.15am, at which point we knock back the last of the Bombay Sapphire and take turns to wear Matthew's talking Darth Vader helmet, issuing orders to each other in an impressive facsimile of the Dark Lord's famous basso profundo.

'Obi-Wan has taught you well,' booms Matthew, jabbing a finger into my giggling chest as I film him using my new digital camera. 'But you're not a Jedi yet. And ... erm ... the Force is strong in this one. Erm ... and ... er ... What else does he say? I am your father, is it?'

We look blankly.

'Oh sod it, time for bed.'

This last sentence is delivered with such menacing intent that it's difficult to refuse. Retiring once more to the spare room, Sorcha and I strip off to compare our bruises before collapsing together under a blissfully soft duvet. We've got four hours to catch some sleepy respite before the alarm clock once more drags us from the bed, and my torso is so covered in grazes and purple blotches that I have to spend the whole night propped up on my scabby left elbow. I do indeed have a pain in the Teesside equivalent of 'all the diodes down my left-hand side'. Marvin, I feel your anguish.

And, in the fleeting sleep I get, I dream that a sensible, adult, thirty-three-year-old Chris Selden is jumping out at me from behind a Dorset boulder, begging me not to unleash the Sponge of Doom and asking me what on Earth I'm doing with my life. When I look down at myself in shame, I realise I'm wearing his old blue and tan ski jacket, bulging at the waistline and riding up my arms. If this is my subconsciousness's subtle manner of telling me to grow up, sleep in and head home rather than spend all day tomorrow at a *Prisoner* convention on the remote Welsh coastline, then it's got another thing coming. In five hours' time we'll be in the car, once again engaging the Starlet's Infinite Improbability Drive.

Providing Sorcha can find her shoes. And her hair doesn't 'look funny at the back'. And neither of us mentions *The Hitch Hiker's Guide to the Galaxy* movie.

THE BATTLE TO SAVE EARTH

By Robert Fischer (Aged Eight And A Half)
Sunday 10 May 1981
PART EIGHT

Not far from our ship, an Imperial patrol was being set out. Robots were guarding a camp and Captain Zero was having some target practice with his laser gun. He was shooting at a round board that was nailed onto a tree. In the centre of the board was a small circle, and that was what Zero was aiming at. Suddenly a Birdman came out of a tent. 'Somthing's been picked up on the radar,' he said. Zero whirled round. 'What is it?' he asked. 'Well send a patrol out if you don't know,' Zero shouted. 'Yes sir,' the Birdman said, and ran back into the tent. Richard, Dirk and I were trying to find some shelter in the jungle. We had walked through miles of swamp and mud without sucess. Suddenly I heard footsteps behind us. I said to Dirk, 'What was that?' 'What?' Dirk asked me. 'Listen,' I said. But we did not have to listen for a blue laser shot over our heads. I turned round and saw a group of Birdmen and robots behind us. I warned Dirk and Richard and we started retreating down into the jungle. Then we ducked behind some trees. The Imperials ran straight past us. Then we ran in the oppisite direction. We had got about half way to our ship when Richard tripped over. klebba had been in medical centre having his wounded arm seen to when he too had jumped into a spaceship and flew down to swamp world. He had just landed and had heard Richard trip over a stone. He ran towards us and grabbed hold of Richard.

To be continued . . .

THE PRISONER

'I need to get some sleep now, I'm starting to hallucinate.' ✈

IT'S THE SUMMER OF 1989, and it's hot. Staggeringly hot. Not just a little bit hot, but face-achingly, back-breakingly, foot-clenchingly hot. Pavements are cracking. Shoulders are peeling. And nomads from the El Azizia Desert are fainting in Stockton High Street. But that's just because they've seen the price of the ice cream on the market.

And I've nothing really to do. I've finished my GCSEs now, and am spending the summer sleeping until lunchtime, watching daytime television and sitting in the bedroom by myself. It's ideal vocational preparation for a budding full-time writer. One sticky, sweat-filled night, though, something happens to puncture my torpor. I'm given to lying awake until the wee hours listening to Metro Radio's brilliant late-night phone-in *Night Owls*, noted for its litany of breathless Geordie callers obsessed with the supernatural. ('Ah swear ah saw a trans-loo-sant figah, standin' at thah foot o' mah bed.') And, when the show finishes at 2am, I switch on the portable TV balanced on my bedside table and watch Tyne Tees's compulsively budget-free 'Night-Time' service (say it in a gruff cinema-trailer voice like the ITV continuity announcer).

It usually has repeats of the weekend's *Chart Show* with Soul II Soul and Jason Donovan, or *America's Top Ten*, presented by the hyperactive Casey Kasem, who – I find out many years later – is also the voice of Shaggy in *Scooby-Doo*. I am as shocked by this revelation as I am on the fateful day that I discover that Shaggy actually has a full name in the show – his bank manager knows him as Mister Norville Rogers. Although it's hard to imagine him being too hung-up on the finer points of financial security.

However, what's caught my attention at 3.30am on this clammy August night isn't Casey Kasem or the *Chart Show*'s clanging mocked-up tape player. ('Don't play this one, don't play this one, don't play this one. Bugger.') It's actually a TV commercial for a car. A Renault 21, in fact. And it's piqued my interest like no car commercial previously, because it seems – in a nutshell – to have an oddly science-fiction-based theme.

'Begin surveillance!'

It starts with a sinister bespectacled figure in a swivelling, circular chair, monitoring on some futuristic CCTV system a livewire figure in a tight black suit, bustling hurriedly through a surreal pastel-shaded village populated by strange, choreographed drones. 'Number 21 shows ambitious tendencies!' shouts Mr Specs, as our hero – sporting a '21,' badge on his lapel – jumps into a red Renault 21 and roars along a treacherous cliff edge, pursued by a giant white balloon that seems to be scrambled from some strange, hidden, underwater sea base. 'Escape . . . to the totally new Renault 21,' barks a severe-sounding voiceover man at the end, as the car swerves through a perilously narrow tunnel and powers away to freedom. The whole kaboodle is accompanied by riveting, clanging, 1960s-style music, the angular guitar lines and stabbing brass a long way away from anything by Jason Donovan or Soul II Soul.

I'm so excited I stay up for an extra hour, and end up dancing to the Tyne Tees Teletext Jobfinder music as the sun comes up over Teesside.

The next day, I mention the advert to my dad, as I'm sure it's a spoof or a homage to something else. 'There's a bloke in a car, in a weird village, being chased by a big white ball to the beach,' I say. It's probably the longest sentence of coherent speech I've offered my parents in the last two years. 'Sounds like *The Prisoner*,' comes the reply. 'Now that was a strange bloody programme, I tell you.'

In this primitive pre-internet era, I decide to make my way to the only resource of information available to me. I pull on my Dunlop Green Flash and tramp a mile in the blistering heat to Yarm Library. There, I browse the 'TV and Film' section, and glean a handful of facts about this surreal, psychedelic 1960s sensation. I'm in a particular 1960s-loving phase of my life, having spent the last year obsessively collecting Beatles LPs – together and solo – from the secondhand record mart at the top of Stockton High Street, and *The Prisoner* sounds right up my street. Especially when I discover that the twanging, brass-parping theme tune was the work of Ron Grainer, whose CV also includes the themes to *Doctor Who*, *Steptoe and Son* and *Tales of the Unexpected*. In the great television Hall of Fame, he's easily up there with Norville 'Shaggy' Rogers.

This is what I learn on that fateful, sun-drenched afternoon.

A BLUFFER'S GUIDE TO . . . THE PRISONER

Perhaps *the* ultimate example of late 1960s TV weirdness, *The Prisoner* was a seventeen-part series shown on ITV between October 1967 and February 1968. In the great British sci-fi family tree, it's the twitchy, paranoid middle brother who had a strange, unexplained breakdown at university and now spends most of time reading UFO conspiracy magazines and constructing trip-wires and listening devices in his bedroom.

The show was devised by and starred enigmatic TV actor Patrick McGoohan as Number Six, a top-level British intelligence officer who – after resigning his post for reasons unexplained – is kidnapped by forces unknown and held captive in a mysterious coastal village whose actual whereabouts remain permanently unclear. As you can probably tell, there's a lot of ambiguity in *The Prisoner*. The village, known only as (ahem) 'The Village' is a surreal, brightly coloured Kafka-esque folly populated by a legion of artificially cheery souls sporting vibrant capes and stripey jerseys, and overseen by the sinister Number Two – whose identity changes from episode to episode. The Village authorities make constant attempts to 'break' a resistant Number Six and discover the reason for his resignation, with the presence of a shadowy Number One overlord being hinted at, but never really confirmed. Early episodes deal with Number Six's repeated attempts to escape by land, sea and air (often being thwarted by a giant, deadly white balloon known as 'Rover'), whereas later episodes are considerably darker, and deal with themes of indoctrination, surveillance, mind control and dream manipulation in such disturbingly psychological detail that the programme was hurriedly ended by concerned ITV bosses, leaving McGoohan a matter of days to write the final, shattering instalment.

That episode, 'Fall Out', reportedly caused such critical and public bafflement that McGoohan and his family had to leave the country for several months. Other reports suggest that this story is a load of old Rovers, and that no such outcry ever existed. Unless you're McGoohan's one-time *Prisoner* collaborator, George Markstein, who later described the episode as 'an absurd pantomime [. . .] a bit of gross self-indulgence by someone who was fed up with the whole thing and wanted to get out of it and wanted to go out in a blaze of something or other'. Ouch.

The show was filmed almost entirely on location in the completely artifical Welsh tourist resort of Portmeirion, a bizarre, Italian-styled village in a remote spot on the edge of the Irish Sea. Notable *Prisoner* catchphrases includes 'Be Seeing You', 'Who Is Number One?', 'I Am Not A Number, I Am A Free Man' and 'Where Does Patrick McGoohan Live? We Need To Find Out What The Fuck That Last Episode Was About'. If you want to annoy a *Prisoner* fan, tell him that Portmeirion looked better in the 1976 *Doctor Who* story 'The Masque of Mandragora'. If you want to spot a *Prisoner* fan at a second-hand car auction, he's the one at the back in the stripey blazer nodding curtly when the Renault 21 comes up for sale.

8.30am. Crossing the Severn Bridge. Me driving, Sorcha glaring noiselessly out of the passenger side window. Ten silent minutes have passed since an argument about Extra Strong Mints.

She yawns, defiantly. We were out of Matthew and Tara's house just after 6am, and free from a deserted Bath city centre less than half an hour later. We're now both so racked with tiredness and the monotony of cross-country driving that we've both lost any kind of grip on reality. It takes two hours driving randomly around the winding county lanes of North Wales before, at a quarter to eleven, we arrive in the village of Penrhyndeudraeth. A sleepy, leafy idyll whose name it's impossible to attempt without first slipping into *Ivor the Engine* accents, this is the nearest 'real' dwelling place to Portmeirion. After driving aimlessly up and down the main street, with another nasty, overtired argument starting to bubble up between us, we eventually see a garish wooden signpost pointing us towards a secluded, leafy track. Glaring at each other and turning the car round, we start to drive the mile to Portmeirion.

The most extraordinary thing about 'The Village' is that it isn't actually a village at all – not in the traditional sense of the word. Nobody actually lives here, and it's no more an organic, natural community than Alton Towers or Chessington World of Adventures. The whole of Portmeirion – including the name – was created from scratch by firebrand Welsh architect Sir Clough Williams-Ellis during a fifty-year spell from 1925 to 1975, making my five years promising to put new tiles on the bathroom floor look pretty bloody shabby indeed. Based loosely on the Mediterranean coastal resorts that Williams-Ellis revered, in particular Portofino, the village incorporates many structures from previously demolished buildings and examples of 'found' art, and has a deliberately nostalgic feel, its pastel-shaded architecture evoking an era of idyllic Edwardian gentility. Bearing all of this in mind, Sorcha is overwhelmed with a desire to pay her own tribute to this most awe-inspiring of large-scale follies, and – after a brief flurry of insults – heads straight for the ladies' toilets by the entrance gate, where she remains for the next ten minutes. She can, in the words of Number Two himself, 'make even the act of putting on a dressing gown appear as a gesture of defiance'. She's a crack shot with a pair of slippers as well.

As I'm waiting, I potter around the entrance gates, chatting idly to the lady in the kiosk (who I half expect to say, 'Be seeing you,' and flick me the traditional *Prisoner* salute, a kind of lazy Scout's honour gesture, brushing the index finger across the temple) before ambling downhill. Sorcha trots down the bank to join me, and we pass the Portmeirion Pottery shop founded by Clough Williams-Ellis's daughter Susan, before emerging into the main village itself.

The place doesn't look quite as I'd expected, and it takes me a second to work out why. It's a testament to *The Prisoner*'s original location-dressers that they managed to take Williams-Ellis's bizarre, unique creation and turn it into something that's even more distinctive. 'The Village' in the show is bedecked with road signs, street plans, shop fronts and taxi stops all displaying the same, unmistakable childish typeface – 'The Café', 'The Town Hall', 'The Bandstand', 'The Hospital' – combining the prosaic with the utilitarian and lending the place a chilling uniformity. It's an impression consolidated by the ever-present Village radio service, piped onto every street corner and heralded with a spine-chilling four-note clarion call before a cheery Fenella Fielding gives notice of craft exhibitions and approaching showers in a smoky voice that's laced with menace. And then there's the ever-present Mini Moke taxis, brightly coloured, horn-parping versions of the ultimate pop art 1960s car. Today, of course, all of that is gone, and what we're actually faced with is a pleasant, sun-baked coastal resort packed with tourists in T-shirts and shades.

And then we spot a woman in a cape and stripey stockings striding purposefully towards the green central piazza, and figure that she has to be heading for the convention. And, as we follow her, a uniformed brass ensemble begin setting up on the bandstand, and everything falls into place. As the sun hammers down from a cloudless Welsh sky, the gardens explode into vivid, blinding shades of colour – and the extravagant fountains glisten into sparkling life, like a real-life version of some lurid Hollywood musical. We've arrived.

We pursue Ms Stripey Legs into the Hercules Hall, a strident terracotta building topped with various farm oddments, including a vintage pigswill boiler. Mounting the stairs, we find ourselves in a small, oak-panelled bar, where a tall, dark-suited man with a ponytail grins heartily and asks for our names. 'If you're Bob, then you must be Sorcha! Have I pronounced that right?' he beams, eerily but impressively remembering the contents of a booking e-mail I'd sent the Unmutual website almost two and a half months previously.

He introduces himself as Rick, and his broad smile and easy-going, wealthy rock-star manner reminds me a little of Ray Davies from The Kinks. He ticks our names off his list and presents us with a convention brochure, as we wander through into the main hall.

The Unmutual website itself is splendidly egalitarian. 'Who are The Unmutuals?' it poses.

'Put simply, as a body or group or Society, they do not exist [. . .] Whilst many people may describe themselves as "Unmutual" in spirit (IE non-conformist), there is no "Unmutual" group or collection of people called "the Unmutuals". There is no "Unmutual Society" to enforce any viewpoint [. . .] So: No rules. No "Unmutual Group". No fan club. Just *individuals* who appreciate *The Prisoner*.'

It strikes me as the cult TV equivalent of Groucho Marx's notorious quote, 'I'd refuse to join any club that would have me as a member'.

We take our places among the rows of wooden chairs,

with maybe a hundred or so assorted fans joining us, many wearing subtle tributes to The Village inhabitants' distinctive attire – deck shoes, striped jerseys, Breton caps, bug-eyed shades. We listen to *Prisoner* expert Rob Fairclough speak about his constant attempts to get a definitive biography of Patrick McGoohan off the ground, persistently thwarted by publishers who want to see 'if a new TV series happens'. The latest rumours, he tells us, suggest that the show will be commissioned by Sky One, star former TARDIS incumbent Christopher Eccleston in the lead role, and be helmed by writer Matthew Graham, whose hit time-travelling drama *Life on Mars* – with future evil Time Lord John Simm as a present-day policeman stranded in the 1970s – has taken *The Prisoner*'s themes of alienation, ambiguity and surreality and turned them into a modern-day TV hit.

We also watch *The Prisonbear*, a brilliant home-made spoof created by giant, bald-headed fan Paul Smith.

'Paul will now tell us how he came up with the idea,' chirps Dave, our genial MC for the day's events.

'Basically, I have too much time on my hands,' admits Paul, to thunderous applause. The film itself is both warmly affectionate and hilarious, recreating the opening episode of *The Prisoner* with innocent-looking teddy bear 'Theodore McGoon' brought to The Village (with bits of cardboard occasionally standing in for Williams-Ellis's more grandiose architecture) and intimidated by a Womble in the local shop before being introduced to *South Park*'s Mr Hankey, the Christmas Poo – here, of course, disguised as Number Two.

Arf, arf.

Afterwards, there's a short lunch break, so Sorcha and I wander back into the village, negotiating our way through a stream of tourists to a small, tightly packed gift shop. In 'Arrival', *The Prisoner*'s electrifying opening episode, Number

Six finds himself in a similar retail outlet being rebuffed endlessly by a surly, intimidating shopkeeper whose maps ('local maps only', naturally) show merely 'Your Village' surrounded – with predictable totalitarian vagueness – by 'The Mountains' and 'The Sea'. In the shop today, a huge array of Portmeirion jams and marmalades are for sale at equally vague prices.

'How much is this?' asks Sorcha, turning over a jar of raspberry preserve. 'It doesn't seem to have a price tag on it.'

'It has not a number, it is a free jam,' I reply, as quick as a flash, thus demonstrating in one fell swoop why I'm destined to stay on local radio for ever.

We're both starting to feel the pace of the weekend, a mind-buggering lack of sleep combining with the aches and pains of yesterday's water-pistol exploits to make us as leaden-footed and zombie-like as any of The Village's fictional inhabitants. Twenty minutes later, we return to the Hercules Hall to watch a 1961 episode of McGoohan's vintage spy series *Danger Man*, which also stars, to my delight, the original *Doctor Who* Master, Roger Delgado, cast – as ever – as a sinister, saturnine agent of dastardly foreign forces. Sorcha, however, is considerably less excited, and rummages in her pocket to produce a BBC Tees Biro, scribbling onto the back of my convention programme the immortal lines 'I need to get some sleep now, I'm starting to hallucinate.'

I glance towards her (quickly, though – *Danger Man* was reaching an exciting conclusion) and realise that she isn't joking. As my dad would no doubt put it if he'd been here, 'Your eyes have gone on holiday and left their bags behind.' I rummage in my pocket for the car keys, and we discreetly shuffle out of our seats . . .

CRUCIAL MOMENTS IN FANDOM HISTORY NUMBER SEVEN: TRYING TO WATCH ALL THE EPISODES OF THE PRISONER IN ONE NIGHT

I kind of know how she feels.

It's Tuesday 26 January 1993. I'm twenty years old, and I'm back home from university for the evening. I've made an exhausting six-hour journey from Lancaster to Darlington on three trains, incorporating an enforced hour in Carlisle, which I gainfully spend attempting to find a chip shop where any request for 'scraps' won't result in physical violence. I'm no longer the fresh-faced youth who danced to the late-night Teletext pages; I'm chunky and grizzled with hacked-at rumpled hair, Dr Martens boots and a fortnight's growth of facial fuzz that clings to my pillows like Velcro. And – brace yourself – I'm in gainful pursuit of the pleasures of the flesh.

Providing you're talking about the twenty-two pairs of legs sliding around a frozen pitch in the name of Premiership football. Yes, I'm still at the stage of my life when a twelve-hour round train journey to see my beloved Middlesbrough huffle around a freezing, smoke-filled Ayresome Park seems like the most enticing prospect in the world. Ambling onto the Holgate terrace, I nestle into my donkey jacket and take a pull on a crafty Silk Cut. All around me are men built like oil tankers, shuffling and grumbling and spitting onto a concrete terrace. I'm entirely at home here – an honest, Northern man of the soil. Albeit an honest, Northern man of the soil who has spent the afternoon in his lecturer's rooftop apartment, discussing Benedetto Croce's theory on the nature of aesthetic beauty. It's a philosophy that's at the forefront of my mind when Paul Wilkinson scores the winner against

Southampton and seems so startled by the prospect that he passes out at the near post.

Afterwards, admittedly, I do enjoy some female company. I've spent the last couple of months writing painfully sensitive letters to a pretty teenage brunette in Middlesbrough, and – as she lives only a short walk from the ground – I've arranged to take her for a drink at full-time. I knock on her door, my breath hanging forlornly in the air as she bids good night to her parents and joins me for a nervy date. We actually walk to the Endeavour, the strange, enticing grown-ups' pub which is – remember – round the corner from my gran's old sci-fi bungalow. It's four years now since my gran died, and even longer since I walked through these once-hallowed streets. And it's actually the first time I've ever been inside this pub – I buy a pint of Guinness for me, half a cider for my friend, and we nestle into the corner and warm each other up with chat and furtive glances.

And I start to cultivate illicit thoughts. Thoughts so foul, depraved and unpleasant that I hesitate to relate them in the pages of this book.

I think: 'If I get home early enough tonight, I could watch all the episodes of *The Prisoner* in one go'.

I'm not proud. Especially as my lady friend is lovely, funny, intelligent and kind. But as I walk her home, cuddle her, and jump into a taxi bound for Yarm, I know that there's a video box set with my name on it waiting back home in my parents' sideboard. The memory of that Renault 21 advert has festered in my mind for the last few years, and the previous summer I was still buzzed enough by *The Prisoner* to spend the best part of fifty pounds buying a spanking VHS presentation set from the dusty upstairs video lounge of Lancaster's ancient WHSmith.

Real life (and Webster's Best Bitter) has intervened, though, and I've not yet managed to watch any further than the very first episode. In the taxi on the way back to my parents' house, I make some quickfire mental calculations. 'Seventeen episodes at fifty minutes each, that's eight hundred and fifty minutes, divided by sixty is just over fourteen hours, with toilet breaks say fifteen hours, so if I start at midnight tonight, then I'll be finished at three o'clock tomorrow afternoon and can have a bite to eat before I catch my train at five.' It's one of the most staggering displays of ambition I've displayed since my university career commenced, but I'm willing to give it a go. At the stroke of midnight, with a greasy fried-egg sandwich in my hand, I slip the first cassette into my parents' creaking video recorder.

I get through the first episode, 'Arrival', with no problems. I'm wide awake, still tingling from the Boro result and a couple of hours of female company, and it passes without a problem. I make another fried-egg sandwich. Halfway through the second episode, 'The Chimes of Big Ben', I'm starting to feel a bit woozy. But I convince myself that I'll break on through, and am intrigued by Number Six's attempts to win The Village arts and crafts competition, spurred on and mocked by a sinister Leo McKern.

It's two in the morning when I make yet another fried-egg sandwich and start on episode three, the intriguingly titled 'A, B and C'. I'm now slumped against the sofa, stretching my eyes artificially wide to keep them open against their will. The plot concerns attempts to drug Number Six and induce dreams in which he will ultimately reveal his state-betraying secrets. Appropriately enough, I start to drift into odd, slumbering fantasies myself. The episode gets woven into strange, half-sleeping reveries of my own, and as I hover on the verge between waking and slumber it's Boro's Paul Wilkinson who I see trussed up in The Village Laboratory, and the Endeavour pub is located round the corner from Number Six's house. I manage to snap out of my mental drifting in time to catch the last five minutes, and I bravely change over the video tape and prepare to embark on episode four.

But it's no use. I last thirty seconds into the opening credits before dropping off into full-blown kip. I wake up at half past five on the front-room floor, the TV screen a mess of white-noise fuzz, and my mind in pretty much the same condition. I reluctantly decide to call off the experiment and tramp up the stairs to bed, pausing only to brush the congealed egg from my eyebrows.

It's another five years before I attempt a similar TV-watching marathon, and on this occasion it's a valiant attempt to watch all three original *Star Wars* films overnight, starting at midnight and finishing at seven the next morning. And on this occasion I'm reasonably successful – although, even then, livewire Boro midfielder Craig Hignett makes a brief appearance in Jabba's Palace at the start of *Return of the Jedi*.

'I was staring out of the stained-glass windows and thought I was under the floor at the Leeds Armouries Musuem.'

'Eh?'

'The Hercules Hall has green stained-glass windows, and the Leeds Armouries Museum has a green glass floor, and I started to think I was trapped underneath it, tapping on the underside of the glass to attract people's attention. I had to leave when we did or I was going to start freaking out.'

Blimey.

I'm walking Sorcha back to the car, where she's intending to sleep for a couple of hours. We pass through the cobbled streets of Portmeirion, back up the hill, and she curls into the Starlet's pushed-back passenger seat, making me promise to wake her before part two of *The Prisonbear*. I kiss her gently on the cheek and she's asleep before I've locked the car doors. As I walk back through the Village gardens, the stripey-blazered gents on the bandstand – tubas and euphoniums glistening in the mid-afternoon sun – begin playing a gentle, lilting version of Beethoven's Sonata No. 8 in C Minor. It lifts into the sky with a gorgeous swagger, and transports me effortlessly back to a long-lost childhood of summer scrapes and ginger beer. And then, at its climax, an enormous man in a Swansea City shirt wanders behind me and contributes a belch so loud it makes the Flake sink into my ice cream.

I head back to the Hercules Hall, where we're treated to a talk and slide show from *Prisoner* cameraman Robert Monks who, organiser Rick tells me excitedly as we enter, has discovered a welter of sepia photographs in his loft, detailing the *Prisoner*'s day-by-day location work back in 1966. And they're great – endless shots of chain-smoking crew members sporting pastel-shaded cardigans and side-partings you could drive a Mini Moke through. He reveals that his own bruised fingernail makes a cameo appearance in episode five, 'The Schizoid Man', and that extra scenes of dialogue were written for 'The Chimes of Big Ben' because McGoohan and Leo McKern were 'living the programme' with so much relish.

As the afternoon wears on, I head back to find Sorcha. She's still curled uncomfortably on the passenger seat, snoring gently with her face pressed against the steamed-up window. I shake her shoulder and she comes round with a gentle smile and a slow, yawning stretch, blissfully unaware of the wide red line across her face where the car upholstery has been pressing for the previous two and a half hours.

It strikes me as we shamble back down that Portmeirion has closed to the public for the day, and – devoid of crowds in Swansea City shirts and baggy shorts – the streets have taken on an eerie, Village-like ambience. We assemble for a meeting on a dias outside 'the Ship Shop', a pink, chapel-like building with a chequered courtyard outside. It's used in the show as the programme's café, but now it's the meeting point for our guided Portmeirion *Prisoner* tour. Two dozen of us convention newbies gather around a leafy wall, to be met by organiser Howard, a tall, jovial, long-haired figure in a Breton shirt and Elvis-in-Vegas-style shades. In the keeping with the Unmutual's rock-star affectations, he looks like Mud's Les Gray after a few years in the Marine Nationale. He's a great guide, pointing out 'Fountain House' where Noël Coward wrote *Blithe Spirit* during a blissful week in 1941, and taking us to Number Six's house itself, now predictably transformed into a *Prisoner*-themed gift shop, but still sporting the unmistakable white and blue livery outside. So unmistakable, in fact, that Sorcha and I have walked past it at least six times today without batting an eyelid.

'Do you know the place well, then? How often have you been?' I ask Howard, as we stop for a break to take pictures and slurp cold drinks.

'We all grew up here, really.' He beams, his eyes turning misty with nostalgia. 'A big gang of us used to book the place out and come and get drunk for weeks on end.'

I think back to my own formative drinking experiences, and how most of them were carried out in the concrete playground of Yarm Junior School in the dead of night, brazenly mixing up the dangerous cocktails of Merrydown cider and small-town boredom. How different my life might have turned out if I'd conducted them in Portmeirion, The Village itself, running wild along the white idyllic shoreline and swinging merrily around the statue of Hercules that Clough Williams-Ellis acquired in Aberdeen in the summer of 1960, and drove on the back of a pick-up from Scotland to North Wales. Although I'm not sure where the Merrydown would have come from; The Village doesn't have a Spar.

Afterwards, Sorcha slips her hand into mine and we peel off on our own private tour, walking past the Portmeirion Hotel (where Number Six plays chess against a succession of fusty military types) and down an eternity of winding steps to the legendary Stone Boat. Once a fully operational 1920s trading ketch, the boat broke its moorings during a ferocious overnight storm, and stranded itself on the nearby island of Ynys Gifftan. Clough Williams-Ellis, in the middle of constructing Portmeirion's quay, salvaged what he could of the vessel and concreted it into his spanking new harbour. Sorcha and I jump merrily onto its bow, and pose for photos as a sea breeze tugs at our rumpled, tired clothes. To our left, the village sweeps up into the wooded hills, its sparkling steeples and green-headed domes peeping out of a rustling mass of trees. To our right, a huge expanse of beach sweeps out to the horizon. It's vast and clean and empty, unsullied by litter and tourist trade and dog mess. An impressive bank of dark, grey cloud is rolling across the skyline, but we potter into the squidgy sand where Number Six is repeatedly menaced by rambling Rovers, and I break into a dramatic run for Sorcha's clicking camera. She laughs heartily as I sink up to my ankles in quicksand, and I laugh too, and we steal a kiss by a rockpool before strolling back up to the village.

We're happy.

Faint, exhausted and filthy, but happy.

BLOODY STUPID THINGS I HAVE DONE IN THE NAME OF FANDOM NUMBER SEVEN: TRYING TO WATCH THE FINAL EPISODE OF THE PRISONER WHILE STONED

Look away now, Mum.

No, really.

A disclaimer: I am not now, nor have I ever been, a regular user of illegal drugs. As far as I can tell, the inevitable conclusion of frequent cannabis use is an inability to move from the sofa and an insatiable desire to eat fourteen packets of Flamin' Hot Monster Munch on the bounce, following them up with a king-size Twix. And believe me, I'm more than capable of achieving either of those mental states without resorting to Class B substances . . . although my addiction to Monster Munch is becoming so all-consuming that I'm wondering if it should be reclassified itself. I'm a whisker away from snorting the dust at the bottom of the bags.

On this occasion, however, I find it hard to resist, because – in a nutshell – it's far too funny not to. It's summer 1993 now, I'm in a grotty student front room in Lancaster city centre, and Simon Crabbe has produced a joint the size of the average pogostick.

I'm not joking. The thing is five feet long if it's an inch – a huge, skinny, elongated stogie that must have taken at least four all-night garages worth of Rizla papers to produce. It elicits an audible gasp from all in the room with the exception of Andy Fordham, who has passed out already from a combination of Webster's Best Better, QC Cream and stupidity.

I can't resist, and, despite the fact that I've never done much of this before, take a hearty toke when it reaches my squishy beanbag. 'Doesn't seem to have much effect,' I sagely intone five seconds later. 'In fact it's not a patch on Scandia Gold.' I'm drinking from an eight-pack of this treacly, super-strength lager, purchased in bulk from our friendly corner shop.

Ten minutes and two tokes later, I'm waggling my fingers in front of my eyes and asking why the music is coming out of the cushions.

I'm helped home by my housemates John Jaques and Raf Uzar, both of whom have decided rather sensibly to abstain. It's three in the morning, and by the time we reach home they've had enough of me rambling about cosmic rays and Middlesbrough's complex ley-line system, and abandon me on the sofa while they shamble off to bed. I lie there alone, grinning silently in the spinning gloom, and as I do so my eyes settle momentarily on the front-room shelf. Something exciting is waiting for me there, and with mind-altering substances flooding through my veins (Scandia Gold, I tell you – dynamite), I'm powerless to defy its irresistible lure.

It's my *Prisoner* VHS box set.

Oh yes.

Pausing only to take an entire loaf of Mother's Pride from Raf's cupboard, and filling its slices randomly with raw, crunchy nuggets of Instant Smash, I slip the videos out of their container.

I've had the box set for over a year now, but haven't attempted to watch any of the episodes since my failed all-nighter four months earlier. I decide, wisely, that the best way to appreciate the series fully is to skip the thirteen episodes I've never bothered watching and move straight onto the last bit to find out what happens at the end.

The following fifty minutes prove to be one of the most terrifying experiences of my life. To *The Prisoner*'s fans, the episode is the ultimate final confrontation between authoritarian state control and the fight for individuality, a stirring and breathtaking allegory for the ongoing battle against establishment repression. What *I* see is this: an exasperated Kenneth Griffith in judge's wig and ermine gown presiding over a secret underground cavern and leading a riotous assembly of white-robed figures in harlequin masks who are frequently led by Alexis Kanner's pipe-cleaner-limbed Carnaby Street dandy into manic renditions of the old spiritual refrain 'Dem Bones, Dem Bones' as Number Six looks down from a gold-trimmed throne before instigating a riot with Leo McKern's Number Two resurrected from the dead to take part in a machine-gun-led bloodbath conducted to the distorted strains of The Beatles' 'All You Need Is Love'.

Amazingly, all of this actually happens, and isn't just the product of my drug-addled imagination. And these are the more coherent plot points. By the end of the episode, I'm curled up in a sweating ball on the sofa, pressing my face into a cushion, unable to withstand any further assault on my senses. It's a non-stop, whirling, psychedelic attack, as much a violent product of 1968 as the Paris Riots and *Revolution 9*. I take one last mouthful of raw Smash before stumbling upstairs to my bedroom, where I spend at least twenty minutes opening and closing the curtains repeatedly to ensure that The Village hasn't appeared outside.

I collapse into bed, which reaches up in a semi-circle to swallow me, and grip with white knuckles on to the whirling headboard until sleep finally takes me away from the madness for the best part of fourteen hours. Finally I understand the kerfuffle, the uproar, the anger and bemusement of unsuspecting ITV viewers who first watched the episode on a rainy Sunday night in February 1968, settling down after roast beef and dumplings having just enjoyed The Tremeloes playing live on *The Morecambe and Wise Show*.

When I wake up the next day, I toy with the idea of phoning Patrick McGoohan to find out what on earth it all meant, but he doesn't seem to be listed in the Lancaster and District directory.

Back in a packed-out Hercules Hall, Jane Merrow is giving her talk. In 'The Schizoid Man' she plays Alison, a doe-eyed Village brunette who shares seemingly both a telepathic connection (she's a dab hand with the old ESP cards) and the beginnings of a romance with Number Six. It's an amazing, bewildering episode, in which McGoohan's character finds his life (and house) taken over by the identical-looking Number Twelve, who sets out to prove that he is the real Number Six, and that Number Six is in fact the imposter Number Twelve. Number Six is only able to prove his identity when he discovers that the bruised fingernail sustained during ESP-related flirting at the beginning of the episode (and yes, it's Robert Monks's digit in the close-up) has been captured by Alison on camera. Are you following this? This is actually one of *The Prisoner*'s more straightforward plotlines, before the series got *really* weird.

Jane today is still slim and pretty, like a slightly less ginger Jane Asher, and talks primly and enthusiastically of her years working on cult TV classics from both sides of the Atlantic – from *Randall and Hopkirk (Deceased)* and *The Avengers* to *Airwolf* and *The Incredible Hulk*. She'd worked with Patrick McGoohan on *Danger Man*, and laughs at herself in an onscreen clip, portraying a seductive Spanish revolutionary. She reveals that McGoohan's devout Catholic beliefs and rock-solid marriage gave him a briskly professional approach to actresses: 'Perhaps he thought we were all fallen women,' she giggles, with an irresistible twinkle.

'If Alison was that good, why didn't she find out why Number Six resigned?' asks one caped fan, betraying the brilliantly 'only in fandom' belligerence of someone – like *The Prisonbear*'s director – with far too much time on their hands.

'It's more of a sensual approach than an intellectual discipline,' twinkles Jane. 'She wouldn't have tried to read his mind.'

There is, as Morecambe and Wise would have said, no answer to that.

The room clears a little afterwards, and Sorcha and I, having been crouched at the back, find proper seats next to a trio of twentysomething girls sharing Quavers from a rustling bag. The fans here are all far younger than I'd expected, and I begin to wonder how much influence that late 1980s Renault 21 advert actually had among my fandom generation. Rick takes to the stage to host the inevitable charity auction, and the Hercules Hall is thinning out as long-term Village inmates are slowly released back into society. The final item up for grabs is a bespoke multi-coloured *Prisoner* cape, a beautiful-looking item of 1960s pop art clothing, tied at the neck with a glittering golden cord. It's modelled at the front of the hall by a bespectacled redhead called Erica.

'Any bids for the cape?' asks Rick, eyebrows raised. 'We can start as low as thirty pounds . . .'

A deathly hush descends upon the hall. Sorcha, to my surprise, nudges me in the midriff. 'Go on,' she whispers. 'Put a bid in to get things started.'

I sigh wearily and raise my hand. 'Thirty pounds,' I holler, rolling my eyes with wistful disdain.

'Thank you, Bob!' beams Mr Memory. 'Any advance on thirty pounds?'

The hall falls into a conspiracy of silence that would make Number Six flush with tacit pride. Fifty assorted *Prisoner* fans shuffle, mumble and glower at their feet for twenty seconds before the hammer falls and I become the proud owner of an authentic-looking item of Village apparel. Sorcha helps me tie up the cape at the neck as I hand over three ten-pound notes to Rick, swirling my new pink, purple and sky-blue accessory round me like some psychedelic Orson Welles. 'It's not really pink, it's more cerise,' says Erica, tugging wistfully at the hem. 'It's a much more manly shade of pink than you'd expect.'

'I'll bear that in mind when I wear it around Middlesbrough,' I smile.

As helpers begin dismantling the convention apparatus around us, we bid our goodbyes to Rick and his fellow helpers and wander back through the bar. When we emerge into a deserted Portmeirion, it's almost dark. It's 9.45pm, and the moon is casting strange shadows around the Village's assorted minarets, towers and converted pigswill boilers. It has a magical, unearthly quality in the half-light, and we wander into a sheltered gazebo – which, brilliantly, buzzes and hums to the touch, confirming my suspicions that Portmeirion crackles with a life of its own – to pose for pictures in the swirling cape. Sorcha looks like a bona fide Village denizen, mysterious and elegant and demure and beguiling. I look like Elvis in 1975. The perfect qualification to be a full-time Unmutual bigwig.

As we pelt through the winding North Wales countryside in pitch darkness, I scrunch the cape into a makeshift cushion and doze into slumber propped up against the passenger side window. I actually slip into a heat-soaked, bumbling nightmare where the huge, white balloon of the Rover is pursuing us from Portmeirion on the twisting A487, bouncing menacingly behind the Starlet's back bumper as a screaming Sorcha hammers her foot on the accelerator and tries to make for the safety of Bangor. I wake up with a stifled gasp as we pass a darkened converted caravan selling burgers and hot dogs from an overgrown lay-by. There's no Rover in sight from the back window, just a battered Ford Fiesta. Although, oddly, we pass a vintage clapped-out red Renault 21 chugging along the A55 to Conwy. Now *that's* showing ambitious tendencies.

We reach home at 3.15am, and collapse into a cuddle before fainting into bed. When I wake up, refreshed, shortly before lunchtime, I pull back the bedroom curtains, so indoctrinated by the experience that I expect to see The Village piazza outside the window, peppered with Mini Mokes and sparkling fountains, and hear The Village radio clarion call, and Fenella Fielding's cheery announcer piping up, 'Good morning, Number Twenty-Four, this is to remind you to clean your teeth before entering the kitchen to make breakfast.' Maybe there's even an imposter Bob and Sorcha in the house, and I'll have to dig out pictures of my water-pistol scar to prove that I am indeed the genuine Fischer article. But there isn't – there's just our street, with John over the road digging the garden, and the kids from next door circling round on bikes. It's just a typical, ordinary, mundane Monday morning.

Except for the fact that Sorcha is all smiles.

Yep, my quest is no longer a solo mission, and Sorcha declares that she's had a thoroughly marvellous weekend, despite the occasional hallucination. She's no longer the cynical firebrand who declared fandom to be full of 'geeks and weirdos' and she is, she insists, looking forward to the

Discworld weekend that we're set to spend together in Hinckley.

We leave for Leicester in four days' time.

Be seeing you.

THE BATTLE TO SAVE EARTH

by Robert Fischer (Aged Eight And Seven Twelfths)
Monday 15 June 1981
PART NINE

Dirk and I ran back to our ship. 'That was close,' Dirk said. 'But what about Richard?' I asked. 'Just let me get my breath back and we'll go after klebba,' Dirk answered. Soon we were running back through the wood and after klebba. klebba took Richard to a strange room. Richard was pushed into the room and was locked in. Then klebba walked towards us.

I snapped a strong stick off a tree and tripped klebba up. The Dirk threw a rope to me and I tied klebba to the tree. Then I drew my gun and fired at the door of Richard's cell. But as the laser hit the door, it bounced off into a swamp. Dirk got a small bomb from his pocket and gave it to me. I threw the bomb at the door and stepped back. There was a huge explosion as the bomb hit the door. But when I went towards the door there was not a single burn on it. 'There is only one thing that can destroy those doors,' Dirk said. 'What?' I asked. 'A speicail laser called Bombpower. It can destroy anything,' Dirk said. 'Where do you get it from?' I asked Dirk. 'From the very core of Swamp-world,' Dirk answered. 'The core?' I shouted, 'How do we get there?' Dirk turned round and said 'Follow me'. He took me to a huge tree and kicked part of it open. 'Get in there,' he said and pushed me in.

To be continued . . .

DISCWORLD

DISCWORLD CONVENTION
HINCKLEY ISLAND HOTEL, LEICESTERSHIRE
FRIDAY 18 – MONDAY 21 AUGUST

'Hamwise Beardribbler died today.'

'I'M DAVE, AND THIS is Oscar'.

It's late on a thundery, rain-lashed Friday afternoon, and I'm at the end of a queue of grumbling Terry Pratchett fans in a sprawling hotel foyer in the middle of a Leicestershire industrial estate. I'm wet, sweaty and pissed off, and a tall, bespectacled bald man is introducing me to his pet dragon.

'Say hello, Oscar!' he chirps.

I mumble a hangdog greeting.

''Ello, Oscar!' he replies to himself, in a muffled, high-pitched squeak.

It's a red glove puppet on the right arm of the irrepressible Dave, and he and Oscar are entertaining themselves in the check-in queue by genially harassing the fifty or so people ahead of them, at least sixty per cent of whom are dressed in the seemingly obligatory Discworld uniform of black, floppy-brimmed hat, ankle-length leather coat, bedraggled ponytail and Iron Maiden T-shirt. I'm still exhausted from the previous weekend's mayhem, and for the first time during my quest I start to feel a little resentment. Looking at the welter of identically clad fans ahead of me, I can't help but think of the old *Life of Brian* scene, in which a legion of grinning disciples chant, 'Yes! We are all individuals!' in blissfully un-ironic unison.

I'm a grumpy bugger, I know. I start to swear softly to myself, and Sorcha flashes me a filthy look that any passing paralinguist would readily translate as 'Don't ruin my fucking weekend'.

Then I spy a small boy, who can't be much more than eight years old, watching an episode of Uncle Trevor's old favourite *The Adventure Game* on a tiny laptop, and I can't help but mellow a little inside. Especially when Keith Chegwin gets sucked into the Vortex.

My mood starts to lift, and I offer Sorcha a smile. I'd look good in a leather coat and hat, given the opportunity. And I quite like Iron Maiden as well.

The 1980s stuff, anyway.

Well, the first couple of albums.

The Discworld convention is big. Really big. You just won't believe how vastly, hugely, mind-bogglingly big it is. I mean, you might think there were a lot of people at the *Doctor Who* weekend in Stockton, but . . . No, hang on, I'm still quoting Douglas Adams here. I need to get myself into a Terry Pratchett frame of mind. OK, imagine the Discworld itself: the vast, circular, 'flat Earth' of mountains, cities, deserts and seas in which almost all of Pratchett's novels are set, carried on the back of four giant, star-tanned elephants, themselves transported through the endless realms of infinity on top of the giant space turtle A'Tuin. You could probably fit the whole lot into the Hinckley Island Hotel restaurant, and the venue's entire suite of twenty-six function rooms has been completely block-booked by the 2006 Discworld convention, at which eight hundred fans – approximately 480 of whom are wearing long leather coats and Iron Maiden T-shirts – are here to celebrate Pratchett's works in a sprawling, back-breaking four-day event.

The reason for Sorcha's disquiet, meanwhile, is simple. Discworld is *hers*. As *Doctor Who* belongs to me, as *Hitch*

Hiker's belongs to Doug, as *Star Trek* belongs to a man who creates thirty-two-acre mazes in the shape of the starship *Enterprise*, so Terry Pratchett belongs to Sorcha. There is a corner of our front room that is for ever Discworld, and here she keeps her collection – row upon row of pristine signed hardbacks, row upon row of pristine signed *paperback* editions of the Same Fucking Books (initialled for emphasis, lest I get pigeon-holed as the *sole* obsessive compulsive in the household) and endless trinkets, ornaments, jigsaws and (ahem) 'collectable figurines'. All stacked in a dusty enclave that I'm not allowed to touch, therefore it plays host to a thriving ecological subsystem bigger than anything Pratchett could ever conjure up from his fevered, bearded, leather-coated imagination. Roll up, children of Yarm, and see the woodlouse graveyard.

She's helped me with the following bit.

A BLUFFER'S GUIDE TO . . . TERRY PRATCHETT AND DISCWORLD

Until J. K. Rowling stuck her wand in the air, Terry Pratchett was the UK's bestselling author, and still holds the proud title of the most shoplifted writer in British literary history. His books – of which more than fifty have now been published – are almost always set in Discworld, a mythical, vaguely medieval flat Earth with a central, mountainous 'Hub' and four directions – Hubward, Rimward, Turnwise and Widdershins. It's populated by a motley selection of wizards, witches, thieves and other assorted grotties, and also plays host to a fair selection of gods (who live in Dunmanifestin on the Cori Celesti, a huge, spiky, ten-foot mountain in the Hub) and 'anthropomorphic personifications' of mythical figures, including Death, the traditional Grim Reaper, who – in Discworld – rides a horse called Binky. In the British cult and sci-fi family tree, Discworld is the specky teenage daughter who likes ponies and making things, but doesn't know enough about Iron Maiden to join in with the Dungeons and Dragons boys.

The first Discworld book, *The Colour of Magic*, was published in 1983, and made an instant cult hero of Pratchett. Many of the books are based around the denizens of Discworld's major city Ankh-Morpork (aka 'the Big Wahoonie'), a foul, stinking, pestilent slum that plays host, incongruously, to the Unseen University, a seat of magical learning staffed seemingly entirely by inept super-annuated wizards and a librarian who happens to be an orangutan.

Popular Discworld catchphrases include 'Ook Ook' (as uttered by the librarian as a response to, well, everything, really), 'Where's My Cow?' (a bizarre children's book owned by grizzled Ankh-Morpork cop Sam Vimes), 'The Knuckles ... The Horrible Knuckles!' and 'How Many Has He Written Now? Is It Over A Hundred?' If you want to sum up Discworld in a sentence, then it's ... well, like *Lord of the Rings*, but funny. If you want to find a Discworld fan in a public library, say, 'Ook ook,' and wait for a man in a long leather coat to jump on a table, scratch his armpits and start throwing books at you. If you want to annoy a Discworld fan, turn up at a popular convention in a foul mood and start making facile comments about leather coats and Iron Maiden T-shirts.

I'm sorry.

'What are you reading?'

'You wouldn't understand.'

It's a sunny day around Easter 1988, and my mum – Gawd

bless 'er – is trying to forge a connection with her sulky fifteen-year-old son. We're on a week's holiday in the Scottish Highlands, and my parents have just returned from a shopping expedition in Fort Augustus, returning to the car with tartan carrier bags full of shortbread, knitwear and other assorted tourist tripe. Ever the martyr, I've stayed alone in our sun-baked Reliant Scimitar, marooned in the car park behind the Great Glen Trading Centre, gently steaming and reading my books. I've been embarking on a world record week-long sulk, ever since being dragged kicking and screaming from my fetid, gloomy bolthole of a bedroom and forcibly separated from my beloved ZX Spectrum, right in the middle of Level 14 of *Arkanoid 2: Revenge of Doh*. I'm not happy, and there have been un-cooperative tantrums, extended screaming fits and overheated breakdowns. And that's just from the Spectrum.

To console myself, before we set off, I'd caught the 294 bus from Yarm to Stockton-on-Tees, and bought two books in WHSmith to tide me through the forthcoming Highland horrors. They're the inspiration for yet another Spectrum game I've been playing recently, a 'graphic text adventure' called *The Colour of Magic*, which has won me over by being – get this – like *Lord of the Rings*, but funny. For the past few weeks, I've been happily guiding the wizard Rincewind and his strange companion Twoflower around the beguiling and hilarious Discworld. Until that fateful day in the upstairs book department, though, I'd had no idea they were tie-ins with the books, and I'd instantly snapped up both *The Colour of Magic*, and its sequel, *The Light Fantastic*. It's day four of our holiday now, and I'm nearly halfway through the second book already.

'Why don't you stop being so bloody surly and just enjoy your holiday?'

'Ook ook.'

Eighteen years later, I'm hunched up on our bed in the

Hinckley Island Hotel, flicking through the self-same books. They're yellowed and well-thumbed now, and there are nasty stains on the spine of *The Light Fantastic*. Sorcha is pottering around the bedroom, hanging up her clothes and fiddling around with contact lenses. I have the books set out in front of me, along with the (mercifully non-tartan) carrier bags full of gubbins we've been given at the convention registration desk. The scale of the event is vast – a labyrinthine timetable laid out in impossibly confusing blocks suggests that there are eight different events taking place at any one time, encompassing talks by various Discworld personnel, workshops in juggling, belly-dancing and rune-casting, maskerade balls, lectures on the Knights Templar and 'Creating Your Own Religion', quizzes and competitions including the 'Unseen University Challenge', signing sessions, coffee clubs, charity auctions and mathematics seminars. I'm eerily reminded of my first day at university – removed from my familiar comfort zone in Yarm and plonked in a bewildering, alien environment, given nothing more than a welcome pack containing Pot Noodles, spot cream and contraceptives to guide me through the lonely nights. Except in Discworld, there's no sign of any free condoms – which is worrying, as you wouldn't want the buggers breeding. Especially as I'm not sure you can get leather coats in baby sizes.

I'll stop now.

An hour later, we wander into the huge, main function hall ('the Dysk') to be invested into our guilds. In the Discworld books, everyone – from alchemists to assassins, from gamblers to glassblowers – belongs to a guild. There's even a Dogs' Guild, whose administrators control scavenging rights, night-time barking duties, breeding permissions and howling rotas. Here, Sorcha and I are plonked unceremoniously into the Lawyers' Guild, and whisked away to the Bhang Bhang Duc room with several dozen other legally minded souls for a pep talk. In the Discworld, the guild is headed by Mr Slant, a sallow-faced zombie who joined the realms of the undead in order to claim the financial disbursements involved in conducting his own defence at the trial that led to his execution. In Hinckley, our boss is Peter Morwood, a respected sci-fi and fantasy novellist whose *Star Trek* book *The Romulan Way* was written in collaboration with his wife, Diane Duane, on their honeymoon. Diane is here too this weekend, and heads the euphemistic Seamstresses' Guild, the conglomeration of Discworld call-girls headed in the books by 'Mrs Rosemary Palm and her lovely daughters'.

Peter strides into Bhang Bhang Duc resplendent in grey power suit and shades, and proceeds to briskly regale us – in a litany of cod-Latin legal jargonese – as to the best methods of fleecing rival guilds. Members of each guild have been given a dozen or so small paper tokens, the object of the weekend's fun being to separate rival punters from their currency by whatever means necessary – the guild with the most other guilds' tokens being declared the winner at the end of the weekend. The method of separation is all down to the ingenuity of the individual. Assassins' Guild members can stab unsuspecting punters (metaphorically) in the back and demand tokens in return, seamstresses can pinch them on the bum and demand likewise. We lawyers, naturally, are predisposed to dish out fines and legal fees willy nilly. My favourite clause among Peter's strategy is the Being Bloody Stupid Act 1581 (Stupedessedare Sanguine) which may be invoked by 'anyone who's had it Right Up to Here with junior (and no-so-junior) members of any guild: where enthusiasm exceeds good manners; repeated thefts and assassinations in the bar (and in the toilets) quickly become unfunny'. To summarise: fine anybody who gets on your wick. He has the look of an angry man about him, and I wonder what outrages have been committed against him in previous years' conveniences.

Afterwards, we wander back to the Dysk, where Terry Pratchett himself – clad in his trademark leather jacket and black trilby – is perched, Val Doonican-style, in a softly lit chair, reading from his as-yet-unpublished next novel, *Wintersmith*. He's a gentle and beguiling reader, and before long his voice starts to soundtrack the occasional floaty dream as the rigours of the day begin to catch up with me, and I drift into languid half-sleep. It's only when I start to snore over Pratchett's Granny Weatherwax impersonation that Sorcha nudges me in the ribs.

'Come on, Hamwise Beardribbler,' says Sorcha. 'Pick up thy broadsword and come to bed.'

She knows too much.

CRUCIAL MOMENTS IN FANDOM HISTORY NUMBER EIGHT: THE SUMMER OF DUNGEONS AND DRAGONS

It's May 1988, I'm fifteen years old, and my name is Hamwise Beardribbler. I have sixteen strength points, 185 gold pieces, and am carrying a two-handed sword and a gold statue of a snake-dog. I know this because it's written on my adventure sheet on the kitchen table. Also at the table are Elrond Goldenbow, Flaxman Orcslayer and the Dungeon Master himself, erm . . . Paul Hayes. Yes – brace yourself – we're playing Dungeons and Dragons.

In these enlightened times, of course, it's difficult to imagine a time when teenage boys could gather indoors and abuse their bodies in such a way, now that stringent government anti-role-playing legislation has made it illegal to roll a twenty-sided dice in an unventilated public building. But back in the 1980s we were wild, we were bold, we were dangerous . . . and we knew how to wear an enchanted breastplate without revealing our mystical powers to the angry dwarf chieftain.

I'm not an attractive fifteen-year-old. I'm dressed in a foul, off-white jumper from Top Man – which I'm convinced gives me the dashing air of Peter Davison's cricket-loving Fifth Doctor but, combined with stained, half-mast school trousers and a shoulder-length mop of greasy brown hair, actually makes me look like I should be selling car radios on North Ormesby Market. I also stink permanently of Quinoderm Acne Cream, a pungent over-the-counter glop whose main method of treatment consists of making the sufferer smell so bad that no one gets close enough to notice the spots. I'm nasty, smelly, greasy, badly dressed and with skin the texture of uncooked pork. So in Dungeons and Dragons circles, I'm considered something of a heart-throb.

Actually, this isn't true, as our gaming session is being conducted at the house of Neil 'Elrond Goldenbow' Braithwaite, who is – no, really – a *genuine* school heart-throb. He's tall and handsome with perfect skin and hair, and looks like some strange *Smash Hits*-sponsored experiment to create a genetic hybrid of Andrew Ridgeley and George Michael. I've still no idea to this day how he ended up playing Dungeons and Dragons, when he should by rights have been shagging supermodels on the Sunset Strip and enjoying a string of Top Ten hits. He's clever and popular, with wealthy parents, and lives in a huge house in a secluded corner of Yarm. And, despite this staggering welter of evidence to the contrary, he's actually really likeable.

Flaxman Orcslayer is, in reality, Phil Slack, a brilliant teenage anarchist who buys underage cigarettes from our local VG shop and listens seemingly permanently to the works of Iron Maiden. And our Dungeon Master Paul Hayes is a strapping, slightly evil teenager who speaks fluent *Blackadder* and *Monty Python*. I like them all a lot, right up until the point that Hamwise Beardribbler dies.

'Fucking *what*?' I holler.

'A boulder falls from behind the Monkey Icon, and crushes you full in the chest. Lose fifteen hit points,' reiterates Paul, with a nasty sneer.

'But that means I'm dead!'

'Pffffft.'

'You're fucking *joking*!'

'Keep the language down – my mum's in the conservatory,' whispers Neil, with all the gung-ho derring-do you'd expect from an elfin warrior on 10,000 XP points.

I throw my character sheet onto the kitchen table and slip into a vile grey ski jacket from Burtons, presumably part of a job lot inherited when the off-piste revellers of St Moritz decided they'd rather stick with Dolce & Gabbana instead. Flaxman Orcslayer giggles into his coffee as he slips Iron Maiden's thunderous *Killers* album onto the stereo, and I storm off home to my beloved ZX Spectrum.

I get very attached to my Dungeons and Dragons characters. Later that evening, when I've left half my oven chips and still haven't spoken to my fussing, concerned parents, my mum takes me to one side and asks me what the problem is – no doubt with fears of teenage pregnancy, AIDS and drug dependency forefront in her fretting, middle-aged mind.

'Hamwise Beardribbler died today,' I mutter.

I've never heard my mum say, 'Oh, for fuck's sake,' but I suspect this is the closest she's ever got.

This is my world, though. I am of course, back at the D&D table the following Sunday, starting from scratch with a brand-new character (Bathrigg Ballslasher), and laughing along with Haysie and Slackie and, erm, Braithwaitie as we crack on to the next Iron Maiden album (*Number of the Beast*) and while away another six hours of our vibrant teenage years. When I'm not playing role-playing games, I'm reading Terry Pratchett or

Douglas Adams, and when I'm not doing that, I'm gathering together with future *Star Wars* compatriot Wez to meet our friend Gaz Norman and play three-man *Gauntlet* on his Atari ST. And yes, forty-five per cent of Teesside blokes do have names that end in the letter 'z', a proud statistical boast only narrowly defeated on a global scale by the men of Mexico City.

I'm still immersing myself in this strange world of swords and sorcery a year or so later, but then, in the summer of 1989, when I enter sixth form and discover punk rock and indie, it all seems to drift away. Almost overnight. I can't help but wonder, though, that if I'd kept playing (as indeed Slackie actually did, and he regales me with hilarious stories of the latest RPG madness whenever I bump into him) whether I'd be like some of the Discworld attendees this weekend – utterly lost in this mythical world, wandering around a Leicestershire industrial estate sporting skimpy leather armour and a broadsword and referring to the hotel staff as 'stout yeomen of the bar'. Shortly before I'd set off for Hinckley, John Jaques – the old university chum who helped me home during the *Prisoner* dope-smoking debacle – had told me that he once worked at a call-centre in Burnley alongside a role-player from Hebden Bridge who had changed his name by deed poll to match his favourite character. And thus spent his working hours answering the phone with the immortal line 'Hello, Affinity Insurance, you're through to Gandalf Pendragon, how may I help you?'

There, but for the grace of God, go I. Although at this stage I'm not sure if it's Offler the Crocodile God or Zephyrus the God of Light Breezes.

It's Saturday morning, and the convention's Hub is . . . well, a hub of activity. A vast open space in the centre of the hotel, it seems busier than most Saturday-morning shopping arcades, although the average Debenhams or Virgin Megastore probably plays host to slightly fewer customers dressed in the skimpy tartan and blue body paint of the Wee Free Men. The guilds are out in force, setting up trestle-table HQs and writing updates on their latest activities on large free-standing flip charts. 'Inhumed Before Your Time?' blares one Priests' Guild notice, in hastily scribbled permanent marker. 'Try Resurrection! Approach the Priests' Guild for a Speedy Life Inhalation. One Token Per Emergency Call-Out – Visit the Back of the Hub.'

I'm amazed at the endeavour and ingenuity that's gone into making Discworld the only convention to date where unprompted fan activity pretty much matches the organised events stride for stride. Sorcha and I wander to the back of the Hub where we're delighted to find Judith, water-pistol fight Judith, selling tarot-card readings and official redemption certificates from behind a velvet curtain. Sorcha thinks ahead to the evening's activities and buys, for two guild tokens, a disclaimer promising that 'all gods small, great and economy-sized grant her the indulgence of drunkenness'. Judith proudly signs the testimony, and I show her my duelling scar from my tumble into the Winspit Quarry crags. Everybody's happy.

The Saturday passes in a first-day-at-school blur. We wander into the 'Unseen University Challenge', a Discworld-based quiz, in which a terrified Sorcha is pressganged into joining a team captained by a man dressed as Dios, the High Priest of Djelibeybi, complete with orange lampshade on his head. It's chaired by the unlikely Discworld Paxman that is Brian, bravely dressed as *Sourcery*'s weedy Nigel the Destroyer and sporting nothing more than a loin cloth and Womble boots. 'Which team gets to go on top?' he asks a bumbling lunchtime crowd. 'The seamstresses,' replies one wag, to a ripple of ribald laughter. Sorcha's team get hammered.

We also see Terry Pratchett onstage again. He emerges before a packed Dysk to rapturous applause and talks warmly of his new role in Sky One's forthcoming adaptation of *The Hogfather*, in which he has a cameo alongside such thespian heavyweights as David Jason, Ian Richardson, Nigel Planer and recent *Doctor Who* star Marc Warren. Pratchett has a blink-and-you-miss-it role as a kindly toymaker – 'It was either that or the Hair Loss Fairy,' he explains. After heart surgery in 2004, he halved his traditional literary output to one book a year, and now claims to have a cholesterol level so low that he's 'allowed to swallow a pound of lard a day'.

He's treated with an overwhelming reverence by the packed hall, and I notice towards the end of the panel that one fan has even come to Hinckley dressed as Pratchett himself, sporting a wide-brimmed black trilby, stick-on white beard and (yep) long leather coat. The adulation with which Pratchett is bestowed in the fantasy community is illustrated by the fact that stage adaptations of his books have now been produced on all seven continents, including Antarctica, where Australian research scientists performed *Wyrd Systers* on their snow-whipped base. He mentions this in passing, along with his long-standing admiration for the ZX-81 and Spectrum computers, which I make a mental note of as potential conversation ice-breakers should our paths cross during the remainder of the weekend.

And then it's time for the Maskerade Parade.

I have, of course, seen fancy-dressers at every proper convention I've been to, but nothing quite on this sort of scale. The fans have once again taken the baton and . . . well, not just run with it, but clambered over the athletics stadium wall and commandeered a light aircraft to fly them to Pseudopolis. We cram ourselves into The Dysk and watch as several hundred fans – including a multitude of Deaths, wizards and Wee Free Men as well as a cracking drag act called Davina Dress who looks like a considerably butcher version of Penelope Keith take their turn onstage, often providing their own musical accompaniment, including a splendid version of 'Morpork, Morpork' to the tune of a particularly well-known Frank Sinatra standard.

Afterwards, we return to the bar and settle in with lashings of Old Speckled Hen, where I see a man in full belly-dancing costume and veil buying a pint of Tetley's Best Bitter using coins stored in his skimpy, tasseled bustier. We stay there, admirably, until a quarter past two in the morning, at which point we stagger past a gaggle of French wizards to bed, only stopping in the Hubward corridor to examine a few more recently added guild notices. 'Has someone spilled your drink? Been hit by one custard pie too many? Had eggs produced from unmentionable places? Let us help you – the Assassins' Guild is offering special rates for inhumation at the convention.' As we read, a shadowy figure idles down the corridor in the corner of my vision, a blurred mish-mash of fluffy grey beard and dangling convention dongles.

'G'night,' I mumble casually, not paying much attention.

'HelloTerry,' gabbles Sorcha, behind me. 'CanIjustsayhowmuch-I'velovedyourbookssinceIwasakidandaskifIcanposeforapic-turewithyou?'

I whirl round. It is, indeed, the man himself. Terry Pratchett. He looks exhausted, and has bleary, red eyes, but poses merrily for the picture and asks if we're enjoying ourselves.

'Yes,' I reply. 'Just looking at all this guild stuff.'

'Incredible, isn't it?' says Terry. 'The fans here are extra-ordinary. You give them an idea and they just take the baton and run. It's amazing.'

I open my mouth to offer a pithy reply about light aircraft, but a look visibly descends upon his face, a kind of 'whatthe-fuckamIdoingit'stwothirtyinthemorningandI'mgoingtogetwoken atsevenbygnomes' look.

'Anyway, I must get some sleep – I'm sorry. Have a fun night!' He grins, and dashes off to the winding Hub staircase.

'Oh my God, we've upset Terry Pratchett,' gasps Sorcha. 'The poor bloke, he was desperate to get to bed.'

'Don't be daft, we only spoke to him for thirty seconds,' I reply. 'He's probably been stuck with the French wizards since eight o'clock.'

But it's no use, Sorcha is inconsolable, convinced that her literary hero has now placed her on some kind of Fan Death List, and will be arranging secret early morning meetings with the Assassins' Guild to have her discreetly inhumed before the juggling workshops start. She tramps to our room racked with torment at having 'ruined' her big moment to finally meet her idol and repay him for all the stolen hours of joy his writings brought her during her lost and lonely adolescent years.

'And he knew I was drunk,' she moans.

'You should have showed him your certificate of redemption from the Priests' Guild,' I offer unhelpfully.

It's a hazard of the job for any convention newcomer. How do you actually go about meeting your heroes? There seem to be three distinct types of celebrity approaches. Firstly (and this was my favoured tactic until my actorphobia started to recede), there's the 'mumbler'. Keep your head down, mutter bashfully, tug a forelock if necessary, move on as quickly as possible. Secondly (and this is the method Sorcha chose to adopt), there's the 'gabbler'. Attempt to encapsulate all that they've ever meant to you in your entire history of fandom in a single sentence so fast and garbled it requires an Enigma machine to slow down and decipher. Thirdly (and this is the Holy Grail), there's the 'slapper'. Slap your hero firmly on the back and treat him or her as an old friend, enquiring confidently about their well-being and cracking the occasional joke. It's an approach that convention veterans seem to have down pat – a kind of Tenth Dan, Black Belt Celebrity Meeting discipline – but Sorcha and I are mere amateurs. Whichever tactic you adopt, you are, of course, at an immediate disadvantage. For many fans, the celebrity meeting is often the culmination of years, even decades, of hero worship – a transitory moment that will stick in the memory for the rest of their fandom lives. For the celeb, it's half a minute out of a gruelling weekend schedule, and they've likely forgotten about it in half that time again. You can't win.

Over a sobering cup of tea in the bedroom, I expound these theories patiently and compassionately to Sorcha, who then debunks the whole lot by revealing she's met Terry Pratchett at half-a-dozen book signings over the course of the last ten years, and always got on swimmingly with him. At which point I ask her what the fuck all the fuss was about, and go to sleep with a clear conscience.

And kick myself repeatedly for not having brought up the ZX Spectrum.

BLOODY STUPID THINGS I HAVE DONE IN THE NAME OF FANDOM NUMBER EIGHT: TRYING TO BE THE NEW TERRY PRATCHETT

It's a bit later in the summer of 1988, probably around the beginning of August, and I've just about managed to discard that bloody awful grey ski jacket, although the bleary Teesside sunshine is working up the stench of Quinoderm to levels that have put ICI Billingham on Yellow Alert. And, with Discworld-related fantasies still dribbling from my unwashed ears, I've started work on my latest million-selling novel. Only providence, laziness and a succession of badly timed school holidays have stopped *The Battle to Save Earth* and its numerous abortive sequels from being *New York Times* bestsellers and, this time, things will be different. I might even get beyond the end of Chapter Two.

The new book is called *Fictional Reality*, and I'm utterly convinced that it's a work of inestimable genius – a triumph of contemporary literary art, and the herald of a superstar author in the making. So much so that I've written those very words on the front cover of the grey Conyers School exercise book in which my masterpiece is being constructed, just underneath the legend 'Drama Class 1C2 Mr Harrison'. There's not a hint of irony about any of these predictions, and I'm actually taking it as read that I won't be sitting my GCSE exams in a year's time, because I'll be busy squandering millions on sports cars, swimming pools, supermodels and private jets. And a diamond-studded ski jacket and a Jacuzzi filled with Quinoderm.

The book, in short, is a shameless Pratchett rip-off. It concerns Inspector Humphrey Pendringham of Scotland Yard, a moustachioed, pipe-smoking detective who arrives in the village of Little Hodcombe to investigate a series of disappearances, accompanied by his assistant, the fresh-faced Middlesbrough master of disguise, Arthur Drumbolt. '*Little Hodcombe and its many mysteries now await our honourable presence, and tantalise us with their fascination. Let us proceed,*' says Humphrey as they arrive at the railway station. Reading it back now, I want to hammer my fifteen-year-old self around the head with a large plank of untreated timber.

Little Hodcombe is home to a bestselling author, named only in the book as 'the Author' and based quite clearly on some twisted, fantasy version of how my fifteen-year-old self envisaged his millionaire lifestyle. The Author has discovered the secret of creating dimensional gateways between the real world and the parallel dimensions of fiction, and is kidnapping village residents to put them in fictional situations – thus allowing his books to write themselves. Confused? Don't worry, it makes more sense if you read the following extracts. Actually, scratch that – it doesn't. It's all bollocks. Here's the Author's introduction:

> *Elsewhere, a brooding evil yawned, switched off its alarm clock, and climbed out of bed. Pulling on a black shirt and neatly pressed trousers of a shade normally associated with coal and the colour on a dartboard that's not yellow, it combed its hair, brushed its teeth and washed its hands before stumbling downstairs in a non-alcoholic haze and pouring itself a small glass of grapefruit juice and a bowl of cornflakes, and switching on the television to watch* Lucky Ladders *with Lennie Bennett.*
>
> *It was truly an evil to be reckoned with.*
>
> *When the programme had finished, it washed up its breakfast dishes, rolled up its sleeves, read the latest issue of* Your Storage Jars *for an hour and then decided to write a new novel.*

It's seven years since I wrote *The Battle to Save Earth*, but I'm still using my fictional exploits as an opportunity to make in-jokes about my favourite real-life things. In this case, grapefruit juice (of which I drink gallons, in between feeding a voracious and bizarre teenage addiction to Smarties) and *Lucky Ladders*, an early morning ITV quiz show that I've become obsessed with, setting my alarm for 9.15am all through the school holidays and watching with religious fervour. The *Storage Jars* bit is a tribute to the Monty Python sketch of the same name, and I've already earmarked Graham Chapman to play Humphrey in the inevitable blockbuster film adaptation.

Humphrey and Arthur predictably end up kidnapped by the Author and transported to a fictional dimension that is – hey, guess what! – loosely based on the world of Dungeons and Dragons role-playing. Here's Humphrey indulging in some swords and sorcery in a dreadful pseudo-Pratchett-esque spoof of a famous *Lord of the Rings* encounter:

There was the Troll, the creature of the underworld, the legend alive. Its hair blew fearsomely in the roaring wind, its eyes glowed dimly in the fiery darkness. It threw back its head and roared, a hideous bellowing roar that filled the cavern with noise and resounded around the bottomless chasm.

Humphrey felt something fall down his leg and hoped it was sweat . . .

The Troll advanced, baring its fangs. It raised its jagged blade in the air, ready to strike. It roared once more . . . then dropped its sword and looked pitifully up at its half-Orc master.

'Oh, good grief,' it said. 'Do I have to do this?'

Beads of sweat appeared on the half-Orc's forehead.

'W-w-what . . . ?'

'Well, you know, day in, day out, I throw people off this bridge to their deaths many miles below. Tends to get a bit monotonous after a while. Not really what I'd call job satisfaction. Just a thought, y'know . . .'

'Yes!' gibbered Humphrey. 'Yes! What a good idea. Yes. Give him the day off . . . Erm . . . tell you what, I'll come back tomorrow and . . . erm . . . we'll try again, OK? Right, bye!'

The noble coward turned and was about to break into one of the fastest sprints ever known to Orc-kind, but as you should well know and I certainly do know, life just isn't like that, and so for the benefit of several readers I shall prolong this chapter with the following words: 'Stop! We do the fight . . . now!'

> *In about three seconds.*
>
> *One, two, three . . .*
>
> *'Stop!' commanded the half-Orc. 'We do the fight . . . now!'*
>
> *Told you.*
>
> *'Oh, all right,' said the Troll, picking up its sword. 'Just this once . . .'*

It goes on. And on. And on. It's said that the UK is currently afflicted with the highest rate of under-age pregnancies in the European Union. Government officials looking to tackle this thorny problem could do a lot worse than issue every British male, on his thirteenth birthday, with a complimentary set of Dungeons and Dragons and a tube of Quinoderm Acne Cream. At any given point, there wasn't a single teenage female within two hundred yards of that bloody awful grey ski jacket.

'You have a seemingly incomparable ability to provide the gentler gender with ample justification for avoiding you,' as Humphrey Pendringham would no doubt have put it.

The twat.

With a name like Vadim Jean, is it possible to grow up as anything other than a successful film director? It's hard to imagine Vadim Jean the flood control officer, or Vadim Jean the canteen sandwich-maker. Surely anyone called Vadim Jean is destined to be a suave, bronzed, sharp-suited playboy with an effortless air of Mediterranean savoir faire and a cardboard box full of Palme d'Ors near the Jacuzzi in the west wing. So, naturally, there's a bit of me hoping that the Vadim Jean currently onstage in Dysk will transpire to be a wild-eyed slob, with egg mayonnaise stains all over his Council Works Department overalls.

But, ultimately, I'm relieved that he more than lives up to the chisel-jawed, yacht-owning stereotype. And he's introducing an exclusive two-minute preview from his lavish movie adaptation of Terry Pratchett's *Hogfather*.

As the film rolls, the tension in the room is palpable. After all, Discworld is perhaps *the* ultimate fantasy example of producer and fans in perfect harmony. Pratchett gives – endlessly and regularly – and the fans take, with rapturous enthusiasm, creatively and industriously manufacturing their own unique spin on the phenomenon, which then seems to feed back to its creator, pushing him on to even greater endeavour. A slick, smooth-talking interloper in this mutually fulfilling relationship could prove disastrous.

Thankfully, as much as it's possible to judge a three-hour TV movie on the strength of a 120-second clip, it looks great. And cheers rise from the crowd whenever their favourite characters appear on screen – including Tony Robinson as smarmy shopkeeper Vernon Crumley, quirkily endearing newcomer Michelle Dockery as Death's grandaughter Susan and a cameo appearance from the Eater of Socks – a stripey-trunked gremlin inhabiting the areas around washing machines – which elicits more cheers and fevered applause from the audience.

Afterwards, Vadim further wins over the fans by revealing that the production team commissioned the manufacture of half a million fake plastic teeth to occupy the Tooth Fairy's Castle, and that he's brought a couple of thousand with him today – in a clear plastic bin bag – for us to help ourselves. In something akin to the 1848 Californian gold rush, a tidal wave of wizards, barbarians and Wee Free Men stampede to the Hub where the Discworld's equivalent of Maundy Money is already being distributed to the needy. Sorcha, with her superior experience of the Teesside January sales, elbows her way to the front like a strawberry-blonde prop forward and emerges from the scrum with two impressive molars in her hand. I inspect both of them closely to ensure that they're definitely film props, and haven't been dislodged from the palette of some poor, trampled deity.

It's at this point that I realise that we haven't seen daylight for over forty-eight hours.

To remedy this, we push through a fire-escape door and find ourselves standing at the side of the hotel's car park in blazing sunshine, swapping bon mots with a gargantuan, bare-chested, tattooed barbarian in viking horns who has popped outside for a Marlboro Light. We ruminate on how long the convention would be able to sustain itself as a self-perpetuating eco-system should we all choose never to see daylight again, instead cultivating root vegetables on the windowsills of our bedrooms and brewing Discworld ale (including the splendid Black Hogswatch, of which Sorcha has already bought a crate) in our spacious en-suite bathrooms. Horrified by the prospect, we decide to make a break for a few hours, and vamoose to a country pub in nearby Kibworth Harcourt for lasagne and chips. When I say 'we', I do – of course – mean Sorcha and myself. Our barbarian friend seems happy enough to stay on the Discworld for ever.

When we return, both hotel bars are packed with hundreds of devotees, all in full, magnificent costume. There are *no* exceptions, and we stand at a high table in Mr Hong's Three Jolly Luck Coffee Bar swigging Old Speckled Hen and chatting genially to ageing warrior Cohen the Barbarian and Josiah Boggis, head of the Thieves' Guild. Cohen in particular has excelled with his costume. He's a wiry, tattooed, bald-headed figure who looks as though he may – just may – have spent time around motorcycle enthusiasts in his time. He has a long, tangled grey beard, an eyepatch, and when I ask to examine his impressive leg tattoos in closer detail, he swings a foot onto the table top and shows me cartoon illustrations of Terry Pratchett, Ankh Morpork stamp designer Bernard Pearson and various assorted other members of the extended Discworld family jaunting merrily around his inner thighs. It's by the far the most impressive sign of fan devotion I've seen on my travels, and I curse my cowardly failure to have grinning caricatures of Russell T. Davies and David Tennant tattooed on my buttocks. I'm a part-time fan, and I know it. Although heaven knows where the Sonic Screwdriver would fit.

As the clock speeds headlong past midnight and the evening becomes a blur, we chat to Kris, a dignified, well-spoken lady in blue chiffon evening gown and tiara. We'd spotted her earlier in the day running the merchandise-room post office, flogging meticulously designed Discworld stamps in the guise of Discworld's Miss Iodine Maccalariat. She tells us that Sunday-night convention tradition demands that we stay up all night, downing increasingly flamboyant alcoholic concoctions before moving straight to the breakfast table. At which point Cohen the Barbarian arrives carrying a tray of seemingly random shorts, wines, beers and beverages. 'I 'adn't gorra clue who ordered what, so I just gorra mixture,' he beams wickedly.

Kris also, fantastically, introduces us to Davina Dress, the muscular, six-foot drag queen sporting the Penelope Keith hairpiece, spangly tights and a figure-hugging little red number. I say hello, and realise after a minute or so that I'm chatting to the man mountain Dave, whose pet dragon Oscar tried to bite me on the nose in the hotel reception queue two nights ago. He's delightfully down-to-earth company, delicately adjusting his bosom and telling us in a gruff, Southern accent how difficult it can be to find diamanté slingbacks in a size eleven in Reading. Meanwhile, his petite, attractive wife, who introduces herself as Columbina of the Fools' Guild, holds up a home-made sign proclaiming the legend 'This Is SO Wrong.'

'So, Davina Dress,' I say to him, 'where does the name come from?'

'Dave in a dress,' he grins, and takes a gulp from his pint of Best.

It's the last thing I remember.

And as it was in the beginning, so shall it be in the end. So claims the Latin 'Gloria Patri'. And Paul Weller in 'Beat Surrender'. And me – hot, sweaty and pissed off, standing at the end of a queue of grumbling Terry Pratchett fans in a sprawling hotel foyer in the middle of a Leicestershire industrial estate.

It's Monday morning. Check-out time. I am hungover, deathly white and dead on my feet. We didn't quite make Kris's all-night swigathon, but the last photograph on my camera is timed at 3.45am. We've already seen Kris at breakfast, wearing enormous wraparound shades and looking delicate, in a refined and dignified manner, of course. Now, in the queue, there's no Dave, Oscar or – indeed – Davina Dress, but there is a plummy-voiced Cohen the Barbarian getting increasingly and noisily frustrated behind me.

And, for the first time in a few weeks, I feel like I've let myself down. Discworld is the best convention I've been to for fans actually *living* in the world – talking it, dressing it, walking it and just . . . well, *being* it. And I can't do it any more. In 1988, the fifteen-year-old youth who sulked over Hamwise Beardribbler's death spent more time on the Discworld than he did in Yarm and Middlesbrough – and you couldn't blame him, the Discworld was less violent with slighter better shopping facilities. But, after almost four days back in downtown Ankh Morpork, I can't wait to get home. I can visit here and enjoy myself, but I just can't *live* it any more. It's not shyness and actorphobia any more; it's lumpen grounding and lack of imagination. Maybe I have been pushed down more by the mortgage statements and the gas bills than I'd ever previously conceded. Maybe the real world does impinge on my imagination just that little bit too much to let it really fly. Maybe I just can't face the prospect of traipsing around Stockton on a Saturday afternoon looking for diamanté slingbacks for my own size-eleven feet.

I realise, on this final day, that I haven't even taken part in the guilds, my sole concession to the battle being to take two alchemists' tokens from a softly spoken Northern Irishman called Alan, in return for an interview for his online Discworld podcast. I'd babbled for two minutes about my Pratchett-worshipping youth into a microphone protruding gently from his *Farscape* holdall. 'I am a geek,' Alan had told me, in his candid Ulster accent. 'I make no bones about that. I accept the term completely, and am unashamed in my geekdom.' I'd always thought that I was too, but perhaps I'm far more normal than I'd ever previously considered.

Shame.

We go to a few events during Monday's seemingly endless daytime, but I can't remember the half of it. By the time the closing ceremony comes round, I'm taking a leaf from Sorcha's book and hallucinating in the main hall. Nothing particularly trippy – just my own bed, and a long bath, and a nice fresh pot of tea.

And the credit-card statements.

I'm not even sure why I'm doing it any more.

THE BATTLE TO SAVE EARTH

By Robert Fischer (Aged Eight And Seven Twelfths)

Monday 15 June 1981

PART TEN

The tree was hollow and could hold about three people. Down the centre of the tree was a long chute like a slide in a playground. But this one went down for miles down and I could not see the end. Dirk came into the tree and told me to slide down the chute. I sat on the top of the chute then took my hands off the sides. Dirk came down after me. I was on the chute for about a quarter of an hour before I finally came to the end. I was on a high platform made of what looked like ice. Sticks of clear ice surrounded the platform. In the middle of the room was a huge round glowing red core. The room seemed to stretch for miles. Suddenly I heard someone behind me and turned round. But only to see Dirk standing behind me. 'What is it?' Dirk asked me. 'It's buitiful,' I answered. 'What is this place?' 'It's called the crystal fortress,' Dirk answered. 'All these are crystals?' I asked Dirk. 'Every one of them,' Dirk answered. I noticed a glowing blue crystal just above the red core. I asked Dirk what it was. Dirk answered, 'It's a crystal that can give you super powers. If you touch the blue crystal you can have super powers untill the end of 1981. But if you come back before midnight on December 31st I can give you super powers for all of 1982'.

To be continued . . .

ROBIN OF SHERWOOD

LEGEND CONVENTION
YE OLDE BELL HOTEL, NOTTINGHAMSHIRE
FRIDAY 25 – SUNDAY 27 AUGUST

'I'm finding it difficult to be positive about your life.'

NOTHING IS FORGOTTEN. Nothing is ever forgotten.

Although I've never been good with faces.

Four days PD (Post Discworld) and I've barely recovered. It's seven o'clock on a balmy Friday evening, and I'm sitting by myself in the bar of Ye Olde Bell Hotel in the charming Nottinghamshire hamlet of Barnby Moor. It's a beautiful sixteenth-century coaching inn, all ivy-coated doorways and traditional oak beams, and I'm drinking a pint of John Smith's bitter and reading the convention brochure. I'm also trying to work out where I know the bloke on the right from.

I've no difficulty in recognising the man on the left. It's actor Phil Rose. In the twenty years since he last squeezed into Friar Tuck's proverbial filthy habit, he's barely changed – he's a big, genial-looking bloke with a mop of silver-flecked hair (sadly now grown over at the back) and a friendly, welcoming aura. He's sipping on a large whisky and chatting amiably to another man whose face is familiar but whose name is just evading me. He's older and slimmer with a streak of snow-white hair and a generous, wizard-like beard. I turn the possibilities over in my mind as Matthew pulls up in the car park outside.

'Evening,' grins the *Bath Chronicle*'s finest as he strides purposefully into the bar, shoots me a wink and buys himself a frothing pint. 'Who's that with Richard Carpenter?'

Richard Carpenter! Of course it is. The creator and writer of *Robin of Sherwood*, and before that the brains behind arguably *the* summer holiday TV show of the 1970s: the brilliant *Catweazle*. Known to all – for reasons no one seems willing to explain – as 'Kip', he's now in his early seventies and still held in high esteem in the industry. He's chatting amiably with Phil, and the two of them are soon joined by two women in medieval wench's costumes who bring to the table a couple of gin and slimline tonics and an armful of Nobby's Nuts.

Matthew, meanwhile, has a confession to make.

'So when did you get to see *Robin of Sherwood*?' I ask, knowing that Matthew is a couple of years my junior. 'Were you old enough to catch it first time round?'

'Oh, I've never seen it,' he replies, nonchalantly sipping on his bitter.

'What??!'

'I've never seen it. John Paul lent me the DVDs, but I've only had time to watch the first ten minutes.'

'So what the hell are you doing here?'

'I just wanted to see what sort of people came to a *Robin of Sherwood* convention.'

I turn into Ray Winstone and chin him with a single right hook.

I don't really, I'm actually proud to be in the company of a man who has single-handedly invented the phenomenon of fandom voyeurism. I fully expect him to be in the car park after midnight, panting at the car windows of fans flicking innocently through their *Robin of Sherwood* autograph books. Clearly what he needs is a hastily written crib sheet detailing the show's salient points to guide him through an otherwise potentially troublesome weekend.

Funny, that.

A BLUFFER'S GUIDE TO . . . ROBIN OF SHERWOOD

Mixing the traditional Robin Hood elements of swords and swashbuckling with lashings of sexy sorcery and pagan mysticism, *Robin of Sherwood* was a glossy Saturday-night ITV series launched in April 1984, aiming to bring a new, mature grittiness to a legend that had become overwhelmed by prancing Hollywood camp. In the British cult and sci-fi family tree, *Robin of Sherwood* is the flouncy earth mother, baking hash cakes in the Aga and consulting her runes before driving to Waitrose to collect her weekly supply of sunflower seeds and organic yoghurt. And all the while cultivating an unhealthy crush on Ray Winstone.

The title role was taken by the unknown Michael Praed, a sculpted twenty-three-year-old with hair so heavily conditioned it looked permanently in danger of actually taking off. Also in his gang were the aforementioned Ray Winstone as a growling, cockney Will Scarlet, looking for all the world as though he had a sock full of billiard balls in his scabbard; a pre-*Casualty* Clive Mantle as the bearded, grizzled Little John, who starts the series possessed by demons and doesn't calm down much afterwards; genial, rotund Phil Rose as a mad, mead-swigging Friar Tuck; and teenage newcomer Peter Llewellyn-Williams as the permanently confused Much, the medieval peasant equivalent of Harry Enfield's Tim Nice-but-Dim.

The series also broke barriers by introducing – thirteen years ahead of the formation of the Muslim Council of Britain – an Islamic Merrie Man into the mix. Nasir Malik Kemal Inal Ibrahim

Shams ad-Dualla Wattab Ibn Mahmud (Nasir to his friends) was a shadowy Saracen assassin captured during the Crusades and hypnotised by the dark arts of the evil Baron de Belleme before eventually being liberated by Robin and his men. Nasir was the coolest member of the gang for two reasons – firstly, he fought with two swords simultaneously, dancing gracefully between perplexed Norman soldiers like some homicidal version of Frankie Goes to Hollywood's Paul Rutherford. Secondly, he didn't speak. In the entire first series of *Robin of Sherwood*, he doesn't say a single word of dialogue, which must have been a godsend for actor Mark Ryan, whose command of the Saracen tongue was probably not helped greatly by his upbringing in the unlikely Arabic stronghold of Doncaster.

In this version, Robin is the adopted son of Herne the Hunter, a mysterious, antlered nature god, the embodiment of the spirit of the trees. He appears to Robin regularly through a cloud of *Top of the Pops*-style dry ice, and gives the show many of its most enduring catchphrases, including the spine-chilling 'Nothing is forgotten' and the cryptic 'You are a leaf driven by the wind'. Robin is also frequently driven into the arms of the willowy, flaxen-haired Marion, played with a deft touch by former ballet dancer Judi Trott. And when Praed left the show in 1985 for a fleeting, ill-advised stint as *Dynasty*'s Prince Michael of Moldavia – a role that (sorry, Herne . . . and Michael) has indeed been completely forgotten – Marion wasted no time in transferring her attentions to replacement Jason Connery. The pouting, blond-haired son of the original James Bond (Sir Sean that is, not Bob Holness), Connery had already gained his cult TV credentials by stripping topless opposite Colin Baker in the 1985 *Doctor Who* story 'Vengeance on Varos'. For one final, bumper series of *Robin of Sherwood*, he more than ably subsidised the entire medieval hair-mousse industry.

So this wasn't just the Robin Hood of bows, arrows and tight green leggings, it was the Robin Hood of stone circles, nature spirits and whispered incantations in gloomy witches' covens. For pale, young children with an unhealthy interest in swords, sorcery, witchcraft and medieval English legend, there was no better time to be alive than 1984.

With the possible exception of 1192.

Matthew and I pick up our pints and wander through to the hotel reception, where organiser Les is dishing out guest packs from a sturdy-looking trestle table. As Matthew signs in, I decide to take the plunge and buy a badge proclaiming one of Herne the Hunter's profound catchphrases, 'You are a leaf driven by the wind'. I pin it to my lapel, and decide this will be my maxim for the convention – I will allow myself to be driven by the fates this weekend, as free as the breeze, blown wherever my destiny takes me. As it transpires, it's a destiny that eventually takes me to a breakdown recovery garage near Mansfield at half past three in the morning, but more of that later.

Matthew and I exchange a brief, unspoken moment of mutual, steely resolve, and enter into the hotel's main function suite to mingle. It's a huge, authentically oak-panelled space with a marvellous, musty, medieval ambience. And it's here we notice something that takes us entirely by surprise.

The convention seems to be populated almost exclusively by women. Attractive thirtysomething women, many of whom are alluringly dressed in revealing medieval costumes. The room is a riot of girlish giggles, heaving cleavages and tumbling tresses on excitingly bare shoulders. I begin to wonder if the pressure of the last few weeks has finally caused my fragile mind to snap, and if I'm now actually trapped in some strange, erotic, cult-TV-fuelled fantasy of my own twisted making. I'll stay here for ever now, while my weeping parents and Sorcha stand around my inert body, strapped to a bed in a secure hospital unit. 'I'm sorry,' the consultant will say, 'we've run some tests and there's no brain activity. But we can't seem to get that weird smile off his face.'

We find ourselves seated at a round table with Emma and Anne, both pretty and chirpy and friendly, and their husbands, John and Richard, slightly less pretty but thankfully no less welcoming. The quiz begins, with Phil Rose at the head of the table as genial, teasing question master and host. 'Question number one,' he intones mischievously, his voice sending a little frisson of Tuck-related excitement through my bones. 'In the opening scene of the very first episode, which year is given by the onscreen caption?'

'1180,' replies Matthew, quick as a flash.

'Blimey, you must be an expert!' exclaims a startled Emma.

'Not really,' smiles Matthew, undaunted. 'I've only seen the first ten minutes.'

She laughs like a drain, and clearly thinks he's joking.

We do unfeasibly poorly in the quiz, Matthew defiantly insisting that every question 'must have happened eleven minutes in'. Emma tells us that a friend of hers is convinced she's the reincarnation of a Roman centurion stationed in Guildford, and I get slightly drunk on John Smith's bitter and manage to elicit a worried look from Matthew when I lumber towards him waving two giant Swords of Wayland under his nostrils. Genuine props from the TV show, these enormous stainless-steel broadswords are lovingly emblazoned with ancient runes and symbols. The two weapons on display this weekend are Morax and Solas, charged with 'the Powers of Light and Darkness' (yep, Herne again, a man you suspect could make an impressive mythological metaphor out of creosoting the garden shed) and with names taken from *The Lemegeton, or the Lesser Key of Solomon*, an ancient (and genuine) book of ceremonial magic, containing instructions for evoking the seventy-two spirits that King Solomon of Israel imprisoned into a brass vessel and cast into a lake. Probably along with a single Dunlop trainer and a stolen Morrison's shopping trolley.

We mere mortals are being allowed to pose for photos with them, so I strike a suitably demonic pose for Matthew's camera, before we exchange places and he lumbers towards me with an evil grimace spread across his face. And then we hand the swords back to their owners before we injure someone, damage something or get mistaken for overgrown schoolboys incapable of picking up a lump of stainless steel without pretending to be the Sheriff of Nottingham.

Herne forbid.

CRUCIAL MOMENTS IN FANDOM HISTORY NUMBER NINE: THE DAY MY AFFECTIONS SWITCHED FROM SCIENCE FICTION TO FANTASY

It's a wet Wednesday afternoon in early 1984, and I'm reaching into my backpack to pull out a phial of dark red liquid. The dragon flaps its wings and roars in agony as I throw the elixir into its eyes. It slumps to the ground and its skin begins to bubble and hiss. The warlock has given me a magical anti-dragon potion, and the fearsome beast lies dying on the forest floor.

I turn to 305.

'Get in!' shouts Ian Oswald, and punches the air with a ferocity that makes Mr Hirst, walking past the entrance to

Levendale Primary School's modest library, peer disapprovingly round the opposite doorway.

'Just reading, sir!' I grin, cheekily. I'm eleven years old, slap bang in the middle of my K-9 project with Doug Simpson, and am getting a little bit lippy in my dotage. I hold the book aloft to show him. It's *The Forest of Doom*, number three in the range of Fighting Fantasy Gamebooks by Steve Jackson and Ian Livingstone. I got it for Christmas, and Ian Oswald and I have been slowly working our way through the dreaded Darkwood Forest, in between PE lessons and practising long division.

Fighting Fantasy books are the latest craze for grubby young boys like ourselves. Consisting of 400 separate paragraphs, they require us to make our own choices throughout, flicking back and forth through the pages depending on how we wish to proceed. 'If you wish to carry on east, turn to 105. If you wish to turn north, turn to 213. If you wish to ever kiss a girl, put the book down now and start washing properly'. They are, let's face it, Dungeons and Dragons for boys too young to buy cider and Iron Maiden LPs. Instead, Ian and I have a pencil, a rubber, two dice and a map of the forest itself, scribbled in Berol Notewriter pen on graph paper shamelessly pinched from the maths drawer.

It's a time of transition in my life as a sci-fi fan. *Doctor Who* has reached an impasse. Peter Davison, *my* Doctor, the only one I've followed from his very first story, has regenerated into Colin Baker, and the series has ended – leaving me at a bit of a loose end. I'm still getting *Star Wars Weekly* reserved, but it's a year now since *Return of the Jedi*, and I'm not really reading it any more. It gets a cursory glance before being thrown onto the bed, where it usually stays, all guilty and untouched, a frustrated wife in a loveless sci-fi marriage.

And visits to my gran's sci-fi HQ bungalow are becoming gradually fewer and further between. For the first nine or ten years of my life I've stayed there pretty much every single weekend, congratulating myself on my multicultural versatility in cultivating friends from both Yarm and Acklam. But now I'm almost grown-up, and my gran – in her mid-seventies – is becoming a bit forgetful, so instead she comes to stay with us at weekends, and three generations of Fischer family spend their Saturday nights together under one roof.

During one of my very last Acklam weekends in January 1984, I had an epiphany. And yes, I closed the bedroom door first. Inspired by having seen the animated version on TV over Christmas, I spent ninety-five pence of my pocket money on a paperback edition of C. S. Lewis's *The Lion, the Witch and the Wardrobe*. Catching the number thirteen bus back from Middlesbrough to my gran's house, I then curled up for the afternoon on the settee as a slate-black sky gathered over Teesside. I was entranced by Lewis's tales of fauns, wicked witches and magic portals, and spent the day wishing beyond all hope for a Teesside snowfall worthy of Narnia itself. On a brief dog walk in the fields around Devil's Bridge – the stone, hump-backed crossing where I'd played Pooh Sticks as an infant – I even told my suspicious mum that I could 'smell a snow-fall in the air'. And I swear to this day that I could – a sweet, tangible, steel-flecked aroma permeating down from yellow banks of cloud. Either that or ICI Wilton had blown up again.

I spent a restless night voraciously reading in between *The Little and Large Show* and Les Dawson, then retired to the spare room to read some more, longingly gazing at my gran's MFI wardrobe in the hope that the doors would somehow fly open, revealing a magical netherworld within. And not just a couple of my gran's old coats and a suit my uncle Trevor bought in 1973. And I fell asleep with the book half-open on my chest, and some point late in the evening my gran arrived to tuck me under the covers. Awww.

And in the morning, when I awoke, Acklam was my personal Narnia.

The snow was a foot deep, I swear – the first flakes had fallen within seconds of me drifting off, and now the streets were filled with a blinding, pristine whiteness, the orange buzz of the street lights and the half-dusk of the morning sky lending Rievaulx Drive a sparkling, eldritch quality. And still the flakes were tumbling down – huge, white lumps of wondrousness, like parachuting Andrex puppies. I jumped out of bed, threw on my parka and jeans, and ran out through the front door, barely remembering to open it first. And yet, for probably the first time in my life, as I ran along to Mr Murray's newsagent's pulling handbrake turns in my wellies and scooping up armfuls of fresh snow to shower over the dogs, I wasn't thinking of science fiction, of *The Empire Strikes Back*'s freezing, snow-covered planet Hoth and *Doctor Who*'s clacky-handed Ice Warriors from Mars. Nope. Instead, my mind was filled with fauns and dwarves and magic and mysticism. Narnia and *The Forest of Doom* (And *The Warlock of Firetop Mountain* – number one in the range of Fighting Fantasy Gamebooks and *still* the best) had pushed me over the boundary from science to superstition, and made me sell my soul to what cider-fuelled men in tightly fitting Iron Maiden T-shirts and long, ginger ponytails were already calling 'fantasy'.

It's a slippery slope. And I don't even have a Spell of Anti-Slipperiness to cast from the Magick Tome the wizard gave me at the entrance to the Enchanted Forest.

After a night of blissful unconsciousness in Matthew's parents' attic, we're back in the main hall for the day's Q&A session. Richard Carpenter takes to the stage alongside his actress wife,

Annabelle Lee, who starred in one episode of the series as Mad Mab, a gleefully insane old hermit living cosily with her family of pigs – including the cheeky porker 'Rutterkin', who gives the episode its title. Richard talks eloquently about the origins of *Robin of Sherwood*, and his desire to update the legend with a young, vibrant cast after being disappointed by seeing a 'tubby Richard Greene' in the role as a young man. Annabelle, meanwhile, reveals that a 'stunt pig' was required to provide her character's trademark oinks.

My actorphobia, I note to myself, now seems to have been completely conquered – in fact, in the homely, close-knit atmosphere of Legend, such conceits seem utterly ridiculous. Afterwards, as Matthew and I potter idly into the hotel's leafy gardens, Phil Rose follows us out and we chat genially about the weather and the weekend, and the theatres he's played in my native North-East. And he reveals to our delight that he's drinking buddies with Nicholas Courtney – Brigadier Lethbridge-Stewart from our beloved *Doctor Who*.

Kip and Annabelle soon wander over to join us, and then the freshly arrived Nickolas Grace saunters out to sign autographs. For us thirtysomething children of the 1980s (even the ones who have only watched the first ten minutes), Grace's portrayal is the definitive sheriff. Eminent American psychologist Dr Robert Hare defines the modern-day psycopath as being an 'intraspecies predator who uses charm, manipulation, intimidation and violence to control others and to satisfy his own selfish needs. Lacking in conscience and in feelings for others, he takes what he wants and does as he pleases, violating social norms and expectations without guilt or remorse.' Add a predilection for narcissistic preening and a tendency to share erotically charged baths with a scrubbing-brush-brandishing Guy of Gisburne, and you've got Grace's sheriff to a tee. 'Lower, Gisburne!'

I shake hands with him gingerly, and he flashes me an electrifying grin. 'To Bob, From the Sheriff and Nickolas Grace,' he writes on the inside page of my twenty-two-year-old *Robin of Sherwood* paperback, then throws his arms around me for Matthew's camera, grabbing my stomach with a manly grip. If he'd asked me to join him for a rub-down in the bath, I'd have been there like a shot with a loofah and some fluffy towels.

The afternoon wears on, and during a lull in proceedings Matthew and I take refuge in the bar, me moving daringly from sugary tea to Guinness as the clock ticks on to half past five. We meet Mark, a tweed-jacketed accountant with the vaguest resemblance to a young Jack Nicholson, who, aside from ourselves, is the only unaccompanied male at the convention. He smokes cigars and drinks whisky and tells us that a tarot reader has set up stall in the hallway.

And so she has.

I've had two pints by half past six, and am in no fit state to resist the lure of the supernatural. Or, indeed, an attractive Scottish tarot reader with flashing green eyes and a gorgeous lilting accent.

She's dressed in a medieval tabard, and is housed in an orange tent in the corner of the hotel's hallway, sitting at a small pub table upon which rests both a silver tankard and a human skull. I'm not quite sure which one she's drinking her gin and tonic from. She introduces herself as Kate, flashes me a nice smile, lays out the tarot cards before me and invites me to flip over the first.

It's Death.

'Death can, of course, mean many things,' smiles Kate reassuringly. 'Not so much physical death as the end of an old way of life, a closing of one chapter in your life and the beginning of another. Shall we try the next card?'

Indeed we shall.

It's the Hanged Man.

'Hmmm,' she says. 'That's a little more complex. This could mean that you're about to make a sacrifice in your life, that something close to you is about to be taken away.' I surreptitiously move my full pint away from Matthew's shuffling feet. 'You maybe feel a little bit outside of events at the moment, and need to take a couple of steps back in order to take stock and move forward. Let's see what your long-term future holds.'

I see what my long-term future holds.

It's the Hermit.

Kate falls silent for a very long time. 'I must admit,' she says to me eventually, picking her words carefully in that lovely Scottish brogue, 'I'm finding it difficult to be positive about your life.'

Reeling from perhaps the most pessimistic tarot-card reading since Father Ted turned over three Death cards in a row ('There's only supposed to be one of those in each pack!'), I take a sip from my Guinness as Kate offers me a small velvet pouch and asks me to take a rune stone at random. I rummage around in the bag and pull out a small, polished black pebble, upon which is engraved a jagged white emblem, like a pointed letter 'R' with a slightly cut-off leg.

'Ah, that's Raidho,' she beams. 'It means a voyage or an evolution – perhaps in your mind, or a physical journey. It's a chariot – keep it in your pocket to bring you good luck on your travels.' She visibly fights the temptation to add, 'You'll need it,' to the end of her sentence.

Elaborate banqueting tables fill the medieval hall, and a procession of flamboyantly dressed ladies are gracefully taking their seats. Matthew and I are, to our shame, the only people in the room not dressed in medieval costume – apart from, ironically enough, Phil Rose himself.

We find ourselves sharing table space with Kirsty, Fiona and

Alison, three outgoing, chatty thirtysomething girls from London. Encouraged in unison to raise our glasses with a pagan cry of 'Herne, protect us', we start sloshing red wine around with wolfshead-style abandon, until silver-haired organiser Pete hushes the hall like a naughty school assembly and – with a transatlantic speakerphone lashed up to a small amplifier – we link up for a live interview with Mark 'Nasir' Ryan.

Now an in-demand voiceover artist, the former Saracen assassin is working in the USA, contributing vocal duties to the new blockbuster *Transformers* movie. Although the telephone line is faint, he speaks with a heartfelt romanticism about *Robin of Sherwood*, and it's clear that Nasir is a character that still moves him. I don't think I've ever heard an actor talk so passion-ately about a role, and it seems the magic and mysticism of that fictional twelfth-century woodland has left an imprint on his psyche. 'Nothing is forgotten. Nothing is ever forgotten,' he shouts, as we cheer him goodbye, and he sounds as though he's fighting back the tears. And, suddenly, to my enormous surprise, so am I. It's as though Nasir, for the past twenty years, has held the essence of my eleven-year-old self bottled in some strange, Arabian elixir, and has now released it into my wine with all the dexterity of a silent assassin. I'm genuinely choked with emotion. Kirsty catches my eye and tells me that, since his involvement with *Robin of Sherwood*, Ryan has thrown himself into researching pagan ritualism and shamanism, and has developed his own revolutionary set of tarot cards – the Greenwood Tarot – based on the ancient English 'Green Man' legend that provided the inspiration for Herne himself. He's clearly a wizard, and I'm under his spell.

I guzzle my medieval banquet (vegetarian option) with greedy aplomb before becoming drawn, predictably, into the traditional convention charity auction, unwisely held on this occasion at half past ten when I've clearly had too much to drink. I find myself locked into a bidding war with a petite woman on the far side of the hall dressed as Nasir, complete with full Saracen assassin's face mask.

The source of our battle of wills is a selection of knitted *Robin of Sherwood* dolls.

I'd spotted them being created by a frilly smocked wench in a whir of needles during Phil Rose's panel earlier in the day. Pretty much the whole main cast is there – all about six inches tall, made entirely of wool, and even sporting the occasional woollen accessory, a bow or a quiver or a longstaff. I can't resist, and find myself punching the air in celebration when I finally clinch the deal for a bargain sixteen pounds.

Half an hour later, I'm in the small bar – arranging my new knitwear chums on the slippery surface and surrounded by an increasing posse of admiring females, despite Kirsty's solemn warning that 'Those dolls have an evil look about them.'

As we chat, Phil Rose wanders through the bar and joins a small gaggle of smokers puffing away in the night air around the side of the emergency exit. On his way back, I can't resist accosting him and asking him to pose with the woollen dolls, which he graciously and good-humouredly agrees to do, despite my repeated attempts to dunk Tuck into the top of a fresh pint of Guinness. I grin alongside him, and we suddenly find ourselves the subject of a barrage of paparazzi flashes from the gathered throng. I feel staggeringly famous and celebrated in a manner entirely unbecoming of a local radio presenter. It's a feeling of well-being and euphoria that lasts at least another hour, until Matthew bursts my bubble with a single well-timed observation on the inside lane of the M1 as we travel back to his parents' house.

'Is it me, or are the headlights getting dimmer?' he asks.

'Eh?'

It's late now, long after midnight, and he's been listening

patiently to me wittering on about spirituality, shamanism and Raidho runes while the dolls glower at us disapprovingly from the back seat.

'Shit, they really are. I'm going to have to pull over.'

'What?'

I look nervously from the windscreen and notice that the Peugeot's headlights are indeed fading down to little more than a glimmer. We're about four miles south of junction thirty, and there's not another car on the road. As the headlights dim into darkness, we judder onto the hard shoulder. The car, effectively, dies in its sleep. Matthew tries the ignition and receives nothing for his troubles but a cough, a groan and an obscene observation from me. We clamber out of the car and sit on a crash barrier at the bottom of a steep, grassy bank leading up to a crown of rustling woodland silhouetted against a pale night sky. Neither of us has a signal on our mobiles.

'I'll walk,' says Matthew. 'We passed an emergency phone about a mile back.'

I nod silently, and stretch out my legs before me. I see him trudge wearily into the blackness, then vanish altogether round a bend in the motorway. It's 1.45am, and the last vestiges of Guinness and wine-fuelled exuberance are rising from me like bubbles and bursting in the cool night air. I plunge my hands into my jacket pockets, and my finger rests against something smooth and cold. It's my Raidho rune, given to me by the delightful Kate to bring me good luck on my travels. A brace of Tesco delivery wagons judder past, their headlights picking out the jagged shards of the rune's pale engraving. I glare up again at the woods as the breeze tugs at my hair and contemplate once more being a Leaf Driven By The Wind. Would Herne protect me if I cast aside my modern-day trappings now, trudged up to the trees and became the first wolfshead in a thousand years to roam the Nottinghamshire forests? I drift off into a strange, drunken, sleep-starved fantasy in which I gather together similarly disenfranchised motorway travellers and construct secret hideaways and rope bridges among the trees, conducting lightning food raids against the Norman stronghold at Tibshelf Services, stealing Ginster's pasties and Flamin' Hot Monster Munch and distributing them among the poor of the local villages, rallying the downtrodden Saxon peasants of Bolsover, Shireworth and Nether Langwith to our spiritual crusade. We would dress in Lincoln green corduroy jeans taken from the men's department in the town's Marks and Spencer, and children would sing 'Rooooooooooooooobert, the Hooded Man' as I gazed mysteriously from beneath my cowl at the busy pedestrianised precinct.

It's not the first time I've flirted with these kinds of sordid fantasies.

BLOODY STUPID THINGS I HAVE DONE IN THE NAME OF FANDOM NUMBER NINE: TRYING TO FIGHT LIKE FRIAR TUCK

It's a hot, sunny afternoon in the summer of 1984, I'm still eleven, and I'm doing secret things in the woods with Doug Simpson.

'Are you ready to start?'

'I think so. Am I holding it right?'

'Not sure . . . hang on, I need a better grip on mine.'

Don't worry, it's not what you think.

I can narrow the date down a bit further if you like. It's Sunday 13 May 1984. I know this because the previous night I watched 'Seven Poor Knights From Acre', the fourth episode of the first series of *Robin of Sherwood*, and at half past seven, when the show had finished, Doug's mum had telephoned to see if it was possible for Doug to spent the night at our house. I've no idea why, as I didn't record the reason in my 1984 WH Smith desk diary, although I did made meticulous notes about having bought the *Doctor Who* book *Snakedance* in Middlesbrough that morning, and having watched *The Grumbleweeds* on ITV, shortly after eating my tea at six o'clock. Doug's need for a bed could easily have been brought about by the cataclysmic destruction of his family bungalow by a freak build-up of rabbit flatulence in his dad's hutch-building workshop, but I wouldn't have mentioned that in my diary because I didn't see it and it didn't directly involve me. It's a curious psychological phenomenon that Sorcha has frequently identified as 'typical fucking only child' syndrome.

Anyway, Doug spends the night at our house, sleeping in my bed while I creak and giggle beneath a flannelette bedspread on a camping mattress on the floor. My diary records only that we 'mucked on upstairs' until ten, which almost certainly means that we giggled into our sleeves while whispering to each other about willies and Frankie Goes to Hollywood. And the next day, we're up at nine, and we take advantage of a warm Sunday morning to traipse the two hundred yards on foot to a small wooded copse near my house, sandwiched between the busy main road and a field of floating, yellow crops belonging to Mr Smith, the burly, bearded farmer whose elderly mother lives next door to us. It's a thick, overgrown pocket of seclusion, and we come here a lot to break wind, talk rubbish and . . . well, arse about with sharp objects. Which is what we're doing now.

Inspired by 'Seven Poor Knights From Acre' – in which Robin and his gang take on a troupe of crack Knights Templar, a psychopathic French fighting force who arrive in Nottingham and curiously fail to mention anything remotely connected to *The Da Vinci Code* – we've created huge longstaffs for ourselves out of fallen branches and are preparing to knock seven bells of each other. And, just to add a frisson of danger, we're doing it on tarzies.

No Teesside childhood in the 1980s was complete without construction of, or at least easy access to, a tarzie. In a nutshell, for the benefit of youngsters and soft, Southern jessies: tarzie [Tarr-Zee] *noun*; a length of rope tied firmly to a high tree branch by means of complicated Cub Scout-style knots, the lower end of which dangles down just above ground level, thus allowing the willing participant to swing backwards and forwards on it, often to great heights, in the style of Edgar Rice Burroughs's aristocratic jungle-dweller Tarzan. Hence the name. Health and Safety, to coin a phrase, would have a field day. But Doug and I care not, and – in recent weeks – have constructed two impressive tarzies on adjacent trees in the copse. Clutching a four-foot lump of jagged branch apiece, we're swinging headlong at each other and screaming our juvenile heads off.

'I'm Friar Tuck!' I shout, swinging my stick wildly, swooshing it inches above Doug's mop-topped head.

'I'm Little John!' he shouts back on the next run, and clobbers me squarely in the testicles with his own makeshift longstaff.

'Oh, shit!'

I crumple to the ground like . . . well, like a smaller-than-average eleven-year-old in a parka, clutching his privates. The breath (and possibly the testicles) have been knocked out of me, and I'm doubled up on the mossy ground, moaning and swearing softly under my breath as Doug brings his tarzie to a halt and jumps energetically to my side. Doug is my best friend, and it's important at this juncture that he responds in an appropriate, considerate manner. Which he does, laughing hysterically and telling me I'll spend the rest of my life singing like Jimmy Somerville.

I'm OK, of course, and my diary records that we cycled home by teatime (Doug on his BMX, me on my Raleigh Chopper) and I spent the evening drawing a *Doctor Who* picture and watching *That's Life*. But I mention this incident because, as far as I remember, this is the very last time that I actually pretended to *be* someone from one of my favourite TV shows. Up until this point, I'd always *been* the Doctor, or Davros, or Han Solo or Captain Kirk during my playtime escapades, but after the summer of 1984, I just became Robert Fischer, often getting up to exactly the same scrapes, but never gleefully and shamelessly assuming these strange, fictitious personas. Perhaps it was my growing sense of maturity to blame, looking forward to secondary school and aware of my own impending adolescence – the changing of my body, the development of my emotions, an increased awareness of the world around me and my own unique relationship with it. Or maybe it was just an innate, burning instinct to protect my cobblers from further assault.

Whatever the truth, once the summer was over, I never really went back to the copse, and within eighteen months Doug had left the country, moving permanently to Western Australia with his parents and his sister. I've barely seen him since, although I still miss him loads, and I hope he looks back on our collaborative childhoods with the same sense of misty-eyed wonder that frequently overcomes me on balmy summer's evenings.

Three days before I set off for Ye Olde Bell Hotel, I make my first visit back to our one-time woodland hideaway for the first time in twenty-two years. It's only half a mile from the house I share with Sorcha now, and I can't think of any reason why I haven't returned here sooner. So, on a blazing Tuesday afternoon – sending the dog in first to test for stinging nettles – I force my way through the hedge and trample amid waist-high grass to the spot where our precious two tarzies had once swung so freely. The air is thick and treacly, just as I remember, with an overpowering smell of wild garlic and a constant mist of feathery dandelion seeds hanging lazily in the afternoon sunlight. Both ropes have long since perished or been cut down by some dastardly agent of the adult world, but the overhanging branches themselves still have a darkened imprint where once our tarzies had clung to their contours. I'm overcome by nostalgia, and find myself entering a *Robin of Sherwood*-style hallucinatory flashback, with images of schoolbooks and Doug Simpson and drainpipe jeans and flabby footballs racing through my head like the flickering of some strange, silent, mind's eye Nickelodeon.

Thankfully, though, I'm now adult enough to resist the temptation to jump up and down in the woods, swooshing a large stick around my head and shouting, 'I'm Friar Tuck!' into the rustling canopy above.

For at least thirty seconds, anyway.

The dog looks on, disapprovingly.

'I've phoned the RAC,' says Matthew. 'They'll be here within the hour.'

It's been half an hour already, and he's crept back without me realising. Fifty-nine minutes and fifty-five seconds later, at 3.15am, an RAC recovery wagon pulls up on the hard shoulder and, amid much head-shaking, sharp intakes of breath and mutterings about something called an 'alternator' (whatever that is), we're towed to R. Staley and Son Motoring Services, five miles north-west of Mansfield on the A617, where a burly man called Lee fetches us both a cup of tea from the machine, and we slump into plastic chairs while we wait for a second recovery vehicle to arrive and take us to Matthew's parents. Lee gives my chest an odd look as he hands over our beverages, and I realise I still have a badge proclaiming, 'You Are A Leaf Driven By The Wind,' attached to my jacket lapel. I toy with recruiting him for my modern-day woodland crusade, as he looks like he might be handy with a longstaff. And, if push comes to shove, he probably knows what an 'alternator' is as well.

We stay there for an hour, watching *Swingers* on Channel 4 on a portable TV in the corner. Eventually Matthew's Peugeot is loaded onto a trailer and, in rapidly brightening daylight, we're driven back to his parents' house in Attenborough. The car is dumped at the roadside, and before we traipse upstairs to bed I gather the woollen dolls from the back seat, and can't help but feel there's a certain malevolent gleam in their eyes. I shove them to the bottom of my overnight bag, and smother them with a towel and a spare pair of jeans. When I crash into bed at 5.30am, sunlight is streaming through the skylight above me.

'Morning, Bob! Hey, where's Matthew?'

It's barely four hours later, and I'm standing in Ye Olde Bell car park blinking hazily and dozily in the blinding early morning sunshine. I strain my eyes to focus, and see Kirsty and Alison waving merrily from the doorway. I tell them the sorry story, and pass on regards from Matthew, who has decided to curtail his convention adventures to seek out brave new challenges (and an alternator) in the intimidating wilderness of the Nottingham *Yellow Pages*. 'It's the dolls!' laughs Kirsty. 'I knew those dolls were cursed!' They offer their condolences as we pile onto the luxury coach.

Yes, we're going on a school trip.

Fiona joins us, and we make up a giggly foursome as the coach pulls away from Ye Olde Bell Hotel and takes us on the half-hour journey up the A1 to Sherwood Forest. It's the height of the school holidays, and the visitor centre car park is teeming with large, red-faced parents and sticky-faced kids who'd rather be at Alton Towers. But I care not.

I have an archery competition to win.

A large forest clearing has been set aside, and four full-sized targets are gleaming in the afternoon sunlight as the fans assemble in a wide semi-circle. We're treated to a terrifyingly impressive demonstration by the Bowmen of Woodland, a four-some of medieval re-enactors who – resplendent in fabulous outlaw costumes and flowing hair – lift up their bows and whistle their arrows into succession of bullseyes with casual aplomb. Afterwards, they troop nonchalantly to a fallen log and watch calmly as the rest of us prepare for our own archery exploits. They look so good that I amble over, introduce myself, and ask them to pose for a photograph. Red-haired Freya, blonde Julie, bearded Jon-Michael and sandy-haired John. As I walk away, I realise with a giggle who they remind me of. It's Abba. I spend the next hour trying to stop 'Thou Art The Dancing Queen' rattling around in my head, only to have it replaced by 'Take a Chance on Thee' and 'Knowing Thee, Knowing Thou'.

And in the midst of all this nonsense, I get to the final of the archery competition.

It's a staggering achievement for a man incapable of walking down a pavement without falling over his own feet, and I'm still not quite sure how it happens. Perhaps I am A Leaf Driven By The Wind, and Herne himself has guided me to this destiny, seeing in me the spiritual qualities essential to spread his nature philosophies through a modern, industrialised world and bring about a quiet revolution of enlightened, mystical thought. Or maybe it's just that everyone else was rubbish. Regardless, I manage to squeeze through three qualifying rounds by closing my eyes, holding my breath and trying to invoke the halcyon summer of 1981, when – remember – I could complete a 501 finish on a dartboard with less than fifteen darts.

The prize for the overall winner is staggering. It's a silver arrow. No, really – just like in the original legend itself. Convention organiser Pete, quite an accomplished bowman himself, has it in his hand, and it's beautiful. As I step up to what I'm going to bloody-mindedly refer to as 'the oche', my heart is pounding. Is it possible I could bring this marvellous prize back to Teesside, the spoils of unlikely victory at a convention that's had more than its fair share of disaster?

Frankly, no. The single arrow I'm allowed in the final spirals pathetically into the white outer rim of the target, and I'm beaten to the prize by an excited American woman called Diane who shoots confidently into the blue segment before punching the air and whooping. As consolation, Pete – a genial cockney with a passing resemblance to *Red Dwarf*'s Norman Lovett – presents me with an almost-as-good plastic silver-arrow-shaped Biro from the Sherwood Forest gift shop. I hold it sheepishly aloft as Kirsty, Fiona and Alison commiserate, and I repay their kindness by falling asleep the second we get on the bus, and snoring loudly all the way back to Barnby Moor.

Back at the hotel, I say my goodbyes, and thank them for adopting me during Matthew's enforced absence. They've been great company, and we share one final round of drinks as Pete conducts us through a bout of traditional Sunday-evening *Robin of Sherwood* bingo, which – in a defiant display of vindication – I win, crossing '36 – the Earl of Huntingdon' from my card and jumping into the air with all the dignified restraint of an *X-Factor* audition. I collect a bottle of South African wine for my troubles, and clutch it proudly to my chest as the girls and I swap e-mail addresses. 'Watch out for those woollen dolls, they're trouble.' warns Kirsty, with a devilish gleam in her eye.

As I climb back into the Toyota horse-drawn carriage, still waiting patiently round the back of Ye Olde Bell in the spot it's occupied since Friday teatime, my mind is reeling. I think this is the convention that has touched me the most, brutally exposing so many exquisite childhood memories, and it's both the nature of the Legend experience – with its homely, welcoming community and intriguing mystical elements – and the essence of *Robin of Sherwood* that have combined to move me in such an unexpected fashion. The show itself is a story about death and sadness and struggle, but it's also a story about faith and belief and togetherness – and I've had those in spades this weekend. Even at 3.30am in a break-down recovery garage near Mansfield.

Nothing is forgotten. Nothing is ever forgotten. Except perhaps the route back to the A1, which takes me three circuits of Barnby Moor's winding country lanes to find. And all the while the malevolent glare of those woollen figures burns into my soul from the back seat of the Starlet.

The Curse of the Dolls is about to strike.

THE BATTLE TO SAVE EARTH

by Robert Fischer (Aged Eight And Seven Twelfths)
Saturday 20 June 1981

PART ELEVEN

Then Dirk said, 'That core is full of bombpower. So I'll give you a container and you can climb down to the core, crack the core and get the bompower into the container.' Dirk gave me a round bowl and I climbed down to the core. I thought it would be boiling hot by the core but it was quite the opposite. I was freezing and I fastened my track-

suit top. Then I kicked the core. Inside was a huge layer of red bubbleing liquid. I dipped the round container into the core and filled it up with bomb power. Then I climbed back up to Dirk. 'Well done Robert,' Dirk said. Dirk opened a hatch on the back of his gun and poured the bomb power in. Then he closed the hatch and put the container back in his pocket. Then he said 'Follow me,' and jumped back onto the chute. I did the same and we both climbed back into the tree. Then we ran to Richard's prison. When we got there, Dirk handed me his gun. I pulled the trigger and a huge flash of light came from the gun. When the smoke had cleared I saw that the door had been blown down and Richard was standing in front of me. 'Thanks Robert,' he said. Then Dirk started running back to our spaceship. We both ran after Dirk. Then I saw why we were running. klebba, Zero and some robots were running after us. Soon we reached the spaceship. It had now rose to the top of the swamp.

To be continued . . .

MONTY PYTHON

MONTY PYTHON DAY
DOUNE CASTLE, STIRLING
SUNDAY 3 SEPTEMBER

'And, after the spanking ... the oral sex!'

BE AFRAID. BE VERY AFRAID.

The first portents of the curse's deadly potency arrive at 10.15pm on the A1, on the way back from Barnby Moor. From nowhere, a biblical-strength storm begins to sweep across the darkened dual carriageway, blattering filthy, West Yorkshire rain against the Starlet windows and buffeting the car between lanes with terrifying ease. It's the first spot of rain I've seen all weekend, and I slow my speed to thirty miles per hour, my windscreen wipers wheezing and panting as they struggle to cope with the onslaught. A spine-chilling thought crosses my mind – I'm the first-born son in my family (a phenomenon Sorcha has frequently identified as 'typical fucking only child . . .' – yes, you get the picture) and I glance nervously over to the hard shoulder to check for frogs and locusts.

As I trundle along the suddenly deserted highway, a pale orange light on the dashboard catches my attention. It's the petrol gauge. I've no idea how long it's been running on empty, but the car is already starting to chug noticeably. I glance over my shoulder to see if there's a canister of fuel anywhere in the back (there isn't, and never has been) and realise with a start

259

that the woollen dolls are glaring back at me intently. They're lined up in formation on the back seat, and exude an air of malevolent evil. I swear a few of them have swapped places since I last checked.

A shiver goes through me, and I throw my jacket from the passenger seat into the back, covering them up with a single swift movement. As I do so, a miraculous change comes over the weather. The rain slows, almost instantly, to a light drizzle, and the wind drops from a typhoon to a breeze. And, instantaneously, the welcoming lights of Ferrybridge twenty-four-hour services emerge triumphantly from the murky gloom.

A day or two later, I e-mail Kirsty, Fiona and Alison to tell them about this strange phenomenon.

A mail comes back from Alison with the unambiguous subject heading 'Burn Those Dolls!' She tells me, as a rising tide of terror engulfs my trembling inbox, that their journey home to London was interrupted by a flat battery in Kirsty's car, and, the following day as she searched for a replacement, the bonnet flew up on the dual carriageway and smashed straight through her windscreen. A few days later, an e-mail from Kirsty herself arrives, describing how her short, post-convention holiday in Rome was beset with incessant flight delays, and when her repaired car returned from the garage, it had a new problem with the 'engine idle speed' (whatever that is). Fiona, meanwhile, has a stinking cold, and – in a fit of temporary blindness brought on by a Strepsil overdose – has fallen down the stairs. It seems all who came into contact with the dolls have fallen foul of their evil intent. It's like the Curse of Tutankhamen, but centered closer to Retford. I suggest we try to contact Phil Rose to ensure he's still alive and healthy, and hasn't been ambushed by Templars on his journey home.

Fiona suggests, through a haze of Vick's Sinex, that the problem might be the lack of a guiding influence to steer the dolls onto the path of righteousness. In a nutshell – there isn't a Herne doll to keep them all in check. Empowered by her suggestion, I gather the dolls on top of my PC monitor, shifting my broadband modem to one side, and print out an A4 picture of Herne himself, looming mysteriously out of the mist with a caption proclaiming, profoundly, 'You are nasty bits of wool driven by the wind.' I pin this to the wall behind the dolls and ask the pagan god of the trees to protect us from their evil ways. Within half an hour, my broadband modem explodes in a modest puff of smoke, and I spend a soul-destroying thirty minutes waiting for NTL customer services to pick up the phone (Nothing Is Forgotten . . . except, perhaps, your reason for living) to organise a replacement. While I wait for the engineer to arrive, I move the dolls onto the top of the PC tower itself. A day later, minutes after my new modem has been installed, my PC makes a tired, groaning noise and shuts itself down completely.

Two days later, after endless anguished phone calls, car journeys and attempts to decipher the arcane language used in my local PC repair shop ('The wiffle lever has caused a shortage in the winky winky generator' – well, it might as well have been), I find myself paying £237 to have a new motherboard installed in my computer. At which point I shove the dolls to the back of the deepest cupboard I can find, and pile a load of sandbags in front of them. I make a solemn vow – for the sake of mankind, humanity and the entire population of Barnby Moor – never to release the dolls from their bondage again, and, when the time comes to sell the house, a United Nations bomb disposal squad will first be summoned to destroy the cupboard and its contents with a small thermonuclear explosion.

And in the midst of their campaign of terror, I'm preparing for a Monty Python convention.

A BLUFFER'S GUIDE TO . . . MONTY PYTHON

As much a part of the collective British comedy consciousness as jesters, Schadenfreude and Income Tax returns, *Monty Python's Flying Circus* began with an explosion of anarchic comedy on Sunday 5 October 1969, although a vigorous and tantalising campaign of foreplay had been building up slowly for many years prior. The team comprised John Cleese (the tall, authoritarian one), Graham Chapman (the tall, extremely silly one), Michael Palin (the nice one that your mum likes), Terry Jones (the little Welsh one who's frequently naked), Eric Idle (the musical one with the scary eyes) and Terry Gilliam (the brash American one who did the cartoons). Cleese and Chapman had studied together at Cambridge, along with the slightly younger Idle, and all three of them had worked together on ITV's satirical 1967 sketch anthology *At Last the 1948 Show*. Meanwhile, Palin and Jones had worked with the trio on *The Frost Report*. Palin, Jones, Idle and Gilliam (a New York animator discovered by Cleese during a Cambridge Footlights tour of the US) teamed up for ITV's hit children's show *Do Not Adjust Your Set*, and *Monty Python's Flying Circus* was born of the BBC's desire to offer Cleese and Chapman their own show, the elongated duo agreeing on condition they could rope in their various collaborators to help.

The initial show lasted for four series – the last of which went ahead without a disillusioned Cleese – and produced four feature films. The first of these, *And Now for Something Completely Different*, was merely a compendium of remade TV sketches intended to break the US market. The other three

– *Monty Python and the Holy Grail* (1975), *The Life of Brian* (1979) and *The Meaning of Life* (1983) have become immortal, untouchable megaliths on the British comedy landscape.

The show's influence has become so all-pervading that the adjective 'Pythonesque' is still used regularly to describe brands of surreal humour that almost always singularly fail to emulate the original series's anger and anarchy. Original Python material mercilessly lampoons virtually any aspect of Britishness – from the class system to religion to celebrity culture to impenetrable bureaucracy and intellectual pretentiousness. It's a surreal, often morbid world populated by screeching 'ratbag' housewives, twisted dirty vicars, sleazy violent spivs and arrogant army generals, and it crackles with a vicious, anti-establishment venom that still feels relevant almost forty years on. And it has lots of cartoons and knob jokes as well.

The most famous Python sketches include 'the Parrot Sketch', in which a pedantic John Cleese returns a deceased bird to Palin's sleazy petshop owner; 'The Lumberjack Song', in which a macho Michael Palin sings a ditty about tree-felling that ends in sexual ambiguity; 'Nudge Nudge Wink Wink', in which a leering Eric Idle presses Terry Jones to reveal details of his love life; and 'the Ministry of Silly Walks', in which a bowler-hatted Cleese portrays a stiff-lipped government minister who walks to work in amusingly absurd fashions. Popular Monty Python catchphrases include 'Nobody Expects The Spanish Inquisition', 'Spam', 'He's Pining For The Fjords' and 'Why Are They Now Doing West End Musicals?' If you want to annoy a Monty Python fan, quote the programme relentlessly but inaccurately paraphrase the most important lines. If you want to find a Monty Python fan in a mature student union refectory, then just ... go in.

'At the end of the day, you can't expect me to live like a monk.'

I say this as I reach the bottom of the stairs, creeping up behind Sorcha as she rummages in the sideboard for the latest electricity bill. We've just had an argument about something or other, probably either money or the fact that I've now been away 'having fun' at conventions for four consecutive summer weekends, during which time the lawn in the back garden has reached Amazonian proportions. We've had to attach a periscope to the dog when she goes outside for her morning constitutional.

Sorcha whirls round to confront me, only to find that I am – indeed – dressed in the full flowing cowl of a medieval monk, complete with hood, sandals, rope belt and air of pious superiority. It's a scene that could have been lifted wholesale from the script of *Terry and June*, were it not for the fact that Sorcha actually laughs.

I'm a master at breaking the ice during conflicts. They should send me into North Korea dressed up in a gorilla suit.

The monks' costumes had been waiting for me when I returned from Barnby Moor. I'd bought three of them on eBay the previous week, determined to become a fully fledged fancy-dresser for at least one convention experience. Wez – *Star Wars* Wez, the chocolate-cake-loving skinhead – had readily agreed to accompany me in costume, and so had his brother Paul, who lives in Wishaw, a mere forty miles from Doune Castle, where much of the exterior location work for *Monty Python and the Holy Grail* took place. Paul is actually one step ahead of us, in that he attended last year's Monty Python Day, breaching the castle boundaries dressed as a Knight of the Round Table, along with his Dutch friend Cristyl Elands, who constructed from cardboard boxes a perfect scale replica of *Holy Grail*'s giant Trojan Rabbit, and promptly won the fancy-dress competition. She also, Paul regularly tells us to hearty guffaws, once received a letter from the bank addressed to 'Crusty Glands'.

The monks themselves feature in *Monty Python and the Holy Grail*, a troupe of medieval puritans led by future Rutle Neil Innes, chanting hymns of austere Latin piety while repeatedly slamming themselves in the face with lengths of timber. They always remind me of Middlesbrough fans.

I pick Wez up from his house on a freezing Saturday lunchtime and we set off for the Scottish border in teeming, driving rain, our three religious habits draped carefully across the Starlet's back seat. It takes us four hours to reach Wishaw, during which time we eat a brace of sticky buns in the car park of Abington Services while a monsoon sweeps horizontally against the steamed-up car windows. And this is what Sorcha calls 'having fun'.

It's early evening by the time we reach Paul's spanking-new house, and he greets us enthusiastically at the front door while his French wife, Marie – graciously playing hostess to our follies despite being eight months pregnant – dashes around fetching coffee and biscuits. Paul is a laconic, dry-witted Teessider who looks virtually identical to his older brother, and he quickly shows us to the shed, where Wez busies himself sawing up a length of timber to make three rough-hewn crosses for us to wear round our necks. He expertly planes a dovetail joint into them and drills perfect holes to accommodate hairy string. Paul and I watch in awe before giving up the ghost and playing darts instead. He consummately thrashes me without a stroke of effort, my one-time oche prowess having dissipated into the mists of time. I might as well have had the *Millennium Falcon* after all.

We troop back into the house and change gleefully into our

monks' costumes, donning sandals and newly hewn crosses before settling onto the sofa to watch *You've Been Framed*. It's narrated these days by one-time surreal stand-up Harry Hill, who – we all comment – is the very personification of Python's surreptitious yet almost omnipresent influence on modern mainstream TV culture. And then we laugh like drains at a dog falling in a paddling pool.

CRUCIAL MOMENTS IN FANDOM HISTORY NUMBER TEN: THE DAY MY MUM BOUGHT A VIDEO RECORDER

It's Christmas morning 1987, I've just turned fifteen, and am opening my presents with a bitter-sweet tinge of melancholy. Time is moving on apace for the Fischer family, and Christmas has lost a little magic. That very morning, I'd lain in bed until ten (proof positive in itself) reading *The Secret Diary of Adrian Mole*. 'Something dead strange has happened to Christmas,' writes Adrian on the day itself. 'It's just not the same as it used to be when I was a kid.'

I'm grudgingly accepting that he's right. But, unlike Adrian, I know exactly where the fault lies. It's me. I'm a gangly youth now, with spots and tufts of facial hair, and am far too surly to stay awake all night. I'd ambled downstairs like a proper Teesside man, made a cup of tea rather than snaffling a Toblerone, and slumped on the settee to sneer at *Christmas Morning With Noel Edmonds*, live from the Telecom Tower for some reason.

Grunt.

And, along with my youthful enthusiasm and *joie de vivre*, another crucial element of Christmas is missing.

My gran.

It's the first Christmas we haven't spent together. She's in her late seventies now and has become incredibly frail, taking up permanent residence a matter of months earlier in a nursing home in nearby Redcar. She's spending the day at my auntie Norma's so it's just me and my parents, and they watch with admirably fixed smiles as I pull open a succession of gleaming ZX Spectrum games, my fingertips still – at this point – grafted to its rubber keys.

And then, out of nowhere, my mum disappears upstairs and emerges with one final gift. It's a large cardboard box, wrapped up in lurid paper and addressed to me and Dad. We remove the paper jointly with manly, patient restraint.

It's a video recorder.

It's a fucking *video recorder.*

I'm stunned.

I had no idea that this was in the offing, and a wave of festive joyousness finally wells up inside me. The early 1980s video revolution had completely passed us by, the Betamax wars being fought and lost without ever impinging on the Fischer household. I lose myself in a haze of wires and cables, attaching the bulky video to our ancient Grundig TV. And then my mum presents us with our first ever video cassettes, their yellow, slab-like cases emblazoned with the logo of Yarm's tiny rental shop.

It's a brace of Python masterworks: *Holy Grail* and *The Life of Brian.*

I've been a Python obsessive for about six months. In the summer of 1987, at the height of my *Hitch Hiker*'s love-in with the cornet-playing Chris Selden, the BBC began to repeat the show on a succession of blissful Saturday nights. From the very off, I was taping Pythons on my portable audio cassette recorder, and playing them back to perfect my impersonations. 'H'why should h'I be tarred with the h'epithet "loony" merely because I 'ave h'a pet halibut?' I'd shriek to myself, although nobody ever answered.

Until September.

Back at school after the summer holidays, a little bit lonely for the loss of Chris Selden and a little bit intimidated at the start of my GCSEs, I was mumbling Python catchphrases to myself in double physics. 'Now, nobody likes a good laugh more than I do,' I'd muttered, in the muted clipped tones of Graham Chapman's silly colonel. 'Except perhaps my wife. And some of her friends. Oh yes, and Captain Johnson.'

'Come to think of it, most people like a good laugh more than I do,' came the reply from behind me.

I'd whirled round.

It was Paul Hayes.

Yep, the future Dungeons and Dragons gamesmaster, the heartless nemesis of my beloved Hamwise Beardribbler. A curly-haired teenager whose path I'd rarely crossed before, we'd suddenly struck up an entire conversation in fluent Monty Python-ese, and we didn't let up for around the next two years. In Brian Eno's splendid 1996 diary *A Year With Swollen Appendices*, the ambient music pioneer chronicles the night he spent watching *Monty Python's Flying Circus* on video, so unable to tear himself away that he saved himself a trip to the toilet and widdled in an empty wine bottle instead. And then – just out of interest – took a tiny, investigative sip. We haven't quite gone that far yet, but – in all honesty – we're really not far off. And I've always had my suspicions about my dad's seemingly endless supply of cloudy home-brewed beer.

Within days I'd been invited to Paul's house to watch *Life of Brian*, and was slightly shocked at the litany of F-words coming from the lips of the previously pristine Pythons. Even nice Michael Palin, who, inevitably, was my mum's favourite. So I'm actually a touch trepidatious on Christmas morning, as my mum slips the film into our spanking-new video recorder's front-loading mechanism. But my dad – who, despite being a long-term Python fan, has probably never seen the film before, concerns about its religious content having so far precluded any UK TV screenings – roars with laughter from the off, and I join him. We make eye contact and guffaw at the rudest of jokes, and Christmas Day lights up again. I've always shared a sense of humour with my dad – a love of the absurd, the surreal, the unexpected release from the humdrum – and even from an early age we've watched *Fawlty Towers* and *The Young Ones* together. The comedic generation gap just never existed for us – I always appreciated his youthful comic heroes, and he's always kept abreast of the cutting-edge new acts. Even today, pushing seventy, he's as happy with *Extras* or *Little Britain* as I am with *Steptoe* and *Hancock's Half-Hour*.

He thinks *Doctor Who* is shit, though, so he loses.

Built at the end of the fourteenth century by Robert Stewart, the First Duke of Albany, Doune Castle sits on a wooded bend of the gentle River Teith, an imposing silhouette against a dramatic Scottish sky. With the use of some pernicious tight-framing and editing, the privately owned ruin was used to depict a variety of different castles in the film, after the National Trust of Scotland withdrew permission to use their own locations, presumably fearing that two thousand years of violent, bloodied history would be fatally tainted by the sight of Graham Chapman clopping two coconut halves together.

Wez, Paul and I are crammed into the Starlet, resplendent in our monks' outfits and sandals. We turn an impossibly tight corner from the windswept village of Doune, and are flagged over by a craggy-faced marshal in the obligatory hi-vis jacket.

'Woah there, lads. Are yez here for the Monty Python Day?'

he enquires slightly grumpily, in the gruff, rough-edged local brogue.

We stare dumbstruck for a moment, pondering momentarily other possible reasons for driving to a medieval Scottish castle sporting three medieval monks' costumes with the hoods up. We react in the only reasonable manner to defuse a potentially awkward situation. We burst into raucous Teesside laughter.

'Aye, well. Can I just see yez tickets?' he persists, stony-faced.

We hold up our tickets and he nods curtly, allowing us to drive up the narrow trackway to the castle grounds. 'That fooled him,' says Paul. 'Now let's get all the lead off the ramparts.'

We'd spent some time at the house over lunch debating what to wear under our habits, and had decided – bravely – to opt for the authentic medieval approach, and just sport the flimsiest of Marks and Spencer briefs. It's a decision we all begin silently to question as we flip-flop out of the car and feel an icy Highland wind tug our nylon costumes across our torsos. As we troop up the hill to the castle's portcullis, another car pulls up next to ours and three guffawing characters in impressive red Spanish Inquisition costumes emerge. 'Ha!' they shout, apropos of nothing. 'HA!'

'The Spanish Inquisition' had been one of mine and Paul Hayes's favourite sketches for double physics re-enactment, Michael Palin being the leader of three frankly rubbish inquisitors, jumping out from behind doorways whenever unsuspecting characters in entirely unrelated sketches proclaimed they 'didn't expect the Spanish Inquisition'. 'Nobody expects the Spanish Inquisition!' they would bluster. 'Our chief weapon is surprise. Surprise and fear. Fear and surprise. Our two weapons are fear and surprise. And ruthless efficiency. Our three weapons are fear, surprise and ruthless efficiency. And an almost fanatical devotion to the Pope.'

I can almost smell the magnesium ribbon. Although I'm not allowed to watch it without my jumper over my eyes.

We tramp into the castle's keep, and our decision to dress up now looks a very wise one. *Everybody* else has made the effort. The blustery, damp-grassed courtyard is filled with knights, monks, lumberjacks, pepperpot fishwives and handkerchief-headed 'Gumbies'. We set up camp on folding chairs, with the Spanish Inquisition still guffawing in front of us.

I've tried and failed in recent weeks to discover where the tradition of convention fancy dress first started. Even the origins of conventions themselves seem shrouded in an impressive air of mystery. In October 1936, half a dozen sci-fi fans, including acclaimed writers David Kyle and Frederik Pohl, travelled by train to Philadelphia, where they met up with six local fans at the house of writer and nuclear physicist Dr Milton A. Rothman. Whether this constituted the first ever convention, as opposed to a few beers round at Milton's gaff, has been the subject of furious fan debate ever since, which seems entirely in keeping with the whole bizarre concept. In January 1937, the Brits had a go; with twenty fans, including Arthur C. Clarke, gathering in Leeds Theosophical Hall. Although history sadly fails to record whether the future author of *2001: A Space Odyssey* dressed in a home-made Morlock costume, argued that H. G. Wells's latest works were the 'Worst. Sci-Fi. Ever' and got drunk on Samuel Smith's Best Bitter before dancing insanely to George Formby's 'Sitting on the Ice in the Ice Rink'. In the absence of any actual evidence, let's just assume that he did. I'd also like to assume that Dr Rothman is the only convention organiser in history who's been allowed to experiment with accelerating nuclear particles. Please.

I decide to commemorate the day's sterling dressing-up efforts by asking the Spanish Inquisition to pose for a picture with Wez. This seems to trigger them into further madness, and they leap to their feet and begin re-enacting the sketch from scratch. 'Cardinal Biggles, poke him with the soft cushions!' barks their leader, as his flying-helmeted henchman (who's actually a woman, wearing a giant paper moustache) grabs a fluffy, soft cushion from their rucksack and jabs it repeatedly into Wez's habit-covered midriff. Five minutes later, they're tying a grizzled-looking BBC Radio Scotland interviewer to a deckchair with a length of washing line. At which point a jovial lumberjack dashes to the front of the stage and asks us to make our way back outside the castle walls to attempt to break the record for the world's longest coconut conga.

For the uninitiated, the budget for *Holy Grail* (and the patience of the actors) didn't stretch to actually riding horses, so all of King Arthur's Knights of the Round Table trot along clopping half-coconut shells together, a factor that inevitably leads to a pedantic cinematic argument atop the battlements of Doune Castle, as Eric Idle's bolshy guard questions how a coconut could arrive in medieval England, disputing Arthur's theory that it could have been dropped by a migrating swallow. It's a running theme that recurs repeatedly throughout the film, eventually culminating in Terry Jones's immortal line 'Ow deu yeu kneu seu much abeut swalleus?', which is never as funny written down as performed.

So we're cleared en masse from the castle keep and asked to take with us the strung-together coconut halves that we've all been given in our Monty Python Welcome Packs. I totter down the cobbled path in extremely ill-fitting Jesus sandals and we shiver outside as a Japanese woman wearing a T-shirt proclaiming, 'I'm Not Dead Yet,' asks myself and the Wez brothers to huddle together for her camera. As we do so, the opening 'unladen swallow' routine from *Holy Grail* is acted out by three seasoned fancy-dressers at the front – one indeed up on the battlements – before we're given the signal to 'chaaaaaaaaaarge' back into the castle keep, clopping our coconuts as we go. As we do so, a succession of rubber chickens and inflatable sheep are thrown down from the ramparts above us by a man doing a fine facsimile of John Cleese's legendarily abusive French knight who deals primarily in the abusive epithet 'Your mother was an 'aaaamster and your father smelt of elderberrieeez.'

We're followed back to our seats by a glazed, middle-aged female hippy with dreadlocks who I'm not convinced doesn't think the whole thing is actually real.

We fortify ourselves with beer, sandwiches and biscuits as the wind whistles around the keep. The lumberjack's shout-out for Rita Thorpe – who has travelled from Colorado to be here today – is met with inevitable catcalls of 'I'm Rita Thorpe and so is my wife!' from all corners of the castle. And as the crowd breaks into a sing-song of Python favourites (with lyric sheets provided in our Welcome Pack), we decide to explore the castle further. The ruin's walls are a labyrinth of stairs, nooks and crannies, and we hitch up our habits and shuffle to the back of the keep. From here, we amble up the open stone stairwell – the same stairwell from which John Cleese's Sir Lancelot begins a bloodthirsty slaughter of guests at Prince Herbert's wedding – and begin to explore the castle's interior.

We quickly find the kitchen, and the window from which – in 1745, at the height of the Jacobite uprising – loyalist Scottish poet John Home escaped by knotting together bedsheets. Two hundred and thirty years later, the scene was almost re-enacted by Michael Palin's Sir Galahad the Chaste, fearing his purity would be compromised when confronted in the very same room by a legion of seductive 'girlies' led by Carol Cleveland's purring Zoot, culminating in the immortal line 'And, after the spanking . . . the oral sex!' There's no sign of either loyalist Scottish poets or oral sex as the Wez brothers and I enter the room, just a lot of dust and a man dressed as a Python fish slapper, complete with safari suit, pith helmet and giant stuffed halibut. I take a picture of him.

By the time we return to the keep and amble around the castle gift shop (where replica Grails are available for forty-five pounds and bottles of Python 'Grail Ale' for a slightly more reasonable two pounds fifty), the evening's 'Python Idle' talent competition is well underway. Paul, now clearly 'emotional' off the back of a full bottle of wine and some hearty swigs of Grail Ale, mercilessly harangues two young boys re-enacting the film's 'Holy Hand Grenade' sequence with admirable vigour. 'Three shall be the number thou shalt count, and the number of the counting shall be three,' they recite to an awestruck crowd.

'Boooooooooooooooo!' shouts Paul, with comically cupped hands across his mouth. 'They won this last year with the same bloody sketch!' I wonder whether we should call up Crusty Glands to provide independent adjudication.

We cap off the competition with another re-enaction, that of the famous 'stoning' scene from *Life of Brian* – all donning false beards and throwing crumpled-up paper rocks at a skinny man in a lion cloth jumping up and down and shouting, 'Jehovah,' – at the end of which I get chatting to Cardinal Fang from the Spanish Inquisition, who tells me that a rumour is sweeping the castle (and it's about time somebody did) that we may soon be playing host to a Python in person.

Michael Palin is apparently on his way.

BLOODY STUPID THINGS I HAVE DONE IN THE NAME OF FANDOM NUMBER TEN: TRYING TO MEET ALL THE PYTHONS

The Spanish Inquisition don't need to put me in the comfy chair, or – indeed – poke me with the soft cushions.

I confess.

I'm not the Python fandom virgin I've hitherto made myself out to be.

In fact, I've probably stolen a march on most of the Python obsessives running around Doune Castle today, in that – (brace yourself) – I've already met two of the Pythons in person.

It's Sunday 19 October 2003, and Sorcha and I are sitting in the audience at Durham Gala Theatre, on the closing evening of the city's annual literary festival. Onstage, a respected historian in a grey double-breasted suit is delivering an academic lecture about the death of Geoffrey Chaucer, accompanied by slides of contemporary fourteenth-century artwork and looking into the political and monarchical make-up of England at the time of the great poet's demise.

It's a fascinating and intriguing presentation, and it's delivered with great vigour and passion by the historian himself, but there's no question that I wouldn't be here if the man onstage hadn't been Terry Jones. If that makes me a shameless hero-worshipper and a shallow devotee of the cult of celebrity, then . . . well, that shouldn't be a surprise to anyone, really. You're talking, after all, about a man who attended a genealogy seminar with the Sixth Doctor, Colin Baker.

Afterwards, Terry retires to the theatre bar to sell and sign copies of his accompanying book, the unambiguously titled *Who Murdered Chaucer?* We join the back of a short queue, and edge closer and closer to the man himself, who's seated behind a trestle table, chatting amiably with fans. I'm still in the early stages of actorphobia here, and the sweat is already gathering in my palms, running down the edge of the pint of real ale I'm clutching for dear life in my white-knuckled hand.

It's my turn.

'This is a *tewwific* pint of beer,' barks Terry as I arrive at the table, sloshing his drink around in the glass and noting

I'm holding a similarly-coloured beverage. 'What exactly is this stuff?'

'I believe it's called Old Growler,' I smile.

'OLD GWOWLER!' he explodes, laughing uproariously. 'How twemendous!'

It's completely disarming to hear such a familiar voice addressing me directly, a voice that I spent around three of my teenage years imitating every single day during various Bunsen burner experiments with Paul Hayes. And even more so when it's shouting the name of a Suffolk-brewed beer named unashamedly after a female private part. He signs the book for us gleefully, and I ask him kindly if he'll pose for a photo with us, which he does – removing his glasses 'so I don't look like an old fart' and grinning for the camera.

Sorcha, for her troubles, doesn't say a word throughout the entire encounter, and when we move away it's quite clear that she's rigid with fear. And, by her own admission, she's never even said 'Ow deu yeu kneu seu much abeut swalleus?' in an amusing *Holy Grail* voice in the middle of a mock GCSE physics exam.

My next encounter is two years later, on Thursday 3 November 2005, in Leeds's plush Vue Cinema, on the opening night of the city's annual film festival. I'm with Wez and Smudge and one-time Atari ST owner Gaz Norman, and we've just watched the UK premiere of Terry Gilliam's new cinematic blockbuster *The Brothers Grimm*. It's a sold-out occasion, and in attending tonight's event I've managed to complete a devastating triple-whammy of self-indulgent treachery, because a) it's my mum's birthday and I haven't gone round for dinner, b) it's the day before Sorcha's birthday and I've left her to celebrate in London by herself, and c) Middlesbrough are playing crack Ukrainian outfit Dnipro in a crucial UEFA Cup Group D encounter at the Riverside Stadium.

Fuck 'em all, though, I'm going to meet a Python!

And I do. The 'other' Python Terry is here in person to introduce the film and conduct a short Q&A session afterwards, and when I emerge blinking from the darkness of the cinema at the end of the evening, he's laughing and joking loudly in that effervescent Californian accent as a gaggle of fans swarm around him for attention. I join the merry throng, fingering the DVD sleeve from *Time Bandits* that I slipped into my inside pocket before shambling out of the house.

Gilliam's work spears my fandom genes with a two-pronged, pincer-attack-style assault. Firstly, obviously, he's a Python – and his immortal *Life of Brian* line 'We 'ave lumps of it out the back' (to be delivered in a slavering, Neanderthal, brow-furrowing grunt) was another regular Paul Hayes instrument of torture for poor old Mr Dillon in the physics lab. Secondly, though, he's directed some of my favourite films of all time. Back in July 1982, at the very dawn of the home-video age, we were shown *Time Bandits* at Levendale Primary School as a last-day-of-term treat – forty shuffling nine-year-olds piled into a darkened classroom and plonked in front of a huge wood-carved TV on wheels, as half of our exhausted teaching staff retreated to the staffroom for coffee and Silk Cuts. I remember it being stiflingly hot, and the two girls sitting next to stinky Chris Herbert having to be given oxygen, and treatment for ammonia burns. But the film – in which a troupe of time-travelling dwarves ransack surreal mythological set-pieces in search of wealth and celebrity – instantly became one of my favourites.

Within seconds I'm standing in front of the director himself, rummaging around in my inside pocket for a crumpled DVD sleeve.

'One my favourite films of all time,' I stammer, red-faced and sweaty and nervous.

He breaks into a grin so broad it seems to stretch around the back of his head. He's shorter than I expected, but slim and tanned with spiky brown hair tied back in a tiny ponytail, and it strikes me as odd that he's about the same age as my grey, distinguished dad, a man who would no sooner wear a ponytail than paint his fingernails cherry red and audition to join the Folies Bergère. And there's no chance of that ever happening – he's more of a fuchsia-crimson man.

'How old were you when you first saw it?' asks Terry Gilliam.

'Nine,' I reply, in an impressive burst of mental arithmetic.

'Ah!' He beams. 'That's the prime age for watching my films. I always try to keep the nine-year-olds happy, and anything above and beyond is a bonus.'

I tell him how much I enjoyed *The Brothers Grimm*, and we huddle together for a photo, only to discover that the battery in the disposable camera I've given to Smudge is clearly dead, and flashless. 'You'll have two blurs against a pitch-black wall,' smiles Terry, with the world-weary resignation of a frequently troubled film-maker. I give him my thanks (from me and Paul Hayes) and trundle off into the cold Leeds night, wondering what my nine-year-old self would make of *Brazil*, with its themes of surveillance, dystopian bleakness and torture.

He probably wouldn't have batted an eyelid. They breed them tough on the mean streets of Acklam.

It's getting dark now, though not quite dark enough to watch a film on a big screen in the open air on a chilly summer's evening. Still, that doesn't stop us trying. *Monty Python and the Holy Grail*'s cod-Norwegian credits roll ('Moose trained by Yutte

Hermsgervordenbroti') and within minutes we're watching Graham Chapman and Terry Gilliam engaged with Eric Idle in an argument about swallows in a scene that takes place twenty feet behind us. Although it has to be said there's no sign of Michael Palin pulling up a deckchair at the back of the castle keep.

I've never watched a film as part of a rowdy, communal experience before. I'm normally so sensitive to distractions in the cinema that the slightest crackle of popcorn is enough to send me raging, Rambo-style, across the tiers of seats, kicking crisps out of teenagers' hands and crushing mobile phones into twisted shards of metal. But I quite enjoy this. Everyone in fancy dress here today – including us monks – dashes up to the front of the keep and acts out their parts when their namesakes appear onscreen, and every man in the castle joins in with the line 'And, after the spanking . . . the oral sex!'

But it's the late Graham Chapman who, as always, steals the show.

Chapman, for me, is the spirit of Python. I love them all as slightly sinister brothers, but Chapman was the Python who lived, breathed and, erm, died it. Seemingly determined to make every second of his life as fun, shocking and stimulating as possible, he's Python's Lenny Bruce; their John Lennon or Sid Vicious. And not only because he was dead before he was fifty. A dedicated anarchist, a voracious campaigner for gay rights and a raging alcoholic throughout most of his Python years, Chapman was also an active member of the Dangerous Sports Club, and once tried to ski down an Alpine black diamond slope in a 'wretched wooden gondola' stolen from an Italian restaurant. He attempted to hang-glide over an active volcano in Uruguay, and frequently blew up hotel rooms with The Who's Keith Moon. He's also one of my favourite modern philosophers.

'What are we?', he asks in his brilliant pseudo-life story *A*

Liar's Autobiography, which once drove me to an athsma attack on a train travelling from York to Northallerton. 'We are tubes – hollow cylinders of flesh. What is our expectation from life? Regular fulfilment of primitive functions at both ends, coupled with the thought that we must leave at least something behind us, very much in the same way that a dog pisses against a tree.'

Take a hike, Jean-Paul Sartre.

He's also a brilliant actor, and the only natural choice to play the leading man in the two Python films that actually require one. As the sky darkens above us and the stars begin to peep through a thin layer of purple cloud, I strain my eyes and wonder if I can catch a glimpse of asteroid 9617graham-chapman. All the Pythons have one named after them, but Graham's will be the silliest.

By nine, when the film's abrupt end is met by a thunderous wall of applause, I'm faint with the cold. Clutching my monk's robes to my naked chest, I pick up my bags and schlep barefoot (I've given up on the sandals) back to the car. It's 9pm precisely, and the castle's battlements now look sinister and foreboding, menacingly black against a bruised Stirlingshire sky. We're back in Wishaw within the hour, at which point Wez goes to bed and Paul, now happily merry on white wine and Grail Ale, cracks open a bottle of Very Young Ardbeg whisky. It's smoky, peaty and unbelievably expensive, and he proceeds to slosh mugfuls of it into a glass for me as we dance maniacally around the front room to the contemporary progressive rock of Circulus, and their new medieval-themed album *The Lick on the Tip of an Envelope Yet to Be Sent*.

In monks' costumes.

At 1am, an angry and exhausted-looking Marie sticks her head round the front-room door and beckons Paul to join her in the hallway 'for a chat'. I can hear the soliloquy in her charming Parisienne accent. 'Now, nobody likes a good laugh more than I do,' she's saying, 'but that's no excuse for being silly. Your mother was an 'aaaamster and your father smelt of elderberrieeez.'

She isn't really. I don't think any words are really necessary. I turn off the stereo and we shamble off to bed. The course of true love is soon restored to its usual glory, though, and Paul reveals in the morning that, before they settled down, Marie placed a bucket by the bed in case he needed to throw up during the night.

We eat breakfast while watching *The Meaning of Life*, resisting the temptation to follow cornflakes and toast with Mr Creosote's notorious 'waifer-theen meent', and by 10.30am Wez and I are heading back to Teesside, seemingly mercifully free of the dreaded Curse of the Dolls. Until, that is, we reach Abington Services and I discover my mobile phone is missing, and frantic calls from Wez's phone to Paul's house and Doune Castle fail to recover it from the dolls' evil grasp.

Still, in the words of the song, I always look on the bright side of life.

Even if the monsoon is still sweeping horizontally against the steamed-up car windows.

One more convention to go.

THE BATTLE TO SAVE EARTH

By Robert Fischer (Aged Eight And Seven Twelfths And A Bit)
Sunday 21 June 1981
PART TWELVE

Dirk did a flying leap of the
swamp and landed in the drivers
seat. Richard and I did the same
and landed on top of each other on
the co-pilot's seat. Dirk started
the engine up and we were zoomed
out of the swamp. Where are we
heading? I asked him. 'Earth,'
Dirk replied. About half an hour
later, the computer board in spaceship started to smoke and
blew up. 'What was that?' I asked Dirk. 'It's Earth's
atmosphere,' Dirk said. 'Get the parachutes!' I climbed over
the two seats and jumped to the back of the spaceship. But
there was no parachutes. I told Dirk. 'We'll have to jump,'
he said. 'You're crazy!' Richard said. 'I'm not jumping down
there!' 'Chicken! Chicken! Chicken!' I shouted at Richard. He
got mad and jumped. Dirk and I followed him. We landed on
Villa Park, Aston Villa's home ground. Suddenly Gary Shaw
scored the winning goal just as the full time whistle went.
Then the crowd came onto the pitch. A big group of people
started fighting Richard and Gary. I did a rugby tackle on
one of the people and pulled some away. Gary and Richard
slipped free and we all ran out of the pitch. Gary put his
track suit top on. Then we found that we were just on Leven
Bank near Paul Frank's house. I stuck my thumb up at a car
and it stopped. We climbed into the back and found Paul Frank
and Andrew Henry there. 'Frankie! Henry!' I shouted. 'Robert!'
Paul shouted. 'You and Richard are late for the camp!'

To be continued . . .

RED DWARF

'No questions. Except one ... Smeg or No Smeg?'

'A PINT OF FLYING Herbert, a pint of Foster's and a large Diet Coke, please.'

It's 31 October 1996, Halloween, and I'm in the fusty, smoke-filled Tap and Barrel in Middlesbrough town centre. I'm twenty-three years old, with a demonic goatee beard complimented perfectly by wraparound shades, bright red devil horns and an immaculate black and red suit that I bought from Sherry's the Mod Shop on a day trip to London with my old schoolfriend Wez. He's here as well, wearing an enigmatic Zorro mask, and so is Brucie, our future Penrhiwceiber *Star Wars* correspondent, resplendent in frilly shirt and plastic vampire fangs.

'OK,' says the barmaid, flashing me an unsure smile. She's young and really pretty, a lovely, shy redhead with an intriguingly posh accent. She's also, I note with fascination, wearing a delightfully incongruous *Red Dwarf* T-shirt.

Our old friend Robert is drinking at the bar. 'Do you know Sorcha?' he says, waving half a pint of mild around with flagrant, gay abandon. 'Fischer, this is Sorcha. She's a friend of Sharon and Kirstine's. Sorcha, this is Fischer. He's, erm ... dressed up as the devil.'

I smile a semi-drunken smile, and shake Sorcha's hand while she waits for Brucie's lager to pour. 'Sorcha?' I comment. 'That's an odd name. How do you spell that, then?'

'I don't bother,' she replies, with a gorgeous little smile. 'I just tell people I'm called Sarah. It saves time.'

Almost exactly ten years later, I catch the same flashing grey eyes with a grin as I lock the door of our crumbling family home and we climb into the car for our first *Red Dwarf* convention. And she's still wearing that same old bloody T-shirt, although I've long since dispensed with the devil horns and shades.

'You were wearing that the first night I met you.'

'I know,' she replies. 'It's been all downhill since then.'

As we turn the corner of the street, she starts singing with wild, tune-free abandon, and I'm duty bound to join in. 'It's cold outside, there's no kind of atmosphere. I'm all alooooone, moooooooore or less.'

Look at us, having fun together.

Anyone would think we actually loved one another.

A BLUFFER'S GUIDE TO . . . RED DWARF

Launched into deep space on Monday 15 February 1988, and lasting for eleven years and eight series, *Red Dwarf* is a cult BBC2 sitcom about a decrepit mining spaceship – the *Red Dwarf* of the title – whose crew are all but wiped out by a devastating radiation leak. The only survivor is scummy, curry-loving maintenance engineer Dave Lister, who manages to cheat death when Holly, the ship's lugubrious computer, keeps him in suspended animation for over three million years. When he awakes, he finds himself accompanied by the Cat, a preening, narcissistic humanoid feline evolved from his one-time pet moggy Frankenstein, and is soon joined by a hologram of his long-dead bunkmate, the sniffily superior Arnold Rimmer, who wears a permanent 'H' symbol on his forehead as a reminder that he's not actually real.

The show made cult sci-fi legends of all its main cast – Scouse performance poet Craig Charles is endearingly repulsive as Lister, and *Spitting Image* voiceover maestro Chris Barrie makes nasal anal retentiveness an art form as the infuriating Arnold Rimmer. The Cat is brought to life by West End dancer Danny John-Jules, who convinced the show's producers that he was cool enough for the role by turning up half an hour late for his audition, and dressed in his father's zoot suit. And the show is frequently stolen by deadpan stand-up comedian Norman Lovett, whose previous comedy adventures had gained him both a cameo role in the final episode of *The Young Ones* (standing in a bank queue behind a mohican-sporting Jools Holland) and a support slot with the Clash. Lovett provided Holly the Computer's disembodied head for the first and final two series of the show, with the interim Holly being portrayed by equally eccentric stand-up Hattie Hayridge, a former civil servant with Her Majesty's Stationery Office.

In later series, the team are also joined by block-headed neurotic robot Kryten, played with a 'bad Canadian accent' by comedian and novelist Robert Llewellyn, who came to producer Paul Jackson's attention when performing his one-man show *Mammon, Robot Born of Woman* at the Edinburgh Festival. And then there's chirpy ship sex-symbol Kristine Kochanski, the one-time lust of Lister's life, who – as played by *Gregory's Girl* starlet Clare Grogan – makes occasional flashback and holo-gram appearances, before metamorphosing into Chloë Annett's pouting parallel dimension incarnation and joining the crew permanently for the final two series. The show has been out of production since 1999, although rumours of a movie revival persist – so much so that poor Norman Lovett recently placed a polite request on his website, nicely asking the show's fans to stop e-mailing him repeatedly about progress on the *Red Dwarf* movie. It didn't work.

Long-running *Red Dwarf* catchphrases include 'Everybody's Dead, Dave, Everybody's Dead', 'Smoke Me A Kipper I'll Be Back For Breakfast' and 'Is It True There's A Movie Version Coming Out, And If So Wh-Aaaaaaaaargh, Stop Hitting Me, Norman!' The show also introduced to British culture the word 'smeg', used as a futuristic substitute for virtually any swear word in the English lexicon – there's 'smeg', 'smegging', 'smeghead', 'smeg off', 'for smeg's sake', 'smegging hell', 'you smegging smegger', and – deep breath – 'What the smegging smeg have you smegging done? You've smegging killed me!' Writers Rob Grant and Doug Naylor have since denied any knowledge of the word as an abbreviation of the word 'smegma', used for centuries to describe the accumulation of secretions that can gather beneath the male foreskin.

The Italian manufacturers of a range of similarly titled upmarket refrigerators have seemingly yet to comment on the matter.

So this is it. My final convention. It's been nearly three weeks since Doune Castle, exactly ten days since Paul found my missing mobile phone down the back of his settee and exactly eleven days since I'd gone out and bought a new one, thus providing the *Robin of Sherwood* dolls with one final swipe of dark retribution. My (physical and mobile phone) batteries are recharged, I'm really looking forward to this weekend, and I can't help feeling a twinge of sadness that the whole jolly escapade is coming to an end.

Because, despite the odd moment of anxiety, irritation and sheer back-breaking exhaustion, I've had a blast. Some events I've enjoyed more than others, but every single one – and I'm filling up as I write this, and not just with Kit-Kats and Flamin' Hot Monster Munch – has made me fall back in love with my favourite childhood and teenage things. I've been like a deep-sea diver in the filthy ocean of consciousness, dredging up long-forgotten memories from the silt and bringing them to the surface to restore them with a much-needed polish.

All of this surges to the forefront of my mind as we tramp through torrential rain to the Peterborough Holiday Inn reception, and decamp to an entirely beige bedroom. I flop onto the duvet and run through an existential audit sheet in my mind. My finances are completely smegged. The price of tickets to my various conventions and fan events has varied wildly. *Star Trek* was a fiver, *Star Wars* was nine pounds, *Monty Python* ten pounds and *The Prisoner* sixteen pounds. For *Doctor Who* and *Blake's 7* I bought the two together at a bargain one hundred pounds. Discworld was forty-five pounds, *Red Dwarf* was sixty pounds and *Robin of Sherwood* eighty pounds. But one thing that hasn't varied much is the endless cost of traipsing up and down the country in the Starlet, combined with hotel fees – my bill at Discworld was nearly £200, and for *Red Dwarf* we're looking at around £150. Chuck in hot meals, copious amounts of alcohol and expensive items of merchandise subsequently bought in a foolish, drunken haze at charity auctions and the sum keeps mounting. And don't forget that the average price of a packet of Flamin' Hot Monster Munch has risen from forty-five pence to forty-seven pence in the eleven months since November 2005.

On the plus side, I'm getting on really well with Sorcha. And I've noticed something striking – we don't argue as much when we're at sci-fi conventions together. Or, if we do, it's about whether the *Liberator* in *Blake's 7* should have a serial number rather than a name.

I'm not entirely sure why this should be, or where it should take our relationship. Perhaps it's because none of the things we do actually quarrel about – the state of the garden, the bathroom-floor tiling situation, why the dog hair hasn't been hoovered off the stairs – are remotely applicable in the strange, cloistered environment of the convention. And maybe the answer is to sell the house, put the dog into cold storage, and spend our lives swinging merrily around the world, from signing session to celebrity panel to water-pistol fight, without ever stopping to allow real life to intrude. I've read that at any given point, somewhere in the world, a radio station will be playing The Beatles's 'Yesterday', and wonder if the same is true of sci-fi and cult TV conventions – if, given unlimited stamina and air miles, you could actually globetrot from one to the next, like a rock band on tour, but without the associated air of debauched, sexual excess. Unless you count the *Blake's 7* weekends, obviously.

We wander down to the convention's main function room, where a couple of dozen tables are laid out, cabaret-style, with white tablecloths and assorted *Red Dwarf* paraphernalia, including fake Coke cans emblazoned with the Jupiter Mining Company logo and flyers for 'Krytie TV Shower Night – Live' featuring 'the Girls on D Wing as You've Never Seen Them Before'. We're soon joined at the table by a clean-cut, twenty-something London couple in *Mighty Boosh* T-shirts, who introduce themselves as Mike and Katy, and tentatively swap life stories with Sorcha while I'm sent to the bar to buy drinks. When I return, Hattie Hayridge is starting off the Friday-night quiz. She's endearingly nervy and giggly, and admits to us all she knows nothing about *Red Dwarf*. And we're not much better – our table limps along to seventh place, propped up resolutely by the staggeringly detailed knowledge of two fresh-faced early teenagers from Hartlepool, who, when *Red Dwarf*'s last series was hogging the TV screens, can barely have been downloaded from Adobe Babymaker 5.1. Or however it is they do it these days.

We're all pissed by the end, and I wonder if the summer's breakneck schedule has finally caught up with me when the room suddenly seems to suffer from an infestation of penguins . . . until Katy points out that the merchandise room has opened for business, and every third fan in the room has spent ten pounds on a scarily authentic copy of Mr Flibble, the fluffy penguin hand puppet that barks dastardly instructions to Rimmer after a hologramatic virus sends him round the twist. They're everywhere, and even the teenage Hartlepudlians on our table have purchased one apiece to peck at each other's heads. 'Mr Flibble's very cross!' they snipe at each other, in authentically nasal Chris Barrie imitations.

Behind them, I notice with a start, is Chris Barrie himself.

Which takes me by surprise – after all, it's almost ten o'clock. But Chris – in a laudable demonstration of the affection in which the show's stars hold their ever-loyal fans – has raced from London to be here on the only possible break in his schedule, and is pelting back again straight afterwards to resume work. 'I'm normally here on a Sunday when you're all incredibly hung-over; this year I'm here on Friday when you're all incredibly pissed,' he beams. He dives straight into a marathon, quickfire Q&A session, the results of which are so entertaining they make me wonder if all such occasions should be conducted after ten in the evening.

Q: 'If you were forced to go on a caravan holiday with either Gordon Brittas or Arnold Rimmer, which one would you choose?'

A: 'Brittas, he'd keep the place tidy. Rimmer would try to kill me during the night.'

Q: 'Did you get your septic tank sorted out?'

A: 'Yes, I now have a soakaway septic tank, and the summer has thankfully been a pong-free zone.'

Q: 'You and Jesus go out to dinner. Who pays?'

A: 'Well, I would offer, but if the Big J. insists . . . '

Afterwards, we stampede into the merchandise room for autographs, and Sorcha drunkenly shakes Chris's hand as he signs her treasured DVD sleeves for posterity. Knowing his football allegiances, I apologise rather too smugly for Middlesbrough's staggering 2–1 victory over Chelsea a few weeks earlier.

'I don't get many chances to gloat, so I seize them when they come around.' I smile.

'Don't worry, you'll get hammered tomorrow.' He grins back, before reassuring me that Gareth Southgate is the man for the job, and asking what I think the rest of the season holds. The two hundred fans in the queue behind me, eager to ask Chris to demonstrate the minute-long Space Corps salute that Rimmer designs in episode two of series eight, exude an air of tangible impatience.

Afterwards, I decide to pay tribute to Sorcha and our new-found sci-fi happiness by darting to the front of the room and taking part in the convention's drunken karaoke singalong. I've flicked through the laminated song sheets at our table, and chosen a timeless pop classic whose concise dissection of the correlation between religious, sexual and emotional ecstasy has always struck me as a rare beacon of intelligence in an often facile commercial pop universe.

'Gawd 'elp us, it's got to be the King,' says the karaoke master, as I bumble to the rear of his PA system. 'What is it, "Suspicious Minds"? Or "Heartbreak Hotel"?' He's clocking my sideburns and drunken, swept-up quiff with something akin to his own unique take on religious, sexual and emotional ecstasy.

'Oh, no,' I beam. 'It's number twenty-seven. "Like a Prayer" by Madonna.'

The room has thinned out now, and with six pints of Boddington's bitter sweeping through my bloodstream (I'm sure Madonna goes through similar pre-gig preparations) I throw myself into the opening bars. I hit every note with powerful precision, a telling combination of heartfelt passion and camp delight, letting my voice ride with religious purity on the crest of a pounding bassline, feeling the music, letting it surge through me and explode with adrenaline, and love, and soulfulness. This one's for her. For Sorcha. The love of my life.

And then, as I hit the chorus, I notice Chris Barrie standing at the back of the room, arms folded, watching me intently with a gleeful, bemused smile across his face.

And the whole thing turns to shit.

CRUCIAL MOMENTS IN FANDOM HISTORY NUMBER ELEVEN: THE REVENGE OF UNCLE TREVOR

It's Tuesday 14 November 1989, the day before my seventeenth birthday. It's a dark, wet night in Stockton, and the air is thick with the musty tangs of autumn – mouldering leaves, leftover fireworks, rotting conkers and a Boro relegation fight. And I'm at Uncle Trevor's house in the suburban sprawl of Fairfield.

Oh, yes.

I look and feel different to how I did even six months earlier. I've ditched the gawky ski jackets and jumpers and have decided to gear up for the 1990s with forthright, fashionable aplomb. Yes, I'm dressing like early period Elvis. Or, rather, as early period Elvis would have dressed if he'd lived on Teesside and shopped at British Home Stores. I'm wearing jet-black shirts with floral embroidery, tight Levi 501s and dangerous winklepickers from Dolcis that occasionally require small dogs removing from the toe-ends. My hair's been cut and brushed into a towering, rockabilly quiff and I've sculpted some whiskery facial hair into sneering, jagged sideburns. Against all the odds, almost two decades on, the sideburns are still in place. I can't get into the 501s any more, though.

And I've pretty much abandoned science fiction and fantasy. Music is my new passion, and it's a matter of weeks since I bought a secondhand acoustic guitar from my old Monty Python comrade-in-arms Paul Hayes. I'd strummed my very first chords in his front room, and, as I'd done so, the TV had burbled in the corner. And what it had been showing was brand-new *Doctor Who* – episode one of 'Battlefield', the start of the final classic series before that sixteen-year hiatus. And I really hadn't been bothered. The times, as one of my new heroes might have said, were a-changin'. Although obviously I'd asked my mum to tape it, and I'd watched it when I'd got home later.

It's not the same, though. We've outgrown each other, me and *Doctor Who*. And *Star Wars*, too – I can't remember the last time I even thought about *Star Wars* and its sequels. *Robin of Sherwood* has been and gone, *Blake's 7* is nothing but a dim, distant memory. I've heard rumours of a brand-new *Star Trek* series, but haven't got round to watching it yet. I'm into 1960s psychedelia, and vintage punk rock, and something that I've read about on Teletext called 'indie'.

It's time for one final fling, though. And just as he had been a decade or more earlier, Uncle Trevor is the unwitting match-maker in this budding sci-fi romance.

He's older now, of course, in his late thirties, and living with his wife, Rose, as well as Christopher and Rachel, their two hyperactive primary-school-age kids. He's a little greyer, and wider, and has a big, bristling beard, but he's still the same old Uncle Trevor, and still as enthusiastic about technology as always.

And we're round here, me and my mum, looking at his new computer. And while we potter around the dining room, admiring the chunky grey keyboard, Trevor snakes a hand onto a nearby remote control and spurs a whirring, clunking video into life.

'Don't want to miss *Red Dwarf*,' he grins.

I affect the mocking, eye-rolling sneer that every teenager in the world somehow masters without effort about a week before their sixteenth birthday. 'That's *rubbish*, isn't it?' I ask him with a smirk. 'The poor man's *Hitch Hiker's Guide to the Galaxy*?'

He fixes me with a steely gaze and a breathy, superior laugh. 'Hardly,' he tuts disparagingly. This art of the effortless one-word dismissal is a centuries-old Teesside tradition made famous in the 1970s by our cultural ambassador to the world, Brian Clough.

I shrug with silent indifference and slurp noisily on my coffee. I make a mental note, though, that he might just have a point. He may not even realise it until he reads this book, but Uncle Trevor brought *Doctor Who* into my life. When a man's got that kind of impeccable track record, you've got to cut him some slack from time to time.

Over the next few weeks, silently, stealthily, I start to watch *Red Dwarf* on a Tuesday night. And I'm slowly drawn into this strange, claustrophobic sitcom – a witty, imaginative, break-neck-paced romp that – despite its sci-fi trappings, clearly lashed on with a deep and heartfelt love for the genre – shares the same themes and premises of many a classic British sitcom. Like *Porridge*, *Rising Damp* and *Steptoe and Son* before it, it's about entrapment – disparate, fractious characters bound together by circumstance and forced to live in each other's pockets despite their deepset intolerances. It just happens to have more talking toasters than its predecessors.

I even find a little support group at school, and – on balmy

Friday evenings, fuelled by Archers Peach Schnapps – me and my new friends Scott Doran and Gavin Wilkinson gather in the kitchen of fellow teenage *Red Dwarf* fan Jennifer Williams, a tall, boisterous fifth-former who becomes the first person I've ever seen get noisily enthusiastic about science fiction while drunk, and thus seems cut out for a lifetime of convention-going. I'm only amazed I haven't seen her at Dimension Jump already.

So thanks, Trevor. After a wobbly beginning, I make a small number of new friends, and don't miss an episode of *Red Dwarf* until university sweeps me away to philosophy, pretentiousness and shameful sci-fi denial.

But that's another story.

'He won't come.'

'I bet he does.'

'He won't, there'll be paparazzi everywhere.'

'He will, he can't resist it, I tell you.'

It's Saturday morning, and we're having a gentle, post-coffee debate with a fresh-faced Mike and Katy. The subject of our discussion: Craig Charles. Ever the *Red Dwarf* enigma, he'd been listed as an attendee when I'd first discovered the Dimension Jump website. But he hadn't been mentioned on any of the pre-convention blurb we'd received through the post, so I'd assumed he'd discreetly withdrawn from proceedings. But now, on a whiteboard in the Holiday Inn reception, his name has been added to the Sunday-morning schedule.

It's not been a brilliant summer for him. On 20 June, as I was preparing to travel to Swindon to meet Britt Ekland, the *Daily Mirror* led with the lurid headline 'Corrie Star on Crack' – detailing how Charles, aka *Coronation Street*'s 'loveable cabbie Lloyd

Mullaney' had gone on a 'crazed crack-cocaine bender' during a four-hour taxi ride from London to Manchester. The stories instigated police inquiries, and in August Charles was formally arrested on suspicion of possessing a Class A drug, before being released on bail. On Friday, as we were driving through a thunderstorm to Peterborough, news broke on the radio that he had accepted a caution for possession and was receiving treatment for his addictions in a rehabilitation clinic. Sadly, no mention was made during the one o'clock news of whether he would be gaining a day-pass from the Priory to attend Dimension Jump, and I'm reserving the right to remain entirely cynical.

Everyone else, though, seems energised by a wave of fandom positivity. The main reason for which is currently onstage, fiddling around with a video camera, chatting amiably to fans, and confessing to his addiction to YouTube, the online video-sharing community. It's Robert Llewellyn. 'Hello, YouTubers, it's me – live at the *Red Dwarf* convention in Peterborough!' he cheers, beaming into the camera lens and encouraging a cheery 'Yay!' from his audience.

'What's the most important thing to have in comedy?' asks one leather-coated fan at the front.

'An enormous penis,' he deadpans unflinchingly. 'That's what's held me back.'

He tells us about his love for domestic equipment – he owns five vacuum cleaners, 'including the new Philips, and that baby *really* sucks' – and also expresses his delight at the high proportion of female fans at the convention. 'It must be seventy per cent girls here today,' he beams. 'Do you know why that is? It's because *Red Dwarf* is about love. It's essentially a good fart joke, but with love wrapped all around it.'

He's possibly overestimating the percentage – after all, this isn't *Robin of Sherwood* – but it's a valid point. If, back in October 2005, I'd been asked to compile a police photo-fit of the stereotypical convention-goer, I'd have selected a forty-five-year-old male in a cagoul, with terrible skin, jam-jar glasses, an inbuilt resistance to the Lynx Effect and enough dandruff to keep Craig Charles's crackpipe in operation all the way up the M6, possibly even as far as Carlisle. Would I have been alone in my unfair preconceptions? Probably not. In the interests of research, I'd delved onto the least sci-fi friendly internet message board I could find (Middlesbrough FC's *Fly Me to the Moon* fanzine site) and asked grizzled football fans what kind of people they envisaged attended conventions. 'Geeks,' came the first answer. 'Tall, thin, skinny men that don't get out much.' The next wasn't much better. 'Men dressed up badly as their favourite characters with a noticeable damp smell,' it sniffed. And still they came. 'Don't forget the monobrow,' warned another. 'And the bad dentistry as well. Lives with his mum but bans her from entering his room. Puts down "Klingon" in the religion section of the census.'

And so on, and so on. Not a single punter even vaguely alluded to the prospect of female science-fiction fans, which suggests that some serious sociological redressing of balances needs doing here. Of the events I've been to, *Blake's 7*, *The Prisoner*, *Robin of Sherwood*, Discworld and now *Red Dwarf* had at least as many women as men in attendance, and any lurking skinny men with monobrows had their pervasive damp smells completely overwhelmed by the ordinary families that turned out for both *Star Wars* and *Star Trek*.

Norman Lovett takes to the stage. 'Apparently we've lost six members of the Peterborough Keep Fit Club,' he deadpans, to raucous laughter and applause. 'No, really, we have,' he protests. 'It's not a bloody joke. The hotel have asked me to mention it in case they've wandered in here.'

I wonder whether the missing keep-fitters have seen the error of their ways and defected, like 1960s Soviet dissidents – crawling under the sci-fi iron curtain and hastily swapping their jogging tops and Nike Airs for Ace Rimmer T-shirts and fluffy Mr Flibbles before blending into the heaving throng.

Meanwhile, I realise that I still have a mission to fulfil.

Back in November, at that very first *Doctor Who* convention, I'd vowed to improve my convention performance next time round, 'maybe – just maybe – summoning enough courage to put my hand up and ask a question to a panel'. Ten months and as many fan events later, I realise with horror that I still haven't done it. However, as Norman chats amiably with the crowd, I hear my calling. This – in the almost verbatim words of Martine McCutcheon – is my moment. This is my perfect moment with Norman.

I stick my hand in the air.

Norman Lovett catches my eye.

This is it.

I clear my throat.

'Norman, I just wanted to ask . . . how did you end up being linked to the part of Davros in *Doctor Who* last year?'

The room falls silent, and all eyes turn to me. Then to Norman. Then to me. Then back to Norman. Then round in dizzy circles a few times, before finally settling on me once more, realising that I'm too embarrassed to say anything else, and beating another hasty retreat for Norman.

'I haven't got a clue,' he protests. 'But I wish people would stop bloody asking me about it!'

It was one of my favourite sci-fi rumours of 2005. As the first revival series of *Doctor Who* had reached its peak, one bright spark on Outpost Gallifrey had spotted a tantalising addition to IMDB, Internet Movie Database, the online repository of all film and TV trivia. Added to the cast list for the forthcoming episode thirteen, 'The Parting of the Ways', was, implausibly, 'Norman Lovett as Davros'. The prospect seemed preposterous. After all, they're such disparate characters: one of them is a bald-headed, twisted megalomaniac noted across the sci-fi world for his grumpiness and desire to exterminate all inferior beings, and the other one . . . nah, sorry, I can't bring myself to do it. The other one is Norman Lovett.

'Have you any idea who started it?' I continue, undaunted, and taking an unprecedented second bite at the question-asking cherry.

'No!' he laughs, before his eyes become clouded over with suspicion. 'It wasn't you, was it? It was! It was you!'

I open my mouth to offer a swift denial, before a hairy man in a leather coat twenty feet to my left sticks up his hand and shouts, 'No, it was me!' The room descends into chaos, and the culprit is carried shoulder-high by his friends. Thankfully Norman takes it all in his stride, and proceeds to treat us to an extract from his Edinburgh Festival slide show, whistling through brilliantly quirky photos of his dogs, socks and kitchen appliances accompanied by a trademark hangdog commentary. Oddly enough, he seems to share Robert Llewellyn's fetish for vacuum cleaners, offering us several photos of his various upright models and a *Which?* magazine-style performance comparison in which – I'm sad to report – the Fischer family favourite Dyson feels the force of his ire. Norman also reveals, to a slight ripple of good-natured disquiet, that he 'can't really stand science fiction, to be honest'.

I hang my head in sympathetic shame.

BLOODY STUPID THINGS I HAVE DONE IN THE NAME OF FANDOM NUMBER ELEVEN: TRYING TO DENY I LIKE SCI-FI AT ALL

'But it's bollocks! All of it. Tacky juvenilia for knobheads who've never grown up. I want my art to speak to me about life, about love and the human condition. I don't need bloody robots and spaceships and little green Martians trying to invade Earth.'

Before you start briefing a crack sci-fi militia squad to conduct a 'hit' on whichever of my childhood friends is spouting forth, prepare yourself for a shock.

It's me.

I'm sorry.

I'm twenty now, and I know it all. No, really, I do – I'm convinced I have life, politics, religion and art all sorted, and my God-given mission for my remaining years on the planet is to bring the world around to my way of thinking. I have *NME* under one arm, a battered acoustic guitar under the other, and spend the hours in between sociology seminars plotting to construct an anarcho-Marxist commune in central Lancaster, preferably within staggering distance of the Wagon and Horses and the Stonewell Inn. Yes, I'm at university and almost halfway through my degree now, majoring in philosophy with a minor in sociology – a textbook combination for the idle, belligerent gobshite. My head is filled with Wittgenstein and Derrida and Jean-Paul bloody Sartre, and I'm always keen to demonstrate my new-found knowledge at the drop of a Breton cap.

As my new housemates will no doubt wearily testify. I'm sitting in the front room with Raf Uzar, an amiable Pole from Derby who wears a bandana and listens to Queen, John Jaques, an affable, bespectacled, comic-book fan from Burnley, and Gareth Johnstone, a shy Cumbrian *Doctor Who* fan with an enviable collection of videos and books in the attic room of our four-bedroomed terrace. I'm drunk, after a night with Jaques in the Stonewell, and spouting forth with venomous aplomb.

'What about *Doctor Who*?' asks Gareth. 'You like that, don't you? You watch my videos enough.'

'I liked it when I was a kid, but it's really cheesy and crap. No one over the age of ten should ever be taking it seriously.'

'*Star Trek*,' says Raf. '*Star Trek*'s good fun, surely?'

'American imperialism writ large,' I splutter. 'Alpha-male macho men conquering worlds for Uncle Sam. They shouldn't be allowed to show it to kids.'

'*Star Wars*, then,' smiles John Jaques. 'Everyone loves *Star Wars*, it's great.'

'So facile it hurts,' I spit. 'Soap opera in space, like *Crossroads* but with funny hats.'

Looking back, I think lots of sci-fi fans go through this rite of passage at some point in their lives. It's the overwhelming desire to look more grown-up than we actually are, a hunger especially strong in students, for whom it ranks alongside eating Pot Noodles and stealing items of traffic management as an irresistible, primal urge. As Paul of Tarsus writes in Corinthians 13:11; 'When I was a man, I put childish things behind me.' Nowadays, of course, I'd counter that with a quote from the Teachings of Tom Baker, 'Robot', episode four: 'There's no point in being grown-up if you can't be childish sometimes.' But in 1993, in the front room of 33 Ashfield Avenue, Lancaster, I'm firmly sticking to the biblical maxim. Despite the fact that I'm still given to breaking wind over Zippo lighter flames at particularly sophisticated student parties.

I mean it, though. For three years at university, I immerse myself in the works of Morrissey, Quentin Tarantino, Martin Scorcese and Joseph Conrad, and anything with a *Doctor Who* logo gets stuffed in a box in my parents' dusty attic. And, I'm ashamed to say, in 1993, *Red Dwarf* is bearing the brunt of my particular brand of bile. The reason is simple – T-shirts.

I've taken an entirely unfair dislike to a particular brand of student. They're all skinny (which I'm not), they're all intelligent (which I'm not), they're all studying maths or computing or molecular physics (which I'm not), and they all spend every daylight hour in the university campus's dingy computer department, squinting at pre-Cambrian-era clockwork internet pages through jam-jar glasses while small mounds of dandruff turn to crystalline stalagmites on their shoulders. Which, thankfully, I don't. And they all – seemingly to a man – wear *Red Dwarf* T-shirts.

And this makes me angry.

At the time, I rationalise this by convincing myself the root of my anger is a heartfelt concern for the advancement of the human soul, that these people shouldn't be locking themselves away in front of green-screen monitors, spouting sci-fi sitcom catchphrases and releasing flakes of Pityriasis capitis into the atmosphere every time they grease their centre partings. They should be out there in the real world, drinking beer, advancing their minds, meeting soul-mates and getting some gamma rays on their acne scars. Now, however, I think the root of my anger was more selfish. I reckon, deep down, I thought that sci-fi deserved better than this. The most imaginative, boundless and forward-thinking of fictional genres was being dragged down into the gutter by association with these morbid geeks, when it should be rising to the metaphorical and literal stars.

I probably start to break free of these mental shackles and embrace my sci-fi heritage at around the same time that I meet the first person in years that I've seen actually wearing a *Red Dwarf* T-shirt, and she's a beautiful, slate-eyed redhead pulling pints of Flying Herbert in a Middlesbrough town-centre pub.

But that's another story, too. And it's already been told.

By the time the inevitable signing session comes round Sorcha and I are inevitably already half-drunk, but we shake hands and pose sweatily with all the main cast of the day – including

Danny John-Jules, the Cat himself, an effortlessly cool figure who looks, talks and dresses like a Premiership footballer. He's probably not *quite* exotic enough for Chelsea, but he'd easily strut into West Ham's first-choice XI. He's certainly a firm believer in the *Red Dwarf* youth policy, being accompanied all weekend by his thirteen-year-old nephew Alexander John-Jules, who played a baby Dave Lister in the series seven episode 'Ouroboros'. 'This is Craig Charles – living proof that rehab *does* work!' grins Danny, slapping his young charge on the back and demonstrating the Cat Shuffle to a wave of very female shrieks.

Early evening descends into, well . . . late evening, and Sorcha and I decide to consolidate our newly revitalised relationship by plonking ourselves on a table-top by the bar and spending the next four hours there chatting amiably to anyone who passes. And, as I squint through blearily Boddingtons-soaked eyes, a tall, thirtysomething blonde woman comes pelting at me through the crowd.

'Sorry, but I can't resist,' she cries. 'Don't I know you from somewhere?'

'I don't think so,' I mumble back. 'Where did you think you knew me from?'

'Yarm,' she says. 'Conyers School. We used to sit in my parents' kitchen and talk about *Red Dwarf.*'

It's Jennifer Williams.

Yep, fittingly, the first person I ever saw getting noisily enthusiastic about science fiction while drunk. And, I suppose, the most recent person I've seen getting nosily enthusiastic about science fiction while drunk – although admittedly there's some stiff competition for this title. I jump to my feet and she throws her arms round me. It's the first time I've seen her for over fifteen years, and we introduce each other to our partners before swapping tales of long-lost friends and youthful exuberances. She's an accountant now, based in Peterborough, and it's fantastic to see her. I'm overwhelmed with the wash of heart-bursting, head-filling, mushy, everything-is-perfect life-affirming soulfulness that can only be attained by the very, very drunk. Or the very, very religious ... but I've already defeated Paul of Tarsus with Tom Baker.

We decide to celebrate the fact that we're so drunk by drinking a lot more, and we're joined by an utterly lovely young Scottish couple, Steve and Jen, who are here celebrating Jen's twenty-first birthday because her parents bought them both tickets as a present. Jen likes *CSI Miami* and Syd Barrett, and Steve is the drummer in an Edinburgh blues band called Ayahuaska (and yes, he writes it down for me), and a dead ringer for John Gordon Sinclar in *Gregory's Girl*. It's possible that I end the evening in the bar at 4am, shouting, '*Bella, bella,*' at him and debating the correct way to spell 'Caracas', but I prefer to dismiss the whole experience as a cruel example of false memory syndrome, brought on by lack of sleep and far too much life-affirming exuberance for one day.

11am. Back in the hall.

Life-affirming exuberance conspicuous by its absence.

I pour myself a pint of mineral water. Scottish drummer Steve, with steely Caledonian resolve, is sipping gingerly on his first beer of the day. Sorcha looks pale. Jen looks tired. I have to play Smeg or No Smeg.

'Some dubious-looking prizes; twenty-two identically sealed boxes. And no questions. Except one ... Smeg or No Smeg?'

Yep, in front of a largely equally hung-over audience, my number has been called at random to make me a box-holder in the *Red Dwarf* equivalent of *Deal or No Deal*. I have box number twenty-two, which turns out to contain a metaphorical £35,000. And a Jupiter Mining Corporation fizzy drinks can. All I can remember is staring fuzzy-headedly at my filthy fingernails on the edge of the black box and wanting to be at home, on the settee, with a blanket over me and a cup of Typhoo steaming on the coffee table. I'm too old and too feeble for this sustained and vigorous alcohol abuse, and I start to wonder how Craig Charles can actually hack it. If it was me on that fateful taxi ride to Manchester, I'd have passed out before we reached Heathrow.

'He's here.' says Katy.

'I'll believe it when I see it.'

He is, though. After passing through a guard of disbelieving fans in the hotel foyer, the erstwhile Dave Lister enters the main hall and is treated to a thunderous wall of applause – a unanimous standing ovation that makes the (substantial) hair on the back of my neck stand up, and brings an entirely unexpected lump to my throat. He looks *fantastic* – he's slimmer than I've ever seen him, clean-shaven and short-haired with shiny, glowing skin and an immaculate black suit that hangs perfectly from his slender frame. He grabs a microphone and strides around the stage, swapping cheeky one-liners with the fans at the front, as a murmured buzz of excitement still continues to circulate around the room. 'I've just come out of the Priory,' he chirps, his Scouse drawl as treacly as ever. 'And I'm now addicted to PG Tips. And my wife now has to wear make-up to go to the shops 'cos she knows she'll get photographed all the way there and back.'

He talks openly and candidly about his addictions, excesses and treatments, before requesting sincerely that we never repeat any of his stories online or in print, as 'the papers will just have a field day – this is for you lot, the fans, and not for them.' So I won't. Although I wish I'd managed to snap a picture of his face when one entirely innocent-sounding lady asked, 'How many lines do you normally get on *Corrie*?' Afterwards, he races straight to the merchandise room to give autographs, and even Sorcha is shaking at the thought of meeting him. Tired of spelling out her name to sci-fi celebrities, she hands him her name-tag from work, which he finds hilarious, and he's still laughing when I push my Smeg or No Smeg cardboard box onto the table for him to sign. 'No Deal!' he scrawls across the label. 'I bet it's the first time you've said that for a while,' I joke, momentarily taking leave of my senses. He catches my eye for a nerve-shredding half-second then bursts into raucous laughter. I notice that he does, indeed, have a steaming cup of PG Tips next to his overflowing ashtray.

And then we're gone.

Unlike the final episode of *Red Dwarf* itself, Dimension Jump doesn't end on a cliffhanger. The Peterborough Holiday Inn doesn't get infected by a chameleonic microbe (or, as the opening credits have it, a 'weird shape-changing space thing'), and I don't find myself, like Arnold Rimmer, backed into a corner of the breakfast bar by the Grim Reaper himself before giving him a swift kick to the smeg receptors. So, this seems pretty final. We swap hugs and e-mail addresses with Steve and Jen and Mike and Katy, and I put my protesting NatWest debit card through one last hotel check-out routine.

I don't really know how to feel. It's as if a whole new way of life – an incarnation, if you like – has come to an end, and I wonder if, as I step through the hotel door one last time, I'll collapse into the ornamental borders around the car park and begin to regenerate. Just like Tom Baker in 'Logopolis' back in March 1981. A halo of light will surround my head, and the faces of my convention companions – Nathan and John and Matthew and Tara and Wez and Smudge and Doug and Judith and Kirsty and Fiona and Alison and Mike and Katy and Steve and Jen – will float into the air in a kaleidoscope of cheap 1980s computer effects. 'Don't go, Bob,' they'll say, in eerie unison. 'You can't leave us now, the world of sci-fi and cult TV fandom needs you too much. Besides which, you haven't paid off your Visa bill yet.'

And then my face will go all wobbly and wiggly and, after a modest BBC budget explosion, I'll sit bolt upright and be a completely new man. Perhaps I'll regenerate into the ultimate sci-fi geek, all skinny and freckly and wan with rheumy eyes from building *Farscape* forums at four o'clock in the morning. Perhaps I'll become a macho sci-fi hater – beating up *Blakes's 7* box sets in back alleys and kicking sand in the faces of weakling action figures on the beach. Or perhaps I'll still be me, and just go home and carry on where I left off – writing, broadcasting, quibbling with Sorcha – before this whole crazy business took over my life.

That's the trouble with regeneration – you never quite know what you're going to get.

We sing again all the way home – the *Red Dwarf* theme, Madonna and the Shangri-Las – and when we get back to the house I make a cup of tea, slice up some cake and we collapse onto the sofa together. I've had fun, I tell myself, but I don't think I'll ever go back to a convention. And then Sorcha looks me in the eyes, and says something that makes my heart melt into gooey lumps of space debris.

She says, 'I've never played Dungeons and Dragons. Can we get some of your old mates round to try it one night?'

I dash to my address book to find a number for Flaxman Orcslayer.

And then, weeks later, when the family Dyson breaks into pieces, she idly turns the shattered valve pipe over in her hand

and muses, 'What hoover did Norman Lovett say he had? I wouldn't mind giving one of those a try.'

So I troop upstairs to the PC (with *The Battle to Save Earth* still plonked unceremoniously on my desk) and e-mail Norman Lovett's website to check, hardly expecting a reply. But I get one, within a matter of hours. 'Hi, Bob, it's a SEBO Automatic Extra,' he tells me. 'They cost a bit more than most models, but in the long run they are cheaper.'

I expect this is the beginning of a deluge, and within weeks there'll be a polite message on the front page asking fans to stop e-mailing him with vacuum-cleaner enquiries.

The End?

The smeg it is.

THE BATTLE TO SAVE EARTH

y Robert Fischer (Aged Eight And Two
    Thirds)
unday 26 July 1981
ART THIRTEEN

The camp?' I asked. 'Yes!' Paul shouted.
  'You know, that camp in the summer!'
That one?' I asked. 'How come only Henry's here?' 'He was the
only one who turned up,' Paul answered. Then Dirk pushed me.
'What?' I asked. Dirk brought a small box from his pocket
  and opened it. Inside was a kind of white cheese. 'Want
ome?' 'What is it?' I asked. 'Davrock cheese,' Dirk answered.
I took a piece and chewed it. 'Quite nice,' I said. Then I
turned away and spat the cheese out. A few minutes later we
rrived at Paul's farm. We had just got in the house when I
said to Richard, 'What did you do with those tapes?' 'Oh,
  Dirk gave them too Ronnie,' Richard answered. 'Ronnie?' I
sked. 'Who on Earth's Ronnie?' 'Ronnie Robot,' Dirk answered.
Want to see him?' 'You bet!' I said. Dirk opened a big case
he had been carrying around and a big shiny robot came out.
  'What time is it?' I asked Paul. 'Half past nine,' Paul
replied. 'Another half an hour and we'll go to bed.' 'Well we
  might as well make the most of it,' Dirk said, and called
Ronnie over. He pressed a button on Ronnie's head and a hatch
  opened. Dirk took a pocket space invaders out of the hatch.
Ronnie closed the hatch and went to sleep. 'Where's Nigel?' I
sked Paul. 'He's staying at Gran's for the night,' Paul said.
  Then Paul noticed my gun strapped to my belt. He asked me
what I had it for. I said 'I use it for space battles and
it's a laser gun'. But Paul did not believe me. I told him
to come outside on the field and I would prove it. We ran
ut onto the nearest field and I fired the laser. A blue bolt
hot out over the field. 'Believe me now?' I asked Paul. 'Yes,'
  Paul said, and staggered back into the house in amazement.

IT'S THE END...

THE FOURTH DOCTOR, 'LOGOPOLIS', EPISODE FOUR,
BROADCAST SATURDAY 21 MARCH 1981:

'It's the end, but the moment has been prepared for.'

FOUR THINGS I'VE LEARNED recently about my thirty-four-year-old self:

1. I don't have a number for Flaxman Orcslayer any more.
2. The most effective way to lose weight is to subsist entirely on a diet of Flamin' Hot Monster Munch and Kit-Kats. I've shed a stone since the beginning of July, and will shortly be marketing this regime as the FHMMAKK-Plan Diet.
3. I love my girlfriend more than I did before we spent a weekend in a Peterborough hotel with Craig Charles and Danny John-Jules.
4. I'm completely self-deluding about stopping going to conventions.

November 2006. It's a bitterly cold evening in Stockton-on-Tees, and I'm sitting by the window of a first-floor hotel bar watching a scuffle break out between two women in the High Street below. Thankfully, should the violence escalate,

313

reinforcements are at hand. Rucksack Man is over by the toilets, and Sylvester McCoy is queuing at the bar.

Sound familiar? It should. I'm back. My journey might be officially over, but I can't resist coming home to Dimensions. After all, it's only up the road. And Nathan and John and Damon and Sean and Neil are here. And Sorcha, who hasn't bought a ticket but has wandered up for Saturday-night drinks because she thought 'It'd be nice to see everyone again.' I'm drunk, obviously, and I'm having a fabulous time. And tomorrow is Remembrance Sunday, when I'll have the pleasure of seeing two tentacle-faced Ood in grey overalls observe the two-minute silence in the bar, lowering their dome-like heads to the floor and switching off their fluorescent translation globes as a mark of respect to the fallen.

Have you ever been to a science-fiction convention?

Really, I'd recommend it.

And for those who are eager to read more of my 1981 opus *The Battle to Save Earth*, well . . . sorry, but you can't. That's it. There *is* no more. The story stops exactly where we've left it, and the rest of my WHSmith exercise book is blank. The final date on the top of the last chapter is Sunday 26 July 1981 – the first weekend of the school summer holidays. I wasn't cooped up at home any more writing about Richard Moxham and Paul Frank and Andrew Henry; I was out racing around with them on endless sunny afternoons, jumping around in Frankie's barns and throwing *Star Wars* figures from open bedroom windows. I did interview former Aston Villa midfielder Gary Shaw for BBC Tees some years later, but I didn't mention his involvement in the Terran-Davrockian war.

Twenty-six years on, though, precious little has changed. I might now be thirty-four years old, but I'm still writing sci-fi stories over beans-on-toast and *Doctor Who* and telling my mum they'll get published. The WHSmith exercise book is a

Microsoft Word document, my mum lives in France rather than Teesside, and *Doctor Who* has spiky hair and an extensive female following, but the principle remains the same. The beans-on-toast, for the record, are unchanged. I eat them every day for my lunch, and tell myself it's what my gran would have wanted.

And, fantastically, I've found Richard Moxham again. I haven't seen him for twenty-two years, but a quick trawl of Facebook turns him up in Alberta, Canada. He's married with four kids now, and intrigued to hear about *The Battle to Save Earth*. Don't judge me too harshly, Richard. I'm older now, and I'm sorry.

In the meantime, sci-fi life goes on. *Doctor Who* is still railroading through the TV schedules, Norman Lovett makes two appearances on my radio show to talk about vacuum cleaners, and Tom Pearcy e-mails to tell me that his 2007 Maize Maze is a thirty-five-acre portrait of Roger Moore, celebrating the thirtieth anniversary of the release of *The Spy Who Loved Me*. And, two days before Christmas, Sorcha and I spend a fabulous Saturday at Matthew and Tara's wedding in Bath, where the groom and his chums dress in Converse All-Stars trainers as a tribute to David Tennant, and the reception tables are all named after *Doctor Who* monsters. We spend all night at the Cyberman table, talking about *Torchwood* with a man called Angus.

Resistance – to coin a phrase – *is* useless.

And I wouldn't have it any other way.

AFTERWORD

It's 2018 now.

Jodie Whittaker is the thirteenth *Doctor Who* (fourteenth if you count John Hurt in the 50th anniversary special, fifteenth if you count the second David Tennant incarnation, when he regenerated into himself after being partially exterminated by a Dalek ... it's a long story); there have been four new *Star Wars* films in the last three years (and Mark Hamill, Harrison Ford and Carrie Fisher have all made me cry into my Monster Munch on separate occasions in a cosy North Yorkshire cinema), and *Blake's 7* has returned as a series of audio episodes starring the original cast, produced by stalwart keepers of the childhood flame, Big Finish Productions.

There have been three new *James Bond* films, three new *Star Trek* films, a new *Hitch-Hikers* book (written by *Artemis Fowl* creator Eoin Colfer) and an ongoing series of Radio 4 adaptations. *The Prisoner* returned in 2009 for a six-episode series starring Jim Caviezel, and the original *Robin of Sherwood* cast (including both Praed *and* Connery) has also reunited for audio adventures. *Red Dwarf* returned in 2009, and – at time of writing – the fifth revival series is in pre-production. Perhaps most astonishingly of all, in 2014 the five surviving members of the *Monty Python* team reunited to play ten sold-out nights at the O2 Arena in London. I was there for the fifth of them, and I cried at that as well.

It's extraordinary and heart-warming to contemplate the fact that every single one of the cultural milestones that helped shape my childhood has once again become current, contemporary (or at least very recent) concerns. What sometimes seemed, back in 2006, like the last flickering embers of middle-aged fandom, have not just reignited but turned supernova, attracting a whole new generation of fans whose fervour and ingenuity frequently shames those of us who grew up during the original era of cult TV. DIY dressing-up has become super-slick and impressive 'Cosplay'. Modest conventions have become sprawling, big-money 'Comic-Cons'. The social media explosion has fuelled a youthful, vibrant generation of new fans for whom *Doctor Who* (and the rest) plays constantly on their smartphones and tablets; carried in pockets rather than tucked away on dusty shelves; the stuff of Netflix and hashtags rather than battered paperbacks and DVDs.

I'm still friends with everyone that I counted as companions on those extraordinary adventures of 2006; including Sorcha, despite the fact that we stopped being a couple in 2010. I feel guilty about the selfishness that I displayed when we were together, and about the way that I depicted some of our stormier episodes in this book, but I texted her today to ask if she had a message for you all. She replied; 'I might never visit another convention now that I've found the answer to Life, The Universe and Everything, but I certainly enjoyed attending them with Bob. Always remember . . . The Turtle Moves.'

I assume that last bit is a Terry Pratchett reference, but I can't check now because she took all the books with her.

My parents and my uncle Trevor are still alive and well, and even Teesside itself has regenerated into a much more welcoming and vibrant area ... although the Swallow Hotel in Stockton closed down in 2009, and – while it awaits conversion into student accommodation – stands like an eerie, deserted monument to those distant, freewheeling Teesside conventions. There's probably still a broken, dust-covered Dalek plunger lying next to a mould-coated half-pint of John Smith's Bitter in the corner of the bar, and a crumpled convention timetable signed by Gareth Thomas.

Who, sadly, is no longer with us. And neither are David Brierley, Peter Tuddenham, Robert Monks, Terry Pratchett, or Richard Carpenter. Here's to them all, and the parts they all played in these strange and beautiful adventures.

Anything else I need to tell you?

Yeah.

I'm 45 now, and – obviously – my childhood has receded even further into the realms of vague memory and faded Polaroid photographs. I'm not as cocksure and flippant as I was when I wrote *Wiffle Lever to Full!,* and I certainly don't drink as much. But the wistful daydreams and fantasies of my childhood continue to sustain me, and the further passage of time – and the loss of some of those who forged and shared those memories – has only given them an extra piquancy.

Thanks for letting me share them.

ACKNOWLEDGEMENTS

First of all, some very sad news. I'd like to dedicate this book to the memory of my old friend Doug Simpson, who tragically passed away shortly after the first edition of *Wiffle Lever to Full!* was published. Doug was a brilliant, larger than life character, and the last time we spoke was when I called him to ask if he minded me including a few of our old childhood scrapes in the book. When I told him what I'd written about him, he thought it was hilarious, and so I've left everything intact as I'm sure it's what he would have wanted. Deepest and heartfelt sympathies go to all of Doug's family and friends. I miss you, Dougster.

For the rest of you horrible lot . . . I'd like to offer huge thanks to the friends who gave up weekends, spare rooms and healthy lifestyles in order to help me on my quest: Simon Westwood, Chris Smith, Andy Bruce (and Charlotte and John), Matthew and Tara Pardo, Stuart Downing, Mike and Angela Pardo, Paul and Marie Westwood, and not forgetting Allie the dog. Woof.

Love and gratitude to the old friends who allowed their childhoods to be ransacked for the sake of a few giggles: Richard Moxham, Doug Simpson, Ian MacDonald, Chris Selden, Paul Hayes, Neil Braithwaite, Phil Slack, John Jaques, Gareth Johnstone, Rafal Uzar and Jennifer Williams. I promise I'll keep in touch more in future.

A hearty shout to all the friends that I made along the way – to Nathan and John, Neil and Sean and Damon and John Paul, Will, Doug and the entire Proctor family, Rick and Howard, Kris and Davina Dress, Kirsty and Alison and Fiona, and Mike and Katy and Steve and Jen. And those are just the names I know – there are countless others who strutted their stuff, drank their beers and told their tales, and it was lovely to spend these silly weekends with you all. And thanks to Dave Price, he knows why.

Heartfelt thanks to the celebs as well – the countless actors, writers, directors and behind-the-scenes workers who made the films and books and TV shows that have taken over my life for the last thirty years. It's a well-worn cliché that you should never meet your heroes, but the heroes I met at conventions and signings were just that – heroic. Which goes equally for the organisers as well – the tireless, enthusiastic fans who put these things together. I don't know how you do it, and even if I did, then I'd never have the energy.

I'd also like to say a word of thanks to those people who, over the years, have encouraged me in various ways to write for a living. Eric Harrison, Graham Parker, Terry Benton, Mark Clemmit, Robert Nichols and Harry Pearson all spring to mind, but there are others and I'm grateful to you all. And little slitty-fingered Vulcan salutes go to Euan Thorneycroft at A. M. Heath, and Lisa Highton, Heather Rainbow, Nick Davies, Joey Hi-Fi, Thorne Ryan and the rest of the team at Hodder & Stoughton for making all my dreams come true.

A big shout goes to my uncle Trevor Atkinson, who's now inexplicably claiming that he 'never really watched' *Doctor Who* in the 1970s. Like all the best science fiction fans, he's clearly going through his period of denial.

Oh, and my gran, Mary Eliza Atkinson, 1909–89.

She was there at the start.